GOURMI

IAIN CRAWFORD

GOURMET GOLF

*A guide to the best golf courses
and restaurants in
Europe*

LOCHAR PUBLISHING · MOFFAT · SCOTLAND

For my in-laws Jack Mainland and Roberto Rinaldi and my sons Michael, Douglas and Neil who have cheerfully played this maddening but fascinating game with me. Lang may yer ba' fly!

© Iain Crawford 1992

Published by Lochar Publishing Ltd,
MOFFAT, SCOTLAND, DG10 9ED

A catalogue record for this book is available from the
British Library
ISBN 1-874027-01-3
Typeset in Perpetua by Blackpool Typesetting Services Ltd,
and printed by Billing & Sons Ltd, Worcester.
Designed by Paul Minns

'Golf in the Midnight Sun' courtesy of the Swedish Tourist Board.
'Little Island, Co Cork, Eire' courtesy of the Irish Tourist Board.
Other photographs by the author.

Contents

AN AULD ALLIANCE

The link between golf and good food is not just some PR-person's dream—two plugs for the price of one—but is an essential and historical component of the 'antient and healthfull exercise of the goff' as the game used to be called in its old Scottish days before it was dragged into designer courses, buggy carts, swinging haute couture and computerised clubhead path analysis.

All these glitzy, adman-world additions have been tacked on to the Royal and Ancient game but food and drink have been there from the start. The first golf clubs were formed in taverns and the first prizes were almost always dinners. The first golf club in the world, the Honourable Company of Edinburgh Golfers, met in Luckie Clephan's inn at Leith for refreshments and sustenance both before and after matches.

Indeed in the eighteenth century the eating was considered to be as important a part of the matter as the playing. In his excellent and entertaining book *Muirfield and the Honourable Company*, 1972, George Pottinger quotes from the minutes of 1753:

> Mr David Lyon, ane Eminent Golfer, after subscribing and engaging himself to play for the Silver Club this day has not only not started for the Club But contrary to the Duty of his Allegiance has withdrawn himself from the Captain and his Company and has dined in another house after having bespoke a particular Dish for himself in Luckie Clephan's. The Captain therefore appoints the Procurator Fiscall to endyte the said David Lyon for the above offence and hereby orders the Culprit to be cited to answer here on Saturday next.

For not eating his dinner, David Lyon was obliged to resign.

The Silver Club referred to in Mr Lyon's indictment is the world's first golf trophy which led to the first written rules and provides the first recorded evidence of a golf Club. The game had been played on Leith Links and elsewhere since at least the fifteenth century but in 1744 the Gentlemen Golfers of Edinburgh (as the Honourable Company was at first called) had presented to them a Silver Club by the City of Edinburgh to be played for annually, the winner to be declared Captain of the Golf for the year.

Until that date matches had been played for wagers, sometimes money but often legs of mutton, gallons of claret, port or whisky or dinners for which the loser had to pay the bill. The Silver Club of 1744 launched championship golf in circumstances which turned out to be at least as dramatic as the tensest Open or Masters tournament ever played.

The winner in 1744 was John Rattray, Surgeon in Edinburgh, who was victorious again in 1745. But in September of that year he was roused from his bed to be Surgeon-General to Bonnie Prince Charlie's army at the Battle of Prestonpans, where the Stuart prince's Highlanders routed Sir John Cope and the Hanoverians. From that victory Rattray accompanied the

Jacobite army south to Derby and back to final defeat at Culloden in 1746. Taken prisoner on the bloody field of Culloden, he was in danger of being executed and only the intervention of fellow Edinburgh golfer, Scotland's senior judge, Duncan Forbes, Lord President of the Court of Session, saved his life—possibly the first instance of the advantage of belonging to a good club!

He resumed office as Captain of the Golf in 1747 but had the tact not to win the Silver Club again until 1751.

So with Rattray the tradition of playing for tropies rather than wine, food or dinners was begun but the association of good food and golf remained. The Silver Club is still donated by the City of Edinburgh and the trophy is still played for at Muirfield, the Honourable Company's home since 1891 and the venue for thirteen Open Championships. But dinner matches go on and golfers on holiday or on business touring in strange parts of what is now the world-wide territory of golf still look for top-class food and drink to round off their enjoyment after a struggle with the challenge and complexities of a first-class golf course.

With gastronomic standards rising all over the world, the simple haunches of mutton, beef or venison washed down with a few bottles of claret of eighteenth-century Scotland have given way to more subtle fare—more subtle and much more expensive. The bill for a dinner at Leith for fourteen in 1801 came to £12.14s and included twenty-three bottles of port, sherry and claret plus rum, ale, toddy, gin, brandy and spruce (the latter was a kind of beer made from spruce fir shoots).

In the experience of playing more than 500 golf courses all over the world I have been compiling material for an international golf gourmet's guide for years—a field of research which has turned many of my erstwhile friends into small bright-green gamma rays of envy.

Undeterred, I offer the entrées, plats du jour, desserts and fruits of my studies to those to whom golf is not just a searing examination of moral fibre and a kind of pilgrim's progress of the soul. This is a book for golfing hedonists, a guide to the most delightful and rewarding places in Europe to play golf and to where you can discuss amiably and repletely afterwards why the round you had in mind didn't quite go according to plan, tried and trusted suggestions for good courses on links and moorland and at well-managed tables nearby.

SCOTLAND

Scotland is where it all started. Although my late and lamented friend Steven van Hengel produced fascinating documentary proof that a street game called colf dated back in the Low Countries to the fourteenth century, the game seems to have been played on open ground in Scotland about the same time and the first recorded ordinance against it (because it was interfering with the practice of archery needed to keep the English at bay) is dated 1457. Naturally, when Steven produced his splendid book *Early Golf* in 1982, it was seized on with whoops of vengeful joy by all the English golf writers and scholars who have never been able to understand why a little troublesome country like Scotland should have been allowed by a blind providence to invent such manifest delights as golf and whisky when a much worthier centre of origin for matters affording such universal pleasure exists just south of the Solway.

The truth of the matter seems to be that no-one knows who invented golf. The twelfth century Senzie Fair at St Andrews brought ships and traders from the Low Countries to Fife for the 15-day Eastertide Fair. Something other than cloth and trinkets may have been exchanged then. What is certain is that Dutch colf disappeared in the seventeenth century, the Scots invented the first recorded rules of the game in 1744 and Scots soldiers and traders exported it to England and, in the nineteenth century, all over the world.

The game has a tradition and atmosphere in Scotland which exists nowhere else. It is not a game for snobs, the wealthy or the socially elite as it is in many countries. It is inexpensive (although getting 'terrible dear' by the standards of 30 years ago which permitted all St Andrews ratepayers to play on the town's four courses free) and there are more golf courses per head of the population than in any other country in the world.

General de Gaulle said in 1962 'How can you be expected to govern a country that has 246 kinds of cheese?' and just as we make selections from the vast array of French cheeses to enrich our menus, so this is a choice from the 430 golf courses in Scotland, beginning in the north.

A guide to restaurant prices is approximated by a star system which applies to the lowest priced *table d'hôte* menu (if any) on offer. The price structure is per person and does not include wine.

Under £12   *
Under £17   **
Under £25   ***
Over £25   ***

Highland

ROYAL DORNOCH, Dornoch, Sutherland IV25 3LW tel: (0862) 810219
6577 yards SSS 72

RESTAURANT
The Bishop's Room, Dornoch Castle ＊＊

Those of us who belong to the long summer nights of the far north have always known about Royal Dornoch but it took an American golf magazine to give it international fame, when it was named by one far-flung golfing scribe as one of the six best courses in the world.

The official date for the formation of the club is 1877 but historical references show that golf has been played there from at least 1616. And there is the Dornoch-born bishop, castigated in St Andrews in 1570 for spending 'the kirk's rents at the golf, archerie, guid chier etc,' who probably learned the game farther north.

Like many great links courses, Dornoch does not make its charms and challenges immediately visible to the eye. Cunning use of the natural terrain means that it is only as you play that its greatness becomes apparent. Various people, including Old Tom Morris, had a hand in its making, and it was here that the famous golf architect Donald Ross, creator of some of America's finest courses, learned the skills which made him the designer of Pinehurst.

The springy turf, the sharp, clear, gorse-scented air, the sweeping views over the mauve Sutherland hills and the wrinkled pewter of the North Sea provide a euphoric golfing atmosphere which not even the dreaded Foxy, the 14th can quell. This 459-yard double dog-leg is typical of Dornoch's fiendish ingenuity. It needs two massive shots to reach the plateau green if there is any wind, and just to complicate matters one has to be drawn and the other faded. There are no bunkers—that would be adding agony to injury—but if you get a 4 here you definitely deserve a large dram of Glenmorangie, the fine local malt whisky, when you get back to the hospitable clubhouse.

If you also make par at the tricky downhill 17th, with its tremulous second shot over ridged bunkers, you definitely deserve a second dram—perhaps Dalmore this time from the distillery just down the coast at Alness.

The main problem with Dornoch is accessibility. It is 51 miles north of Inverness and more than 600 miles from London, unquestionably the most northerly great golf course in the world. The bridge recently built across the Dornoch Firth makes it easier to reach but it is quite definitely in the category defined in the *Guide Michelin* as *vaut le voyage*. There are three other good courses at Brora, Golspie and Tain nearby and the Dornoch Hotels organise a Golf Week in September. Ring Michael Ketchin at the Dornoch Castle Hotel (0862-810216) for full details.

There is no better golfing bargain. After all, if you start at 7am you can easily play three rounds a day in the long northern summer light—with plenty of time between them to sample the splendid Dornoch cuisine.

The Bishop's Room, Dornoch Castle Hotel, Dornoch, Sutherland IV25 3SD
tel: (0862) 810216 **
Dornoch Castle, on the main street of the town, was formerly the Palace
of the Bishops of Caithness and was built in the late fifteenth century on
the site of an earlier palace. Today it is a comfortable hotel personally
managed by its owner, Michael Ketchin, and it has an excellent restaurant
in what used to be the kitchen of the former Bishops' Palace, where
fresh local produce features strongly on the menu. Starters may include
ham and pepper salad or duck and mushroom vol au vent, followed by
lobster Hebridean, herring Rob Roy with mustard sauce, Aberdeen
Angus steaks, venison, salmon or rosemary-flavoured leg of lamb. The
lavish wine list covers eleven countries with more than forty wines at
less than £10 a bottle and yet offering such more expensive splendours
as a 1961 Clos René from Pomerol, a 1976 Leoville-Poyferré and several
excellent burgundies as well as a generous selection of half-bottles and
some bargains in respectably aged Italian and Spanish wines.

NAIRN, tel: (0667) 52787   *6556 yards SSS 71*

RESTAURANT
Golf View Hotel **

In stature Nairn Golf Club ranks second only to Dornoch among the
Highland courses. It lies west of the town along the shore of the Moray
Firth and starts off east to west into the prevailing wind. Essentially a links
course with fine springly fairways, plenty of heather and banks of whin and
few wind-sculpted trees give it character and challenge.
The par is 71 and it is a well-earned score if you and your handicap make
it, for this is a course which calls on all the golfing skills to master its
problems and its subtleties. The first nine is 220 yards shorter than the
homeward half with just one par 5 at the 501 yard 7th. The second nine
opens and closes with holes over 500 yards and there are three long par 4s
at the 12th, 13th, and 16th. There was a time when you could pretty easily
have formed a Cabinet from the summer golfers at Nairn. Viscount Finlay,
president of the club for eighteen years was Lloyd George's Lord Chancellor,
another president, the Earl of Cawdor was First Lord of the Admiralty,
A J Balfour, Ramsay Macdonald, Harold Macmillan and Willie Whitelaw
are other prominent political names. Viscount Whitelaw, still a Nairn
enthusiast, wrote the introduction to the club's centenary book in 1987.
Many important championships have been played here and Nairn claims to
have invented the Golf Week in 1959 with the help of Eric Brown and Henry
Cotton. Nairn Dunbar at the other end of the town is much the same length
as the senior club, rather more sheltered from the North Sea winds except
on the three holes just before the turn but still a fine test of golf.

Golf View Hotel, Seabank Road, Nairn IV12 4HD tel: (0667) 52301 **
This friendly and comfortable hotel which organises its own golf weeks
has an excellent restaurant, which subscribes to the belief that the
Highlands is a haven for gourmets and sets out to prove it with its menus.

Chicken liver tartlet followed by fresh asparagus baked in pastry with chervil butter sauce, red peppers and bay-leaf salad; white cabbage and carroway soup; melon sorbet, cutlets and noisettes of lamb with spinach, walnut and port sauce, strawberry bavaroise, coffee and home-made tablet were on the menu when I was last there. The wine list is splendid, lacking only a proper representation of Australia (but perhaps Greg Norman has been to see them since I last dined there). A modest par 4 from Nairn golf course.

INVERNESS, tel: (0463) 33422   *6226 yards SSS 70*

RESTAURANTS
Culloden House Hotel **** Glen Mhor **

The Inverness course at Culcabock Road is on the eastern side of town, a pleasant parkland lay-out webbed with streams and bordered by handsome trees wih a first nine which has two par 5s but is made 250 yards shorter than the back nine (which has no par 5s) by having three par 3s and two rather short par 4s. There are five holes across the road from the main parkland on the rather different territory of a raised beach which provides holes on two levels finishing with the very tricky par 3 15th, which requires a tee-shot of great accuracy to hold the green. Not too demanding but a very pleasant day's golf.

Culloden House Hotel, Culloden, by Inverness IV1 2NZ
tel: (0463) 790461 ****
This elegant and historic house is where on 15 April 1746 Bonnie Prince Charlie spent the night before Culloden, the last battle fought on British soil. Today it is a beautifully furnished and well-run hotel with a fine restaurant, serving such Scottish delights as smoked haddock and onion soup, grilled scallops with pimento and tomato coulis, seasonal game, long-hung Aberdeen Angus steaks, marinated loin of venison and a fine choice of Scottish cheeses. The wine list is extensive and well chosen and there is an ample selection of half-bottles and, of course, a fine range of malt whiskies.

Glen Mhor, Ness Bank, Inverness IV2 4SG tel: (0463) 234308 **
Nicol Manson's small hotel on the south bank of the River Ness just below the castle has a fine river-view restaurant which runs the whole gamut of Scottish fare in its menu—game, beef, lamb, salmon in various forms, langoustines, mussels, oysters and fresh fish, all cooked to order. Nicol is a very knowledgeable wine enthusiast and his list is both comprehensive and fascinating with lots of interesting wines and some true bargains.

FORT WILLIAM, tel: (0397) 4464   *6218 yards SSS 71*

RESTAURANTS

Inverlochy Castle **** Crannog **

This relatively new moorland course (it opened in 1976) is the only one in the area and has a superb setting. It lies at the foot of Ben Nevis where the mountain path to the steep North Face begins, off the main road to the north of the town. It begins with a stiff short par 4, needing a drive across a small glen and continues through a long and well-designed first half with two holes of more than 500 yards. It eases up on the second nine but it is a good sporting test and the scenery, overlooked by the highest mountain in Britain, is magnificent.

Inverlochy Castle, Fort William PH33 6SN tel: (0397) 2177 ****
This extremely grand hotel has been at a height in the Scottish culinary scene comparable to that of Ben Nevis across the road for many years. Although there have recently been changes in the kitchen, the meticulous standards have been scrupulously maintained and the finely judged compromise between British and European dishes is still there. The superb roasts, the excellent seafood and the list of classic wines are outstanding.

Crannog, Town Pier, Fort William PH33 7NG tel: (0397) 3919 **
A crannog is an ancient Scottish loch-house on stilts and this restaurant in a former bait store overlooking Loch Linnhe fulfils its name well enough. The speciality is large platefuls of seafood, caught by the fishermen of the company which owns the restaurant and markets its harvest from the sea all over Britain. Langoustines come with very garlicky butter, new potatoes and mixed salad. There is splendid fish soup and smoked fish from the Crannog smoke-house. Skate with black butter, pickled herrings, crab terrine and all kinds of other fish, exceptionally fresh and generally simply cooked, are the staples. The wine list is not very high powered but there is a decent house white for £6.50.

GLENCRUITTEN tel: (0631) 62868 *4414 yards SSS 63*

RESTAURANTS
Knipoch Hotel, Kilninver **** Loch Melfort Hotel, Arduaine ***

Oban's only golf course despite its shortness is quite entertaining to play and there are very few courses on the west coast of Scotland until you get to Glasgow or farther south. A full-sized course in Argyll (other than the splendid Machrihanish) has been talked about for years but nothing has happened so far. Glencruitten was designed by the great James Braid and he employed all his renowned ingenuity on it. Laid out in a fertile glen surrounded by cliffs, it demands some decidedly adventurous drives and approach shots to and from tees and greens sculpted from crag faces. Good fun.

Knipoch Hotel, Kilninver, Oban PA34 4QT tel: (085-26) 251 ****
The Craig family's restaurant in this hotel overlooking Loch Feochan, 8 miles south of Oban on the A816, serves five-course set meals of classic quality. The main course might be chicken with local wild mushroom stuffing, duck-in-port sauce, salmon, lamb or beef. Interesting soups are usually the first course followed by a terrine or pâté with a fruit sauce

with cheese and dessert to close. There is an astonishing wine list, exceptionally well annotated, covering a wide spectrum of countries and offering some very distinguished bottles.

Loch Melfort Hotel, Arduaine PA34 4XG tel: (085-22) 233 ***
The coast of Argyll offers some of the most spectacular sea views in the world and the restaurant of the Loch Melfort Hotel, 19 miles south of Oban, has one of the finest of them all: a great sea sweep southwards across Asknish Bay to the green hills of Shuna and Luing and the peaks of Scarba and Jura. Chef-proprietor Philip Lewis makes sure the food matches the setting—superb lobster from their own creels in the bay, delicious oysters, coulibiac of salmon and sole, lamb cutlets with a wild-mushroom sauce. A collection of tempting puds and a good cheese-board are also on the daily-changing menu.
The wine list is extensive rather than expensive—thirty-six wines for less than £12 a bottle and a reasonable choice of halves as well as a selection of modest, decently-aged clarets.

MACHRIHANISH, tel: (058681) 213 *6228 yards SSS 70*

RESTAURANTS
Seafield Hotel, Campbeltown **   Lock 16, Crinan Hotel, Crinan ****

Although it lies 30 miles south of Glasgow by latitude (and 140 miles by the road twisting round the lochs), Machrihanish, 5 miles west of Campbeltown on the Atlantic coast of the Mull of Kintyre, is still in the Highlands and its 116-year-old golf course is one of the finest in Scotland. When it was laid out by Old Tom Morris in 1876, the doyen of Scottish professionals said of the links that 'Providence surely intended them as a paradise for the game.' The present lay-out is that adjusted by J H Taylor in 1914 to allow for improvements in clubs and balls. Each hole has its own character and at the 1st 423-yard part 4 you drive across the Atlantic and agonised decisions involving wind and weather have to be taken before you decide how much of it you can carry. The greens are large but convoluted, there are dips and hummocks and every hole demands thought and correct club selection—not always easy first-time round because there are quite a few blind shots. There is nothing west of you here except America and on a fine day there are wonderful views over Gigha, Jura and Islay and magnificent sunsets as you sip your Campbeltown malt in the clubhouse and reflect on what might have been. Modern scepticism suggests that Old Tom's tribute to the Almighty as a golf-course architect was something he said to every club who called him in as a course designer, but the experience of playing on the springy turf of Machrihanish will mute your cynicism and have you believe that for this superb setting for the 'antient and healthfull exercise' Tom and Providence got it absolutely right.

Seafield Hotel, Kilkerran Road, Campbeltown PA28 6JL
tel: (0586) 54385 **
This Victorian villa on the shores of Campbeltown Loch (famous for the song 'Oh, Campbeltown Loch I wish you were whisky!') was built by the

family which created Springbank whisky, one of the two remaining Campbeltown malts, and its restaurant makes the most of local produce like seafood and salmon, game in season and Scottish beef and lamb cooked simply and well.

Lock 16, Crinan Hotel, Crinan PA31 8SR tel: (054-683) 261 ∗∗∗∗
It is cheating to list Nick and Frances Ryan's great seafood restaurant on the Crinan Canal with Machrihanish when I have tried only to include restaurants within 20 miles of the golf course. But although Lock 16 is more than 50 miles from Machrihanish, I excuse myself on the grounds that unless you fly into Campbeltown or bring your clubs by boat, you will have to pass nearby on your way back and that if you turn west at Lochgilphead it is only 5 miles to the blue-and-white dining room with vast seascapes in the windows and seafood which is landed 50 yards from Nick Ryan's kitchen. There is a five-course menu which offers jumbo prawns which have battled their way through the Corryvreckan whirlpool between Jura and Scarba, sizzled with tropical fruit, mussels marinière from Loch Craignish a few miles to the north, langoustines, lobster, crab, scallops, oysters, locally smoked and wild salmon and, if you insist, Scottish beef or lamb. Good list with some interesting bottles at fair prices. House wine from France at £9.50 a bottle.

MACHRIE, Islay, tel: (0496) 2310   *6226 yards SSS 71*

RESTAURANTS
Kilchoman House, by Bruichladdich ∗∗   Machrie Hotel ∗∗

Islay is home not only to seven of the most flavoursome malt whiskies in the world but also to Machrie, a golf course of a similarly unique status. It was laid out in 1891 and in its early hey-day attracted players like Braid, Taylor and Vardon to compete in its annual tournament. In 1978 it was altered by Donald Steel to bring it into line with modern equipment standards and it remains by far the best course in the Western Isles. Overlooking Laggan Bay, next to the airport, it is no holiday course but a testing links for real golfers with infinite sea-views, burns, bumps and hollows, two tough par 5s and lots of other intriguing problems from fairway to green.
Murdo Macpherson, owner of the course and the nearby Machrie Hotel which doubles as the clubhouse, is so convinced of the virtues and attractions of his remote course that he offers a whole series of bargain price golf packages from Mini-Breaks of three nights upwards which include free golf, bed and Highland breakfast, dinner and air travel from Glasgow, the perfect get-away-from-it-all golfing dream. The food in the hotel has recently been upgraded from solid and substantial to something more subtle and sophisticated. Playing at Machrie is an unforgettable experience. You can get to Islay by air from Glasgow or by Caledonian Macbrayne car ferry from West Loch Tarbert in Argyll.

Kilchoman House, by Bruichladdich, Islay PA49 6UY
tel: (0496) 85 382 ∗∗
Lesley and Stuart Taylor's restaurant and self-catering cottages in the far

west Rhinns of Islay not only merit a detour but necessitate one. There is no passing trade because there is nowhere to pass to, unless you fancy chasing wild goats among the crags of Creag Mhor and Cnoc Dubh, so it is essential to book. The detour is well worth making, not only for the scenery and the welcome but because here is the best food in the island, imaginatively prepared from fresh, mostly local ingredients. Kilchoman House was once a manse and is said to have been built on the site of the summer palace of the Lords of the Isles.

The wild venison with rowan jelly is the best I have eaten (on the neighbouring island of Jura, deer outnumber people by about 20–1), drunken bullock, chicken with Islay cheese, wonderful scallops, lobster and enticing puds make up a seductive menu. There is well-chosen list with some interesting wines at sensible prices.

BOAT OF GARTEN, tel: (047-983) 351   *5672 yards SSS 69*

RESTAURANTS
Auchendean Lodge, Dulnain Bridge ∗∗∗   The Cross, Kingussie ∗∗∗

To complete the Highland region we must go back some 220 miles to the north-east as the eagle flies to find at Boat of Garten, just 5 miles north of Aviemore on the banks of the Spey, what most travelled golfers would agree is the finest short course in Britain. Cut through a birch forest by James Braid with the great 4000-feet peaks of the Grampians, Cairngorm and Braeriach, Cairn Toul and Ben Macdui gleaming on the southern horizon and the salmon and whisky-rich Spey gurgling nearby, this is one of the most glorious places in the world to play golf. Don't let its modest length deceive you, The Boat is no pushover. All that power will get you here is trouble. From the quiet opening par 3 onwards and inwards, it is accuracy that will pay dividends. The second shot to the 2nd, uphill to the gorse-enshrouded green; the narrow drive to the corner of the dog-leg down an avenue of silver birch at the 6th; the huddle of bunkers round the green which awaits your tee-shot at the short 16th and the tough tight finish at the 18th where out-of-bounds hugs the high green will all test your shot-making ability to the full. If it doesn't all work quite as it should, well, there is no better place to sniff the clear air, listen to the river and look at the scenery.

Auchendean Lodge, Dulnain Bridge, Grantown-on-Spey PH26 3LU
tel: (047-985) 347 ∗∗∗
Dulnain Bridge is just 7 miles up the Spey to the north-east of Boat of Garten. This former hunting lodge, with wonderful views over the river and Abernethy forest to the Cairngorms, has an excellent restaurant which makes a feature of using wild products from the woods and hillsides around. Shaggy ink-cap soup, wild-mushroom pâté, steak of venison in rowan sauce and mallard with blaeberries are among the locally inspired dishes. Arbroath smokies in ale and cream and smoked-haddock tartare come from rather farther away but are still decently indigenous. There is a long and interesting wine list and, as befits

Speyside the home of more distilleries than anywhere else in Scotland, a wide choice of malt whiskies.

The Cross, 25–27 High Street, Kingussie PH21 1HX
tel (0540) 661762 **
The Hadleys' highly successful restaurant has people driving for 2 hours from Edinburgh to eat there so the 17 miles south from Boat of Garten for dinner at The Cross is no problem. No-one seems to be quite sure whether it is a top-class country inn or a fine gourmet restaurant which happens to be in a small Highland town. Such delicate distinctions hardly matter when the food is as good as it is here. Soups made with pimento and tomato or chanterelles flavoured with garlic or fennel, pike mousseline, Hramsa mushrooms, local lamb with sorrel cream, fillet of wild roe deer, duck with ceps and ginger, calf's liver with pear purée give some idea of the imaginative scope of the menu and Ruth Hadley's cooking matches the originality of the ingredients. There is a long and lovingly advocated wine list ranging from Bulgarian at £4.95 to 20-year-old claret at £130 with almost everything except Italian wines in between. There are plenty of half-bottles so you can chop and change on individual preferences and courses, and such old-fashioned notions as pudding wines are given proper attention.

MORAY, Stotfield Road, Lossiemouth IV3 6QS tel: (034-381) 2018
Old: 6643 yards SSS 72   New: 6005 yards SSS 69

RESTAURANT
Park House Restaurant, Elgin **

Two splendid links courses, one a centenarian and the other designed by Henry Cotton in 1979, lie behind the dunes on the strip of land between the sea and the RAF base at Kinloss. The Old Course twists and turns so that you seldom face the same wind conditions at consecutive holes and although all the usual seaside hazards present themselves—lots of tricky, steep-faced bunkers, swales and hillocks—the greens are flat and true. The last hole is justly famous for its demands on the second shot which must be struck with real authority and judgement to avoid the gorse and the bunkers and find the raised green just below the grey stone clubhouse. The 17th has a sinister reputation for a different reason for it was on the green of this hole that Prime Minister Herbert Asquith was attacked while on holiday by militant suffragettes. The Scottish Amateur Championship and other important tournaments have been played on this course.

Park House, South Street, Elgin IV30 1JB tel: (0343) 7695 **
Elgin is just 5½ miles from Lossiemouth (and has a fine golf course of its own at Hardhillock). At the pleasing Georgian-style Park House restaurant at the west end of the town, cooking is unelaborate but good with a strong emphasis on local produce from the rivers, the sea, the hills and the fertile fruit gardens of Morayshire. Smoked salmon and avocado soufflé, venison casserole and cranachan are among the specialities. There is a sound short wine list.

North-East

ROYAL ABERDEEN, Balgownie, Links Road, Bridge of Don, Aberdeen AB2 8AT tel: (0224) 702571 *6372 yards SSS 71*

RESTAURANTS
New Marcliffe Hotel ✳✳✳ Silver Darling ✳✳

The first reference to golf in the annals of Aberdeen is in the Town Council Register of October 1598 in a statute against 'playirs on the links during the time of the sermones' but Royal Aberdeen traces it origins back only to the formation in 1780 of The Society of Golfers at Aberdeen, a very exclusive club whose rules stated that not more than twenty-five members resident in Aberdeen were ever to be admitted! The Ballot Box by which this exclusivity was decided is in the clubhouse with a very handsome, intricately carved Captain's chair in which the holder of that august office still sits on ceremonial occasions. Balgownie, where the Club has played since 1888, is a delight, one of these real Scottish golf links found nowhere else in the world. It combines dunes, views over the steel-grey North Sea, bents grass, whins, rolling fairways and bunkers in an amalgam which makes it a very testing course indeed. The first hole takes you towards the sea, with the oil tenders and tugs moving across it to and from the oil rigs offshore. For seven of the next eight holes you play northwards, usually starting from a high tee in the dunes, driving over rough territory to narrow fairways, hummocked and rolling, with tight entrances to greens yawning with bunkers. After the 9th, up by the boundary fence with the Murcar course to the north and the fishermen's bothy with nets drying on rough-hewn trellises outside, you turn south to drive over a wild and menacing hill with an out-of-bounds fence on the right, an invisible bunker to the left and a burn and a valley in front of the green.

The boundary fence haunts you most of the way inwards and there is a long tough road home to the clubhouse at the 443-yard 18th, where after a solid drive, you need a strong second to carry the ridge in front of the green which will bounce anything short off into one of the waiting bunkers. A great course.

New Marcliffe Hotel, 51–53, Queen's Road, Aberdeen AB9 2PE
tel: (0224) 321371 ✳✳✳
This comfortable hotel on the west side of the city has a good restaurant which specialises on Scottish food fresh from the hills, moors, seas and rivers. There are carvery lunches and à la carte dinners which feature such dishes as collops of monkfish with ginger and spring-onion sauce, venison medallions with brambles and port, fillet of pork in a roulade with smoked goose, and asparagus and pavlovas made with whichever fruits are in season. Sound wine list.

Silver Darling, Pocra Quay, Footdee, Aberdeen AB2 1DQ
tel: (0224) 576229 ✳✳
This French-run restaurant by the round pilot house at the end of North Pier specialises in fresh fish and shellfish sometimes barbecued à la

Provençale but also more classical dishes like jumbo prawns with beurre nantaise or mussels cooked with herbs and cream, hot oysters with garlic and shallot butter or a mixed grill of fish or scallops with a wine sauce. Short and not very graciously-priced wine list.

BALLATER, Ballater AB3 5QX tel: (03397) 55567   *6106 yards SSS 69*

RESTAURANTS
Tullich Lodge ∗∗∗   The Green Inn ∗∗

This is Royal Deeside just a few miles from Balmoral, Her Majesty the Queen's Scottish home. The course was opened in 1906 with a classic exhibition match between Harry Vardon and James Braid but the club was formed earlier and has its centenary in 1992. In a magnificent setting on the banks of the famous salmon river, the Dee, there are impressive mountains looming on either side but the course is laid out on the moorland turf of the open glen. The 1st is a testing long hole with a ditch crossing the fairway and there are several other holes in the longer first half where distance is important. Five par 3s take the pressure off a bit, although one or two of them, notably the 9th, are no pushover.

Tullich Lodge, on A93 1 mile east of Ballater, AB3 5SB
tel: (03397) 55406 ∗∗∗
In one of the most delightful small hotels in Britain, a pink granite Victorian mansion built a century ago by an Aberdeen advocate on a wooded hill overlooking the Dee, Neil Bannister and Hector Macdonald run one of the best restaurants in the country. The mahogany-panelled dining room serves a four-course dinner which offers no choice (although vegetarian dishes can be ordered in advance) and everything is fresh. There is salmon and sea trout, grouse, pheasant and venison in season, sea fish comes from the quaysides of Aberdeen and Buckie, meat from the local butcher, most vegetables from the kitchen garden where there is also a smokery. Mussels in white-wine sauce, mushrooms au gratin, marinated smoked herring with avocado, spiced carrot soup, succulent pink Aberdeen-Angus beef, hot-pot with beetroot, braised ox-tail with spring cabbage, home-made haggis are samples of the dishes on offer. There is an excellent wine list at reasonable prices, almost all of it French and a splendid selection of malt whiskies. Closed December to end of March.

The Green Inn, 9 Victoria Road, Ballater AB3 5QQ
tel: (03397) 55701 ∗∗
This small restaurant in the centre of the town, on the green, specialises in local produce. The Chef's Special, which changes every night, may feature salmon from the Dee, game from the hills or venison in season, or the harvest of the North Sea in the form of baked crab with chives and cheese sauce or seafood gâteau. Good puds like hot strawberries in Drambuie sauce with home-made ice cream and Scottish cheeses. Short wine list.

BLAIRGOWRIE, Rosemount, Blairgowrie PH10 6LG tel: (0250) 2594
Rosemount 6581 yards SSS 72 Lansdowne 6865 yards SSS 73

RESTAURANTS
Kinloch House Hotel, Essendy *** The Log Cabin Hotel, Kirkmichael ***

Rosemount, the older course at Blairgowrie has long been known as one of the finest and most beautiful inland courses in Britain. Each hole is separate, carved through forests of birch, larch and pine with perilous heather lurking by the fairway's edge. Driving is of supreme importance here, for, if you do not hit the ball straight from the tee, you will either be in heather or find your second shot blocked by trees or, at least, complicated by having to negotiate a most difficult entrance to the green plagued with bunkers. The 5th is a tough par 5 made even more difficult by the huge birch tree in the middle of the fairway which comes into play on the second shot. There are other good long holes and some tricky short ones and the 16th, a 487-yard par 5 where you drive across the Black Loch to a tree-lined fairway turning left is a lulu. A par here is something of a triumph. The Lansdowne, cut through a pine forest by Peter Alliss and Dave Thomas in the 1970s, is also a challenging lay-out with many long par 4s as well as two 5s well over 500 yards in length and only three par 3s. Two tough but fascinating courses side by side is something not often found.

Kinloch House Hotel, Essendy by Blairgowrie PH10 6SG
tel: (025-084) 237 ***
On the Dunkeld road 3 miles west of Blairgowrie, this delightful old country house, surrounded by rhododendrons and the peace of the countryside, serves beautifully cooked food mostly of the traditional style such as salmon, game and steaks, whole lobsters and sardines grilled fresh from the Atlantic, marinated salmon, good soups and generous sweets, very much country cooking old style but all the better for that. Proprietor David Shentall likes his guests to be well dressed—gentlemen must wear ties—but service is warm and attentive. A fine list with good vintage clarets covering the last twenty years, vintage ports and a good selection of half-bottles as well as an exceptional range of malt whiskies.

The Log Cabin, Kirkmichael, by Blairgowrie PH10 7NB
tel: (025-081) 288 ***
Kirkmichael is 12 miles north-west of Blairgowrie off the road to Pitlochry. This Norwegian-style log cabin high in Glen Derby serves delicious and original food and specialises in game dishes from the local hills along with beef collops, lamb Lady Lucy and exotic sweets like cinnamon-flavoured hazelnut tart with Blair Castle raspberries and chocolate whisky gâteau. Good wine list. A comfortable and interesting place to stay or eat in spectacular surroundings.

PITLOCHRY, Golf Course Road, Pitlochry tel: (0796) 2792
5811 yards SSS 68

RESTAURANTS
Birchwood Hotel ✳✳✳ Dunfallandy House ✳✳

Do not be deceived by the modest yardage. Despite there being no par 5s in sight, this uphill course rising to holes with magnificent views down over Glen Tummel, towards Schiehallion and up the slopes of neighbouring Ben Vrackie, needs every shot in the bag. It was here that John Panton, the doyen of Scots golf professionals, learned the game and you only have to play a few holes to understand how he became such a wonderful iron player. A stream and some cunningly placed bunkers call for careful shot-making at the 1st and there is out-of-bounds on the right on nine holes starting with this one. Although only four holes are more than 400 yards in length the undulating fairways and uphill-downhill nature of the course make it a real test of accuracy and club choice. Naturally there are some demanding par 3s, the best of which is probably the 16th which has six bunkers round the green, out-of-bounds on the right and breathtaking views over the Tay and the Tummel to provide additional distraction from the high tee. A spectacular and truly enjoyable course.

Birchwood Hotel, East Moulin Road, Pitlochry PH16 5DW
tel: (0796) 2477 ✳✳✳
This Victorian manor house in its own grounds has a choice of à la carte and table d'hôte menus and a reputation for fine food and enterprising cooking, which can offer dishes such as smoked venison with pear, creamed Arbroath smokies, trout from the local reservoir, Loch Faskally, Highland steak with a whisky sauce and sirloin stuffed with haggis. There is a long and well-chosen wine list. Open March to November.

Dunfallandy House, Logierait Road, Pitlochry PH16 5NA
tel: (0796) 2648 ✳✳
This Georgian mansion house was built in 1790 for General Archibald Fergusson, son of the famous Scots philosopher of the Enlightenment Adam Fergusson, who was born at Logierait. Set on the west bank of the River Tummel, it commands superb views up the glen and over the elegant town of Pitlochry and it retains much of its eighteenth-century magnificence in its current role as a twentieth-century country-house hotel. It must be doubted if General Archibald or his father ever ate as well as guests may do now by candlelight in the handsome dining room where the menu offers interesting dishes from local ingredients such as wild-duck breasts poached with chanterelles, garden herbs and claret, salmon and trout prepared in different ways, steaks and game and a comprehensive list which takes proper notice of Californian and Australian as well as European wines. Open March to October.

MURRAYSHALL, New Scone, Perth PH2 7PH   tel: (0738) 51171
6446 yards SSS 71

RESTAURANTS
Old Masters Restaurant, Murrayshall ★★★★
Number Thirty-Three, Perth ★★★

Murrayshall, just 4 miles north-east of Perth off the A94, is that rarity in Scotland an interesting golf course attached to an hotel of quality where the pleasures of gourmet golf can be indulged in one place. Designed in 1981 by Hamilton Stutt the lay-out has six par 5s and five 3s with the home nine the longest by some 150 yards. A hilly parkland course with splendid oak, copper beech and chestnut trees and with six holes where water comes into play, it has a few bland and undistinguished holes and one badly-designed dog-leg where you have to hit short off the tee and long for the second shot.

There are some pretty holes and many command sweeping views of the Perthshire countryside among them the par-3 *Schiehallion* from which the famous conical peak above Loch Rannoch can be seen on the western horizon. Golf carts are available but there are several long par 4 and par 5 drags uphill for the walking player and a curiously laid-out finish of 3, 5, 3, 5, 3.

Opening with a fairly straightforward uphill par 4 with an ill-defined green blocked by sentinel pines, you are then launched into two par 5s, one up and one down, the first incorporating a wall and two large mid-fairway bunkers to threaten the drive and the other a fierce guardian set of bunkers across the approach to the angled green. Then it is over the water at the 4th as it is at the 10th, and so on until the finish around the clubhouse. A second course designed by Dave Thomas is currently under construction.

Old Masters Restaurant, Murrayshall Country House Hotel,
Scone PH2 7PH tel: (0738) 51171 ★★★★
Bruce Sangster, Murrayshall's award-winning chef draws on the produce of the hotel's four-acre garden to cook his Scots food with a French accent and to offer such dishes as home-cured gravad lax with dill sauce, puff-pastry pillow stuffed with wild mushrooms and sliced pigeon breast, gratin of Arbroath smokies and smoked salmon, cauliflower and smoked-cheese soup as starters followed by monkfish tails cooked in garlic curry and herbs, gâteau of roe deer with wild mushrooms in Arran mustard, grouse, fish stew or steak. Among the sweets are lemon tart and Murrayshall steamed sticky toffee pudding. There is an extensive and thoughtful wine list.

Number Thirty Three Seafood Restaurant, 33 George Street,
Perth PH1 5LA tel: (0738) 33771 ★★★
Gavin and Mary Billinghurst's restaurant in the centre of Perth is a charming art-deco setting for interesting and delicious mainly seafood meals. The Oyster Bar serves light meals and the mirrored dining room offers the full menu, including Mary's wonderful seafood soup, prawn and whitefish terrine with gruyère sauce, roast monkfish with smokey

bacon and tomato and basil sauce, baked-halibut steak with yoghurt and orange sauce, Mary's seafood casserole and various sweets, including the Perthshire favourite, sticky toffee pudding. A most carefully selected and fascinating wine list and first-class house wine in measures from a quarter-litre upwards. Not large, so it is essential to book but well worth the telephone call. Open Tuesday to Saturday except for ten days over Christmas and New Year.

GLENEAGLES, Auchterarder, Perthshire PH3 1NF   tel: (0764) 62231
King's: 6815 yards SSS 71   Queen's: 5964 yards SSS 69
RESTAURANTS
Conservatory, Gleneagles Hotel **** Cromlix House, Kinbuck ****

The two Gleneagles courses are among the finest inland courses in the world and here great golf and good food come as a package. The King's and the Queen's were both designed by James Braid, the first man to win the Open Championship five times and a new course, the Monarch, due to open in 1993, has as its architect Jack Nicklaus, the only man to win the Masters six times. If they ever decide to build another course at the Glen, I don't know where they are going to look for a designer!

From these two fine tests of moorland golf there are magnificent views over the Grampians to the north, the green Ochil hills to the south and the mountains of the Trossachs to the west. The turf is firm and springy underfoot, the peewits wheel and call overhead, pigeons clatter from the tall firs, grouse call from the heather and roe deer prance across the fairways from the stands of pine and silver birches.

The Gleneagles courses are Braid's finest creations. The King's is a testing 6452 yards off the medal tees, laid out for the most part on the highest ground with fairways of wonderful natural turf and superb, if difficult, greens. Like many great courses it begins deceptively. The 362 par 4 1st offers a huge fairway to the drive from the starter's box beside Ian Marchbank's shop and the second shot from this encouragingly open space to the plateau green looks easy. But the clear air makes distance tricky to judge and you are well advised to take a club more than the one you first thought of if you are not to finish up in the bunker 30 feet below the flag, from where you need a terrifyingly vertical wedge shot to have a putt for your 4. The great holes are not long in coming, the 3rd *Silver Tassie*, where a long second shot to the oval green has to carry a high ridge. *Het Girdle* the 5th, a short hole where your tee-shot must find and stay on the green with nothing but trouble everywhere else. All the holes have vernacular names, an education in the Scots tongue. The most famous is probably the 13th *Braid's Brawest*, 464 yards par 4. The drive has to carry a ridge with a large bunker and if you hit it perfectly, you still need a long iron or a second wood meticulously struck to the elevated well-protected green. The 17th, *Warslin' Lea*, often back into the wind, has probably ruined more good scores than any other hole. After a tight drive menaced by ridge and penal rough, it turns half-left and demands a second shot of canny judgement to catch the high kidney-shaped green.

The Queen's Course is not as long (5964 yards) but it is scenically very splendid with more trees and water than the King's. Very different in character, it has only one par 5, the 7th, *Westlin' Wyne*, a long downhill hole with out-of-bounds on the right and eight strategically sited bunkers. It is a testing driving hole because of the clutch of bunkers on the inside elbow of the slight dog-leg. Even if you do not reach them off the tee they impede your second shot and your view of another clutch of bunkers, short of and around the green, waiting eagerly to gobble up your ball.

Trees are much more of a feature on the Queen's than on the King's, although quite a few holes have a moorland quality. On the closing holes, water comes into play with two of the Queen's five beautiful short holes set around Loch an' Eerie and its forested island at the 13th and 14th and the need to carry another lochan off the tee demanded at the 18th.

These are courses on which it pays to be bold as well as accurate, the brave shot often pays off but there is always a way round for the higher handicap player. Gleneagles is dedicated to the recognition that not all players are tigers and that less bristling monsters are entitled to enjoy their game. For the Monarch, Jack Nicklaus has promised 'an accessible monster'. We shall see.

The Conservatory, Gleneagles Hotel, Auchterarder PH3 1NF
tel: (0764) 62231 ****
You can always be a tiger at the table if not on the course for in Gleneagles's main restaurant the Conservatory everything is cooked from raw. No convenience foods: nothing pre-prepared. All the dishes you eat from the world-ranging menu are prepared on site. The hotel has its own butchery and bakery.

Pâtés, galantines, terrines, butter and ice sculptures, croissants, scones, pastries and bread are all made in house. So there is a seasonal and international menu of some splendour, stressing the use of Scottish ingredients, and a magnificent wine list. Gleneagles is the only country hotel in Britain to receive the AA's highest award of five red stars.

Cromlix House, Kinbuck, Dunblane FK15 9JT tel: (0786) 822125 ****
Off the A9 on the Kinbuck–Braco road, Cromlix House lies in its own 5000-acre estate which has been in the same family for 400 years. In this wonderfully comfortable hotel, a rather forbidding-looking, late-Victorian mansion, the interior belies any external menace and there is a restaurant to match the splendour and luxury of the elegant furniture, porcelain, glass and silver and the family portraits of the Eden family. There are three dining rooms, one dominated by a striking portrait of the youthful Prince Rupert and in them chef Ian Corkhill offers a fixed four-course menu with alternatives. There could be sautéd partridge or breast of guinea fowl filled with foie gras, langoustine timbals with scallops, medallions of monkfish on an aubergine fondue with rosemary butter, fillet of beef, with madeira sauce or salmon en croute and beautifully made and most tempting desserts. There is a long and well-chosen wine list, very strong on clarets but descending as far as Chile, and recommended half-bottles to go with the various courses. Open all year: booking essential.

CARNOUSTIE, tel: (0241) 53249 *6936 yards SSS 74*

RESTAURANTS
Eleven Park Avenue, Carnoustie ∗∗   But 'n ben, Auchmithie ∗∗

Jack Nicklaus called it 'the longest toughest championship course in the world' just before the Open Championship was last played there in 1975 and Carnoustie has always had a formidable reputation as a golfing challenge—particularly when the wind blows. It has been dropped from the Open roster since that memorable play-off for the title between Jack Newton and Tom Watson, largely because of accommodation problems. However, most people who have played this great course will hope that those may soon be resolved and that Carnoustie at its formidable championship length of 7252 yards will once more be back on the top tournament circuit.

In true Scots tradition, this is no exclusive links populated by the gin and Jaguar mob but a course belonging to the Tayside town itself, where anyone can play and where golf has been played for more than 400 years. Carnoustie thinks it knows about golf—with some justification. Most of the 300 professionals who took the Scottish game to America came from the banks of William McGonagall's 'Silvery Tay' and these windswept links with their huddled copses of trees, treacherous bunkers and the dreaded Barry Burn spiralling fiendishly across the finishing holes commanded respect when hotel accommodation for players and spectators was not a key factor in deciding Open venues.

There are no easy holes on this course. The 1st is a long par 4, over the Barry Burn and at the 2nd you have to drive over Jockie's Burn and avoid the notorious Braid's Bunker 240 yards out in the middle of the fairway to set up your second shot. At the 3rd Jockie's runs just in front of the green: at the 6th, a superb long hole with out-of-bounds all down the left, it is too near the tee to be a menace but there is a diagonal ditch awaiting your second if you escape the fairway bunkers. And so the course unrolls, demanding concentration and positive shotmaking until you come to the 16th and the beginning of what is probably the most challenging finish in British golf. The 16th is a 238 par 3 with a tight entrance to the sloping green and six bunkers clustered around it. At the 17th the full menace of the sinuous Barry Burn comes into play.

At both closing holes you have to cross the burn twice. You can just about do it in one at the 17th if you are very long and straight with a following wind and tide. Against the wind you have to lay up on the tongue of fairway between the waters known as the Island. At the 18th, played in the opposite direction, the drive must be steered over the burn between the bunkers on the right and the out-of-bounds fence on the left and then you must carry the burn again 40 feet short of the green to get on in 2. Tough stuff.

Eleven Park Avenue, 11 Park Avenue, Carnoustie DD7 7JA
tel: (0241) 53336 ∗∗
The only drawback with this restaurant in a splendid Victorian house in the centre of Carnoustie is that it does not have a drinks licence. However you may bring your own wine and enjoy the well-cooked food

from fresh local produce which Park Avenue offers. There is game in season, good lamb and beef dishes, terrine made from Arbroath smokies and smoked salmon, ragoût of seafood and Glayva and heather honey ice cream. Open all year.

But 'n ben, Auchmithie DD11 5SO tel: (0241) 77223 **
This fisherman's cottage, 8 miles to the north-east of Carnoustie, on a turn-off towards the coast off the A92 just beyond Arbroath is very concerned with things of the sea and the principal ingredients in its simple but charming restaurant is fresh fish from the Arbroath boats. Naturally the Arbroath smokies are wonderful, for this delicious copper-coloured fish, most delicate of all smokehouse flavours, had its origins in Auchmithie. Fresh fish is also well cooked and there are simple sauces, baked potatoes, salads and vegetarian meals. Short, inexpensive but interesting, good wine list. Open all week except Tuesday and Sunday dinner.

DOWNFIELD, Turnberry Avenue, Dundee DD2 3QP   *6905 yards SSS 73*

RESTAURANTS
Jahangir, Dundee ** Raffles, Dundee **

Downfield is an unusual course for this part of the world. It is parkland, set in rolling woodlands on the north side of the city, tough, long and relatively sheltered. It opens with two long par 4s, both over 400 yards and then a 230-yard par 3, well bunkered with a sloping approach to the green which tends to throw the short ball into sand. Indeed, in the first nine the only holes less than 400 yards are the two par 3s and there is a 535-yard par 5 with a mind-concentrating stream looping across the fairway from 100 to about 20 yards from the green. The inward half is less merciless—there are actually three par 4 holes under 400 yards. At the par 5 11th you can have a go for the green in 2—if you think you can carry the ditch across the fairway 60 yards short of the flag. A number of championships have been played on this course among them the Ladies' Open, Scottish Amateur, the Benson and Hedges Matchplay and various international matches.

Jahangir, 1 Session Street, Dundee DD1 5DN tel: (0382) 202022 **
Dundee has had a long connection with the Indian sub-continent through the jute trade so it is not surprising to find that one of its best eating places is Indian. This exotically decorated restaurant with a splashing fountain in its centre has some interesting and unusual Eastern dishes on its menu, including Afghan Karie, Nepali and Kashmiri fruit curries, Jaipuri, Nentara and Masaledar dishes and an excellent Tandoori fish. There is a short wine list and Löwenbräu on draught.

Raffles, 18 Perth Road, Dundee   **
This relaxed café bistro near the university serves good food in a pale-washed, dark-wood room with lots of trailing plants and plates on the walls and windows overlooking the Tay Bridge at the back. Starters

include avocado with hot seafood, salmon and prawn mousse with fresh fruit and poppyseed toast and main dishes offer grilled fish, pan-fried steak with onions and whisky, served with asparagus and nutmeg-flavoured dauphinoise potatoes, chicken with herbs and the sweets are tempting, Italian chocolate torrone or elaborate sundaes. Good coffee and a decent short wine list with a choice of half-bottles.

Fife and the South-East

OLD COURSE, ST ANDREWS, tel: (0334) 73393   *6566 yards SSS 72*

RESTAURANTS
The Peat Inn, Peat Inn **** Old Course Restaurant, St Andrews ****

St Andrews is known as the Home of Golf, and the Old Course, whose history stretches back to at least the fifteenth century, is properly the most revered stretch of golfing territory in the world. It is just 1 hour and 10 minutes drive from Edinburgh airport and a couple of hours from Glasgow. In summer the only problem is getting on to the Old Course. Everyone wants to play it and, in my opinion, far too many who should not be allowed on it are permitted to play. There are three other courses at St Andrews: the New, opened in 1895 (6604 yards SSS 72); the Jubilee, opened in 1897 (6805 yards SSS 72); and the Eden, opened in 1913 (6400 yards SSS 70); and there will soon be another, the Strathtyrum, currently under construction.

You can easily absorb the atmosphere of the most famous links in the world from the New—and there are those in St Andrews who claim it is just as tough as its ancient neighbour. The courses run alongside with not even the barrier of the wall which separates the Old from the Eden, it is worth considering if you have a problem making a booking on the Old.

The St Andrews courses are public and belong to the town and from April to October on the Old Course, Monday to Saturday, there is a ballot for starting times. Entry to the ballot must be made by application in person or by telephone to the Starter (tel: 0334 73393) by 2pm on the previous golfing day.

The names chosen in the ballot and starting times are shown on the Starter's List which is displayed in the Caddies' Shelter, local golf clubs and the Information Centre in South Street from 4.30pm onwards. You can check your luck in the draw by telephone.

On Thursday and Saturday afternoons, alternate places are reserved for local players. The Old Course is closed in March and on Sundays because, as old Tom Morris said, 'The course needs a rest even if the players don't.' When the Open Championship was played at St Andrews in July 1990, the Old Course equalled Prestwick's record of hosting the tournament for the twenty-fourth time.

Many, many players have been deceived by the Old Course. It is not spectacular; it is not particularly beautiful—although few people can stand on the 1st tee below the solemn grey clubhouse of the Royal and Ancient Golf Club without a thrill and a tremor and the long bay sweeping eastwards to the sea and the gorsey humps and hollows in the blue distance have their own charm.

The 1st looks easy. It has the broadest fairway in the world, shared with the 18th. True, there is a stream, the Swilken Burn just in front of the green but what of that? It is a simple hole if you hit a straight drive (slightly out to the left, for the burn curves back towards you on the right), and a nerveless second over the burn. But wind and pin placement—and nerves—can make it very tricky.

And that is only the start. All the way out to the turn on the banks of the River Eden, there is rolling country, hillocks, gorse bushes and huge double greens where a careless approach can leave your ball 150 feet from the pin. There are steep-sided, deep and terrifying bunkers, often invisible from the fairway.

In the second nine there are tight, menacing out-of-bounds lines to be avoided along the Eden Course wall and the problems of threading your shots through fairways so savagely bunker-strewn they look as if they have been bombed. And of course there is the Road Hole.

'Straight out of a horror movie' is how one distinguished professional once described it to me. The drive at the 17th is hit over the corner of the Old Course Hotel to the fairway bending right. From there it is a long-to-medium iron to a very narrow green lying at an angle of 30 degrees to the fairway with the road behind it and the infamous pot bunker front left.

The Road Hole bunker is now known as 'The Sands of Nakajima' because Japanese champion, Tommy Nakajima took seven shots to get out of it in the 1984 Open. I have always preferred old-time golf writer, Bernard Darwin's terse description of it as 'room only for an angry man and his niblick'. One of the most formidable finishing holes in the world.

Peat Inn, Fife KY15 5LH tel: (033-484) 206 ✳✳✳✳
There is no dilemma when choosing where to eat in the St Andrews area. David Wilson's Peat Inn is not only one of the finest places to eat in Scotland but one of the best in Britain. At this simple but tasteful cottage restaurant 6 miles outside St Andrews at the cluster of houses named after the inn at the junction of the B940 and the B941, the food is superb and the wine list quite exceptional, strong on burgundies and clarets at reasonable prices even for exceptional wines, with some Californians, Australians and others, all carefully chosen.

All the standard Scottish strengths are in the menu. Fine beef and hill lamb, game and wild salmon; scallops, crab, lobster, mussels and sea-fresh fish from Fife's picturesque little fishing ports down the road.

Delicious un-Mediterranean fish soup, oysters in hot butter sauce, pigeon in a pastry case with wild mushrooms, warm monkfish and scallops on a potato galette, mouth-filling Peat Inn venison pie, wild duck with thyme, saddle of hare. The imagination and skill which David Wilson brings to cooking is a never-ending delight. And the puddings created by Patricia Wilson are splendidly extravagant rather than pricey. The great 1930s champion golfer, Bobby Jones once said 'If I had ever been set down in any one place and told I was to play there and nowhere else for the rest of my life, I should have chosen the Old Course.' If you substitute eating for golf that is rather how I feel about the Peat Inn. It merits not only a special expedition but the very real possibility of gettling lost in Nether Fife. Take the risk but phone first (0334 84-206). Naturally it is popular.

The Old Course Restaurant, St Andrews Old Course Hotel, Fife KY16 9SP tel: (0334) 74371 ★★★★
The Old Course Restaurant in the St Andrews Old Course Hotel, the yet again refurbished and reformed architectural monster which stands by the fairway of the 17th on the Old Course, is on the ground floor. Even more sensational views over the St Andrews' courses, the bay and the beautiful old university town can be had from the Road Hole Bar and Restaurant on the fourth floor. Wherever you eat, the food is good, self-consciously Scottish and offers a health menu choice. The menus, masterminded by executive chef Billy Campbell, have been constructed in consultation with international culinary maestro, Anton Mosimann. Mosimann, unquestionably one of the great chefs of our time, created *cuisine naturelle*, which, despite its French name, is a style influenced by both Japanese and English traditions. It avoids heavy cream, buttery sauces, overpowering spices, sugar or salt and conforms in a practical and delicious way to Mosimann's philosophy of living well, eating well and staying well.
The hotel has a built-in health spa and pool with all kinds of massage and treatment facilities and you can eat in either of the restaurants without departing from your regime. However, that does not mean that the food is skimpy or meagre in portion. Those not tied down by regimes can eat hearty grills of meat, game and fish from the rotisserie in the Road Hole restaurant or more subtly concocted dishes at ground level. There is a well-chosen wine list with a choice of half-bottles.

LADYBANK, Amsmuir, Ladybank KY7 7RA tel: (0337) 30725
6641 yards SSS 72

RESTAURANTS
Ostlers Close, Cupar ★★★★ Fernie Castle, Letham ★★★★

Outside Fife, Ladybank is a curiously unknown course which is a great pity in view of its qualities. Tom Morris had a hand in its original construction in 1879 but it has been altered several times since the Doyen of St Andrews laid out the original six holes. Today it is a fine and exacting parkland course set in a forest of mature oak, pine, rowan, chestnut, beech and birch. It begins quite fiercely. A difficult 349-yard par 4 with a lateral ridge in the centre of the fairway and a well-bunkered approach to the green leads to a tough 548-yard par 5 where trees narrow the drive landing area. There is another big par 5 of 543 yards at the 7th with a serpentine fairway with humps and ridges which goes two ways before it reaches the green. The 9th features a difficult second shot usually over trees to a green guarded by a large swale. There is another big par 5 at the 13th and some rugged par 4s all around the 400-yard mark before you get back to the neat modern clubhouse. Ladybank has been a qualifying course for the Open Championship on two occasions and in 1983, to celebrate the conversion of the Old Course Hotel to a country club, there was a memorable exhibition match between Jack Nicklaus and Severiano Ballesteros (Ballesteros won). Ladybank Golf Club is just a mile down the road to the south from the junction of the A91 and the A914.

Ostlers Close, Bonnygate, Cupar KY15 4BU   tel: (0334) 555742 ****
This award-winning small restaurant just off the main street in Cupar makes imaginative use of the fresh fish available just a few miles away on the Fife coast in its Pittenweem seafood dishes, shellfish and such things as Cream of Tay salmon soup but there is also game from Auchtermuchty, ducks and guinea-fowl from local farms and fruit from the Carse of Gowrie plus organic herbs and vegetables from chef James Graham's own garden to make up the interesting menu. A well-selected but rather uninformative wine list which includes several half-bottles. Open Tuesday to Saturday. Seats only thirty people, so best to book.

Fernie Castle, Letham KY7 7RU tel: (033-781) 381 ****
Built as a fortified hunting tower in the sixteenth century, Fernie Castle, about 2 miles north on the A914 from the Ladybank course, is now a comfortable and stylish country-house hotel set in 30 acres of quiet and sheltered grounds, known to be the home from home of a few of the more discerning golf writers when covering tournaments in these parts. The restaurant dinner menu is as enticing as the castle itself. Terrine of grouse and mallard with red-currant jelly; salmon poached and stuffed with lobster pâté; fillet of venison marinated in honey and served in a port and brandy sauce with wild mushrooms and sumptuous sweets using local fruit. Civilised wine list.

THE GOLF HOUSE CLUB, Elie, Leven KY9 IA5 tel: (0333) 330237

RESTAURANTS
Bouquet Garni, Elie **   The Cellar, Anstruther ***

The history of golf at Elie goes back a very long way to the end of the sixteenth century and the course is very much a traditional links with almost no concessions to modernity. The only one comes at the 1st hole where you have to drive over a ridge towards an invisible fairway and the starter uses a naval periscope salvaged from the submarine HMS *Excalibur* to see if the way is clear. Although there are no par 5s and only two par 3s, there are plenty of holes where the wind gets at you and makes scoring awkward. The holes along the sea from the short 11th to 13th have fine views over the bay to Kincraig Point but you may well be more concerned getting to the green in the regulation 2 on the 12th and 13th because both holes demand shots of some power and controlled direction especially when the wind is off the sea. There are two long par 4s at the 16th and 17th as well and the 18th is a fine finishing hole, bunkers all over the place, rough to the left and out-of-bounds to the right and through the back of the green to which you have to play a skilful second shot from a valley several feet below the flag.

Bouquet Garni, 51 High Street, Elie KY9 1BZ tel: (0333) 330374 ∗∗
In the middle of the East Neuk of Fife you would expect a restaurant to specialise in the sea fare which lands daily on the rugged stone doorsteps of the local harbours and of course the Bouquet Garni does just that with its langoustine and tomato bisque and fillet of salmon with langoustine mousse. But the warm candle-lit dining room also serves other Scottish dishes such as game in season, good beef, lamb and duck and particularly delicious vegetables. Open all year, Tuesday to Saturday.

The Cellar, 24 East Green, Anstruther KY10 3AA tel: (0333) 310378 ∗∗
In a village 5 miles north of Elie on the A917 this low-beamed, tiled-floor cellar with its tables made out of old sewing machines, takes itself seriously as a fish restaurant. Although there are lamb, chicken liver pâté and occasionally other non-marine items on the menu, for the most part it is seafood or salmon. The salmon comes with asparagus in pastry with a lemon sauce, there is home-made gravdlax, crayfish and mussel bisque, smoked-haddock pancake, turbot, halibut with hollandaise sauce, Chardonnay sauce to accompany the scallops, garlic butter with the langoustines. Uncomplex puds like spiced apple strudel and pineapple ice with chocolate sauce. The cooking is essentially simple using first-class raw ingredients in unsmothered style. There is a long wine list with an unusual range of Alsatian Gewurtztraminers, lots of New World Chardonnays, substantial Chablis and a selection of half-bottles. Open Monday to Saturday, excluding Monday lunch.

EDINBURGH

There are twenty-six golf courses within Edinburgh's city boundary and another sixty within less than an hour's drive from the centre. Edinburgh is the only place which could possibly challenge St Andrews for the title of the Home of Golf, for it was the Company of Gentlemen Golfers in Edinburgh who wrote the first rules for the game and founded themselves into a club when the city presented the first golf trophy in 1744, ten years before the founding of the Royal and Ancient Golf Club in St Andrews. But being the capital of Scotland and with so much else to boast about, Edinburgh has magnanimously foregone that distinction but you will find no other city where the game is so much a part of the fabric of living nor where the facilities for playing the game are so widespread, inexpensive and of such high quality.

As with the golf, so with the restaurants. Edinburgh, for some reason unplumbed by sociologists, is an eating-out city and there are probably more good restaurants in Edinburgh per head of population than anywhere else in the British Isles. The city has a population of under half a million and the statistics offered by other world-famous food guides support this vaunty claim to culinary distinction.

COURSES

BRAID HILLS, Braid Hills Approach, Edinburgh EH10 tel: (031) 447 6666

Up above the city is the site for two of Edinburgh's municipal courses. The Burgess Society cast covetous eyes on this site before the city bought it in 1893 but moved too slowly, despite receiving a report from one of the investigating committee which said 'The green is spendid.'
Whatever may have been the opinions of the burgesses in the 1860s, no-one now disagrees with that verdict for these rewarding courses set on the foothills of the Pentlands have wonderful sweeping views over the city and the estuary of the Firth of Forth.
Braids No 1 is the stiffer test with two par 5s both well over 500 yards but it is not the long holes but those specialising in the crag-to-crag shot, one being the tee and the other the green, with deep valleys in between, which gives Braids its individuality. There are a number of less mountainous holes but this is not a course for anyone with a coronary problem but for someone who is fit and likes to combine golf with hill-walking, the challenge of making really testing golf shots to difficult-to-catch greens with magnificent views over one of the loveliest cities in the world.

BRUNTSFIELD LINKS, 32 Barnton Avenue, Edinburgh EH4 6JH tel: (031) 336 4050

One of the oldest clubs in the world, Bruntsfield Links Golfing Society had its origins at Bruntsfield on the Boroughmuir, just a mile or so south of Edinburgh Castle, where the Scottish armies mustered to march to Flodden and where golf has been played since the fifteenth century, as the date of 1456 on the Golf Tavern overlooking the Links attests. There is still a pitch-and-putt course there.
The club moved to its present site at Davidson's Mains in 1895 where, as well as having an excellent golf course, it also enthusiastically maintains the traditions of hospitality associated with the game.
The rolling fairways of the course overlook the Forth with views across to the green hills of Fife. After a gentle opening, the 3rd and 4th set up a

challenge with two par 5s back to back, followed by a difficult par 3 and a tough uphill finish to the front nine.

The inward half has only one 5 but there are a lot of good holes including the 11th where the drive must be hit accurately between a wood and a hedge and the uphill 17th where a tired second shot can court disaster. Good food in the clubhouse.

DALMAHOY COUNTRY CLUB, Kirknewton EH27 8EB
tel: (031) 333 1845

The two courses built around the splendid William Adam mansion which was once the home of the Earl of Morton, were laid out by James Braid in 1927 and are now the main attraction of the recently formed Country Club. The East Course has been used for many tournaments, including the Haig Tournament Players' Championship, the Senior Service Wills Open and the Sun Alliance. Both nines begin with uphill par 5s of no great complexity but the 1st is followed by a string of long par 4s all considerably over 400 yards and culminating at the 5th with a hole of 461 yards with a view of the castle behind the green and a number of troublesome problems in front of it. You must keep your drive on the top half of the right to left slope not to run down into rough or trees and the long approach to the tilted green is an unyielding shot.

At the 7th there is a lake along the right but it only really comes into play at the 8th where it can swallow your drive if it is at all faded, and even eats into the right side of the green to catch the mis-directed pitch.

The second nine is more than 200 yards shorter but there are some bothersome holes particularly the 17th where you have to hit your approach to a high plateau green half-screened by a tree.

DUDDINGSTON, Duddingston Road West, Edinburgh EH15 3QD
tel: (031) 661 4301

'A good test for good golfers' someone once called this course and it is a pretty accurate description. Duddingston was originally a bankers and insurance companies' golf club but it shook off these restrictions after the First World War.

As one of the longest and most testing courses in the Lothians, it has been used for several championships and its formidable parkland lay-out certainly poses plenty of problems for everyone. It begins with a 507-yard par 5 and then immediately asks for different skills with a tough par 3 in the opposite direction. There are two more par 5s in the outward half, the longest the 544-yard 8th.

The inward half is shorter although the only par 5, the 17th incorporates a threatening pond. At the 18th the burn which featured at the first two holes comes back into play and when you have holed your final putt here, 'you know you've been on a golf course', as they are fond of saying to you over a drink in the clubhouse.

THE MUSSELBURGH GOLF CLUB, Monktonhall, Musselburgh
tel: (031) 665 2005

Be warned, there are three Musselburgh golf clubs all having their origins in the old Links Course of 1774 which still has nine holes surrounded by the race course to the east of the town. It was there that six of the early Open Championships were played in the nineteenth century (most of them won by Musselburgh golfers) and the player who won the first-ever Open at Prestwick in 1860 was Willie Park, a Musselburgh man.
Royal Musselburgh moved to Prestongrange in 1925 and still flourishes under the auspices of the Coal Industry Social and Welfare Organisation. Like Royal Musselburgh, the course at Monktonhall was designed by the omnipresent James Braid and it is a rugged lay-out with a lot of lengthy par 4s and four demanding par 5s, the most formidable at the 4th and the last, which is played uphill from the River Esk to the clubhouse. This is a good test of anyone's golf and a thoroughly enjoyable course to play, with a lot of variety between the holes on the river side and those on the other side of the railway.

MORTONHALL, 231 Braid Road, Edinburgh EH10 6PB
tel: (031) 447 2411

Mortonhall has had several revisions since the club was founded in 1892, the latest of which in 1979 did away with its notorious 'mountainous' finish along one of the northern ridges of the Pentlands foothills.
The new 6557-yard course has two par 5s in each half all over 500 yards and although the alpine finish may have gone, the hills still come into play by providing shelter from northerly winds. Mortonhall is a good example of getting a lot of golf course into a comparatively small space and its recent promotion to host important tournaments is well deserved.

ROYAL BURGESS, 181 Whitehouse Road, Barnton EH4 6BY
tel: (031) 339 6474

The Royal Burgess Golfing Society claims to be the oldest golf club in the world with a founding date of 1735, nine years earlier than the Honourable Company of Edinburgh Golfers, but the earliest documents in the club's archives go back only to 1773, although it is clear from them that golf was being played by members of the society for a long time before that. Like Bruntsfield next door, Royal Burgess had its origins on Bruntsfield Links and came to its present site just off the main road to the Forth Bridge, via Musselburgh.
This was in 1894 when the course was laid out by Old Tom Morris, with, inevitably, James Braid making amendments later. Mature parkland with many handsome trees and an air of aristocratic seclusion distinguishes the course but this slightly bland air is deceptive. Although there are only two par 5s, six par 4s over 400 yards present enough problems—at the 465-yard 4th, for example, a shot of both skill and power is required to negotiate the narrow entrance to the green. The short 13th is closely bunkered and at

201 yards you need a good long iron to reach and stay on the green and the dog-leg on the 15th needs a powerful drive if you are to avoid a large fairway tree blocking you second shot.

SILVERKNOWES, Silverknowes Parkway, Edinburgh EH44 5ET
tel: (031) 336 3843

Just along the road from the patrician links of Royal Burgess and Bruntsfield is Silverknowes, Edinburgh's newest municipal course, opened in 1947. It has the best views over the Firth of Forth and its islands of the three courses and is a spacious but interesting lay-out demanding accuracy rather than power at most holes, although at the last, at 601 yards the longest hole in Edinburgh, it needs both. The well-rounded fairways and the small greens make precision a real virtue and a good score will be made from well-played approaches rather than long tee-shots for which, with the exception of the 13th where you have to drive over the corner of a stand of trees, there is plenty of room.

RESTAURANTS

L'Auberge, 56 St Mary's Street, Edinburgh EH1 1SX
tel: (031) 556 5888 ★★★★
Daniel Wencker's entirely French-managed and French-staffed restaurant, just off the Royal Mile, is the most elegant and the most accomplished French restaurant in the capital. There is an inexpensive lunch menu which belies its price category but in the evening the food is more elaborate, the choice is wider and the prices naturally reflect this.
The menu and service are impeccably French, there are only French wines on the list and the food is a happy compromise between *cuisine nouvelle* and dishes of substance. It changes regularly but you are likely to be offered starters such as bisque de langoustines, aiguilettes de pigeon sur gaspacho, rabbit with herbs, fish soup, heart of artichoke salad or authentic pâté; main courses can be dishes such as fillet of porc with fennel and anchovies, sweet and sour breast of duckling, rabbit with honey and herbs, grilled shark with butter sauce or beef fillet with saffron and pink peppers.
The wine list is as distinguished as the food, the peach and grey restaurant has great charm and the attention is knowledgeable and friendly. L'Auberge is open seven days a week.

Champany Inn, Champany Corner, Linlithgow EH49 7LU
tel: (050 683) 4532 ★★★★
Clive and Ann Davidson's restaurant (turn right at exit 3 on the M9 to Stirling, just 20 minutes from Edinburgh and 10 miles from Dalmahoy) is dedicated to superb meat and seafood, mostly charcoal grilled. The steaks are hung for longer than almost anywhere else; you can pick your own lobster live from a stone-well nourrice. First courses can be shellfish, gravdlax, one of the in-house smoked meat or fish dishes. Main dishes are the wonderful steaks in various sizes and cuts, charcoal

grilled, for which Champany's is deservedly world famous, steamed lobster or steamed or grilled salmon or the best steak tartare I have ever eaten. There are simple but delicious puds like crème brûlée, Stilton which won the cheesemakers' top award for the UK and a wine list which boggles the mind. The first fifty pages are devoted to burgundies, then there are clarets, fastidiously chosen Rhône, Italian, Californian, Australian and South African vintages and about sixty half-bottles. Nothing is cheap but unless you are very fortunate, you may never have eaten such meat before and the choice on the wine list is dazzling.

There is also the Chop and Ale House next door where the theme of charcoal-grilled beef, lamb, lobster and salmon is pitched at a less expansive key with smaller portions and lower prices. Open Monday to Saturday, except for Saturday lunch.

Indian Cavalry Club, 3 Atholl Place, Edinburgh EH3 8HP
tel: (031) 228 3282 **
An upmarket smart Indian restaurant with the staff in military-style uniforms serving the kind of food you might eat at a regimental banquet in India: subtle and tempting dishes with some unusual accompaniments such as garlic nan and smoked-salmon rice. There is an especially good range of fish dishes—something missing from most Indian and Pakistani restaurants except for the ubiquitous prawn—like East Indian seafood soup, pomfret steamed with fresh coriander and tomatoes, spiced trout with mustard sauce and chilli garlic prawns with bhindi. As well as all the tikkas and tandoori there are Bombay chicken casserole with mushrooms and eggs in a ginger and herb sauce, Red Fort Chicken steamed with mild herbs and yoghurt with almonds, cashews and fresh tomatoes, lamb stewed in fresh spiced lemon juice with chick peas and ginger. There is a good wine list and the menu suggests wines to match dishes.

Kris, Malaysian Restaurant, 110 Raeburn Place, Edinburgh EH4 1HH
tel: (031) 315 2220 **
Kris Krishan's Malaysian restaurant in Stockbridge may be named after a ceremonial dagger but it certainly does not stab you in the wallet and th food on offer is original in flavour, appetising and generous.

Malay food has been subjected to many influences, particularly Indian and Chinese, but has retained flavours which give it a distinctive personality. On the menu are curries like Ikan which cooks fish with Malaysian spices and garlic. There is also Indonesian Nasi Goreng in an unusual mix of seafood, beef, chicken and vegetables with noodles, shredded egg and salad.

There is wok-fried, Chinese-style marinated beef in soy sauce, garlic and pepper and Malaysian satays made with Scotch beef and chicken, served with cucumber, pineapple and the traditional peanut sauce.

And there is a Taste of Malaysia menu which gives you a bit of nearly everything. Prices are reasonable, service is cheerful and there is an excellent list which comes from one of Edinburgh's best wine merchants, Raeburn Wines across the road.

Martins, 70 Rose Street North Lane, Edinburgh EH2 3DX
tel: (031) 225 3106 ***
Martin and Gay Irons' restaurant, stuck away in a back lane off
Edinburgh's Street of Pubs, is worth a search because the food, wine and
service here are accomplished, well thought out and interested. There
are now more cooks in the kitchen but they have managed not to spoil
broths like beetroot and ginger soup, crayfish bisque nor the pheasant in
pastry or with figs and lime sauce, salmon with watercress sauce nor the
other simple but intriguing dishes on the menu. The wine list is enterprising and carefully chosen and for an upmarket restaurant the prices
are fair. Open Tuesday to Saturday, excluding Saturday lunch.

Pierre Victoire, 10 Victoria Street, Edinburgh EH1 2HG
tel: (031) 225 1721 *
There are now three Pierre Victoire bistros in Edinburgh (and one in
Inverness) and the emphasis in all of them is on good, tasty food à la
française and sound basic wine (plus a few luxuries) at cheap prices.
Although if you are looking for a quiet intimate chat to get down to the
realities of what you should have done at the 14th, it could be a bit noisy
and crowded, Pierre Victoire does offer real value for money and the
dishes, especially on the dinner menu, are lively and authentic.
Mussels with garlic and Pernod butter, oysters with red pepper and
more Pernod, mushrooms with smoked salmon in brandied cream, good
and inexpensive lobster and crayfish, roast rib of beef, good portions.
Not smart but animated and good value.

Prestonfield House, Priestfield Road, Edinburgh EH16 5UT
tel: (031) 668 3346 ***
Prestonfield was built for Sir James Dick, Lord Provost of Edinburgh,
around 1685 as a replacement for a house on the same site burned
down during student riots in 1681. Although it has been added to down
the centuries, it has retained the grace and fine proportions of earlier
times. The architect was Sir William Bruce, who restored the Palace of
Holyroodhouse for Charles II, and some of the fine interior seventeenth-
century wood and plaster work bears a strong resemblance to similar
decoration in the Royal Palace.
Dr Johnson and Boswell dined here on their return from the famous
Hebridean tour of 1773 and some other notable guests have been
Bonnie Prince Charlie in 1745 and Benjamin Franklin in 1759. The
dining rooms are exceptionally elegant, the plaster work on the ceilings
is among the most decoratively exuberant in Scotland and the north
drawing room on the first floor, ornamented with embossed red leather
panels made in Cordoba in 1676, is particularly fine.
It is hard for the food to live up to all this architectural splendour but
it does its best. Consommé with poached quails' eggs and scallops,
scampi with lime and raspberry vinaigrette; smoked chicken with salad
and walnut-oil dressing; grilled bacon wrapped around game and
chicken livers and Cullen Skink, the delicious Scottish finnan haddie

soup were recent overtures. Main courses could be pan-fried veal with lime and ginger sauce, pastry horn of creamed sweetbreads, chicken breast and saffron mousseline and sauté fillet of beef in pink pepper-corns and red wine sauce.

With a sumptuous dessert trolley and a notable wine list they show that the kitchen is not too overwhelmed to make positive gastronomic state-ments in this splendid setting. Certainly the most beautiful restaurant in Edinburgh.

Raffaelli, 10–11 Randolph Place, Edinburgh EH3 7TA
tel: (031) 225 6060 ∗∗∗
Bruno Raffaelli, who for years has had the best wine bar in Edinburgh next to his dignified Florentine-style restaurant, has at last improved the restaurant menu which, although worthy and well presented, never matched the excellence and enterprise of the range of Italian wines on offer. Very much a business man's eating place much patronised by investment bankers from nearby Charlotte Square, Raffaelli's is open from lunchtime all through the afternoon to 9pm.

The new menu has starters like carpaccio, the Italian version of steak tartare with truffled olive oil, lemon and reggiano cheese; fresh mozarella with oregano, fresh tomato, basil and olive oil; bresaola, the air-dried ham from the Valtellina, with marinated Italian beans and polenta with wild mushrooms: there is a wide range of pasta and rice dishes, a fine selection of seafood and such piatti central to Tuscan cuisine as loin chop of veal grilled with garlic and rosemary; veal piccata with wild mushrooms; osso buco and medallions of venison with Barolo and polenta. The wine list is as comprehensive as ever, ranging over the Italian peninsula; Cabernets and Chardonnays from the north, superb Barberescos from Gaja in Piemonte, Pinot Grigio, Refosco, Araldo and the fascinating golden Picolit from the Valle vineyards. There are care-fully chosen Chiantis such as Castello di Ama and other Tuscan and Umbrian wines, the great nebbiolo grape vintages from Piemonte, mag-nificent Brunello di Montalcino. Next door in the stylish wine bar you can eat more simply and still drink from the same opulent list.

Skippers Bistro, 1a Dock Place, Leith EH6 6UY tel: (031) 554 1018 ∗∗
Alan and Jan Corbett have the prototype Leith dockside restaurant. For some years they have served the best fish available to the capital's diners-out who revel in, rather than resist, the elbow-to-elbow bistro ambience with the daily change of menu chalked on a blackboard.

Outstanding dishes include sole and salmon paupiettes with fresh herb sauce, red mullet marinated with coriander, herrings in sesame seeds with orange and ginger, pan-fried fillet of trout with lemon and tarragon, smoked haddock in cider, gravdlax with mustard and dill sauce and mussels in a variety of guises including a splendidly garlicky Provençal garnish. The wine list is short but apposite. There is good Sancerre, Leith Bordeaux Blanc, Muscadet and white burgundy to partner the fish dishes and a few good reds as well.

The Vintners Room, The Vaults, 87 Giles Street, Leith EH6 6BZ
tel: (031) 554 6767 ✴✴✴
Down in the ancient Vaults in Giles Street, the oldest commercial
building in Scotland still in use, the monks of the Brotherhood of St
Anthony controlled the wine trade through Leith in the twelfth
century. Today, happily, there is still a host of gastronomic and
vinbibulous experiences housed within its venerable stones. In one
corner is Judith Paris's wine warehouse, Wines From Paris; the top
floors are occupied by the Scotch Malt Whisky Society and beneath
them is The Vintners Room.
The handsome dining room with its seventeenth-century plaster ceiling
was where the Leith merchants who succeeded the monks did their
deals in claret. In this and the long whitewashed and beamed wine
bar next door, Tim and Sue Cumming have given a new impetus to
the restaurant. They came to Edinburgh from Bath, where they met
at The Hole in the Wall, trained under the legendary George Perry-
Smith, and subsequently bought the restaurant from him when he
retired to Devon.
Their menu is comprehensive, ranging from Provençal fish soup with
rouille, the full-bodied Livornese fish stew cacciuco, brains with capers
and venison pastrami with honey sauce, through monkfish like a
pepper steak, noisettes of pork with mustard sauce, coq au vin de
Bourgueil, ragoût of monkfish with peppers and spinach to brown
bread ice cream, crème brûlée and prune, almond and armagnac tart.
There is also a bar menu which offers some of the same dishes and
a reasonably priced and selective wine list.

The Grill, Balmoral Hotel, 1 Princes Street, Edinburgh EH2 2EQ
tel: (031) 556 2414 ✴✴✴✴
Edinburgh's newest restaurant in the completely refurbished and
newly-named Balmoral Hotel at the east end of Princes Street offers
some of the best food in the capital in an elegant and capacious suite
of rooms, beautifully decorated in dark red lacquer, brass, polished
wood and wrought iron. The set lunch menus for two courses and
three courses which both include a half-bottle of wine per person are
exceptionally good value—duck breast with white asparagus salad;
grilled lamb chops with béarnaise sauce or poached beef tenderloin
with herb cream; Bavarian cream with caramel and apple slices and
coffee are a typical menu. The five-course dinner is possibly even
better value—goose-liver salad, grilled mullet, hare fillets in a gamey
sauce, an excellent selection of Scottish and European cheeses, a
strawberry dessert and coffee, for example. There is an extensive à la
carte and the menu says firmly 'Gratuities are not expected by our
staff'.
The wine list is what you would expect of a top class restaurant but
surprisingly reasonable in price. There are 17 wines for under £20 and
a choice of 14 half-bottles. Service manages to be friendly and impec-
cable at the same time, a very difficult feat.

THE HONOURABLE COMPANY OF EDINBURGH GOLFERS,

Muirfield, Gullane, tel: (0620) 842123   *6601 yards SSS 73*

RESTAURANTS
La Potinière *** The Rosebery **

The Lothian shoreline south of Edinburgh is one of the greatest golfing coasts in the world, much of it flat with horizons made up largely of sky and sea. There are more than forty courses in the Lothian region but there is no question which is the peer. The geese flying over Aberlady Bay are part of the wild open northerly feeling of the place and on Muirfield primitive as well as sophisticated elements come into play. Jack Nicklaus said it was 'a punishing kind of perfection' and named his home golf course after it.

There are those who play this unique course who find it difficult to distinguish between these elements but this is only because they cannot tell the difference between savagery and torture. The winds and the deceptively rolling terrain and the wire-like clinging fronds of bents grass are savage, but the depth of the bunkers and the way the small ones, in which you can barely swing a club, are placed next to the green at short holes is sophisticated torture.

Despite these characteristics Muirfield is a golf course for gentlemen. They have only been at Muirfield since 1891 but the Honourable Company is the oldest golf club in the world and at their original home in Leith in 1744 they drew up the first rules of golf ten years before the Royal and Ancient at St Andrews was founded.

The clubhouse offers a gallery of formidable-looking old clubs and balls, portraits of past captains painted by Sir Henry Raeburn, David Allan and Stanley Cursiter, roaring open fires, splendid dishes like mutton with caper sauce, sound claret, good port and a tray of liqueurs by the coffee.

Members are not seen in anything as bourgeois as blazers (the only time I was there wearing one, I was as conspicuous as a canary among falcons). Patched tweed jackets and checked knee-breeches with heavy wool stockings are the rig of the day. The infamous notice 'No Dogs: No Ladies' has disappeared, if it ever existed—this kind of quasi-mythology gives you the tone of the place. The golf course is no less exacting than its members. A cartoon in the clubhouse entrance hall depicts a woebegone golfer up to his cloth cap in bents grass looking at a notice which says 'Muirfield Welcomes Careful Drivers'.

This is not a joke. To be off the fairway here is to be deep in trouble. Even if you put your drive on the fairway you have only won a quarter of the battle at most. At the first hole (par 4) there is a point about 380 yards from the tee with another 60 to go to the flag where the fairway narrows to just 19 yards. There are short holes pitted with bunkers in which Nick Faldo cannot be seen from fairway level and the long holes are trapped with a punishing ingenuity and severity which is murder on the carelessly aimed shot.

The two halves run in concentric circles. The first nine go right round the edge of the limits of the terrain from the great banks of wind-swept buckthorn, blazing with copper-coloured berries in autumn and the pewter gleam of the Firth of Forth to the north, to finish under the clubhouse and the graceful walls of Greywalls Hotel, with one of the roughest finishing holes in golf. The 9th has shattered many an illustrious and seemingly well-founded hope. It is 495 yards long, menacingly narrow at drive length with a fearsome shot over a clutch of bunkers to get near the green.

It perfectly represents Nicklaus's splendid definition of a great golf hole as one which needs the right number of really good shots to make par and one truly great shot to get a birdie.

Having got through all this, however, you are only halfway round. Muirfield's Inner Circle is more eccentric than concentric but the pressure on solid driving and precise shotmaking never lets up. It has one of the best finishes in the game. The 17th is a 542-yard par 5, narrowed as usual by rough and with a row of formidable bunkers across the fairway about 150 yards short of the green set in a duned hollow. The 18th is a par 4. It measures 447 yards but is always farther than you think, especially to clear the malignant bunkers which protect the final green. Muirfield is a great golf course.

Despite all the mythology it is not impossible to arrange to play there. Things have relaxed in the last few years and visitors are no longer regarded with the ingrained xenophobic suspicion they once were. But you do have to book a long time in advance and you must have a handicap of 16 or less. Provided you can meet these conditions you will have something to talk about in your golf-club bar for the rest of your life.

La Potiniere, Main Street, Gullane EH31 2AA tel: (0620) 843214 *****
Rather like Muirfield, La Potinière has developed its own mythology of inaccessibility. Perhaps it has something to do with the name which means 'The Gossip'. People will tell you that you have to book a year in advance to eat there and while this may still be true of certain Saturday nights, it is not true of lunch on weekdays. In addition, David and Hilary Brown now offer dinner twice a week on Friday as well as Saturday.

When you do get there you will probably be surprised to find this culinary legend housed in a small, unpretentious building with inside just a quiet single room decorated with plates from famous French restaurants and framed illustrious wine labels. The food is superbly cooked with imagination and style but there is a heavy leaning towards white meat and the menu is obligatoire and sometimes not announced at all, as if it was the customer's privilege to eat there, an attitude of which I am not fond. But the quality of the food is undeniable and the wine list is superb, if you have an hour or so to spare to read it. It is easier to take David Brown's advice and most people do this. However, no-one's bottle counsel is infallible nectar for everyone and this can be off-putting. If you don't mind being made to feel an uninstructed pleb in search of self-betterment, it is an uplifting gastronomic happening. If you don't fall into this category, it is still an experience.

The Rosebery, 3 Rosebery Place, Gullane tel: (0620) 842233 ****
Anne and John Boyd's newly opened restaurant on the right just after

you pass Jimmy Hume's pro-shop by the first tee at the Gullane One course, is pretty, charmingly relaxed and offers interesting and carefully prepared food and a well-chosen list of more than thirty wines from Australia, New Zealand, America, Germany, Italy, Spain, Chile and France at sensible prices.

Following the seasons, the menu changes regularly and you might start with crab ravioli, mushrooms and onions stewed in red wine, seafood terrine with smoked salmon or prawn, mango and avocado salad. As a main course it could be monkfish with Dijon mustard sauce, roast rack of lamb, salmon with lime curry sauce, duck with calvados and apples or beef with oyster mushrooms. The house wines come from Georges Duboeuf and cost £6.95 per litre and there are half-litres and a choice from 14 half-bottles. Lots of the wines cost less than £10 and the most expensive other than champagne are a 1989 Hawkes Bay Chardonnay for £13.55 and a Côte de Beaune Villages, Les Abesses 1988 for £13.50. John Boyd's cooking is stylish and everything is freshly prepared and attentively served. The Rosebery is an engaging place to eat and drink really well without breaking the bank.

NORTH BERWICK, Beach Road, North Berwick EH39 4BB
tel: (0620) 2135

RESTAURANTS
The Open Arms, Dirleton ✱✱ Greywalls, Gullane ✱✱✱

North Berwick is the thirteenth oldest golf club in the world and one of its original members, Captain Brown, fought at the Battle of Waterloo. Golf had been played continuously over the West Links of North Berwick for at least a century before the founding of the club in 1832 and only at St Andrews can you tread more ancient fairways. Not only is it venerable but it is one of the most attractive and most stimulating links courses anywhere, with every hole setting a different problem of length, judgement, knowledge and direction. There are beautiful views over the great beaches of this coast across to the rocky islets of the Forth estuary and out to the volcanic hump of the Bass Rock and distant May Island. Playing golf at North Berwick on a fine day is one of the greatest delights of the game. On a day with strong winds, it is a struggle but a challenging and enjoyable one. It begins with a curiously difficult hole, just 328 yards long but with the beach on your right and a road across just below the rocky headland on which the green is set. Near the white-painted fence which marks the beach the ground is sandy and offers an unrewarding lie from which to play your second; across the road you are up against a rocky grass slope with a blind shot and, even out to the left and short, you have to make your pitch into a green which slopes away towards the sea and where a wind totally different in strength and direction is blowing from the one you feel standing on the fairway.

The 1st is a good example of what holes at North Berwick are like. You have to think your way around this course. The best route is seldom obvious from the tee and even when you know the course well, everything can be changed by how and from where the wind blows. Getting a 4 at this hole is a psychological triumph which can set you up for the rest of the round.

At the 2nd you drive across the corner of a bay towards a cluster of distant grassed sandhills, then there is a tricky shot avoiding bunkers left and right into a large green. At the 3rd you cross a stream which will worry you more at the 16th than here and then have to fly your second over the March Dyke, the wall which marked the boundary of the original six holes, to a green half-masked by a bunker with the sea wall to the right. The 4th is short in a sheltered valley but with pot bunkers right and left and a long green which can make a whole club's difference when you have determined the pin position.

And so it goes on, with a positive decision to be made on every shot. There is a stream just in front of the green at the 354-yard 7th. At the 9th you play the second par 5 across whatever wind may be blowing that day, over threatening fairway bunkers in the middle and a high plateau green to catch as the hole dog-legs left. The 10th and 11th are played from tees in the dunes high above the beach, one a bunker-ridden par 3 and the other a 500-yard par 5.

The originality of North Berwick is most conspicuous at the 13th where you must set up your tee-shot to give you a pitch across a lateral wall to a green in the dunes by the beach; at the 14th *Perfection*, where the second is played blind over a bunkered ridge to a seaside green; at the short 15th *Redan*, a much plagiarised hole, where the ball must carry a ridge and a huge bunker 20 feet below the flag to find the sloping green; at the 16th, there is a wall in front of the tee, a burn at drive-length, out-of-bounds on the right and a green with a valley in the middle. An unforgettable course—and not just for the views.

The Open Arms, Dirleton, EH39 5BG tel: (0620) 85 241 **
The Open Arms, opposite the ruined twelfth century castle in one of Scotland's prettiest villages, is just 2 miles from Gullane and 2 miles from North Berwick, off the A198. Arthur Neil's welcoming and cosy restaurant has been serving excellent food and first-class wine for several decades. A man of many parts, Arthur, a canny judge of fine wines, an able raconteur and a past captain of North Berwick Golf Club, keeps a good table where the value for money is outstanding. The famous Open Arms's mussel and onion stew has delighted golfers from all over the world for generations but as starters to the three- or four-course set-price dinner you might also have hot chicken mousse wrapped in spinach leaves with a tomato and basil sauce, sliced avocado and mango with a stem ginger dressing, or duck and liver pâté in clove and orange aspic: to follow, a choice of soups and then pan-fried lamb's sweetbreads with bacon and cocotte potatoes, sliced breast of pheasant with haggis and creamed vegetable sauce, baked fillet of sole and leek purée with a shrimp sauce or sautéed calf's liver with spiced raspberry coulis. Sweets are delicious and there is also a savoury on offer and cheese. The wine list is rich in good clarets, expertly chosen burgundies

and good wines from the Rhône, the Loire, Alsace, Italy and California. Open all year, including Sundays.

Greywalls, Duncur Road, Gullane EH31 2EG tel: (0620) 842144 * * *
Greywalls is the most beautiful hotel in East Lothian, designed as a country house by Sir Edwin Lutyens, architect of New Delhi, the Cenotaph in Whitehall and the British Embassy in Washington, within gardens by his almost equally celebrated collaborator, Gertrude Jekyll (although there are those fresh from the Honourable Company's links who swear that her name more readily suggests that she designed the golf course).
It is one of the most distinguished and original twentieth-century houses in Scotland and the only remaining Lutyens's house in the northern kingdom, built of honey-coloured Rattlebags stone with tall Tudor chimneys, a curved front and intriguing pyramid-roofed gable endings—a real eye-catcher of a building for those who wish their eyes to be pleasured rather an assaulted.
Inside it is equally gracious. The library, with its open fire, fine panelling and its books, is one of the most relaxing and delightful rooms in any Scottish hotel and the additions which have been made to alter it subtly from a family home to an hotel have kept faith with the original design and, if not inspiring, are at least, inoffensive.
The food is ambitious and often successful, the wine list is adequate and the setting is so splendid and country-house comfortable that criticism is stilled by well-fed sloth.
Greywalls overlooks the 9th and 18th greens of Muirfield and, like the other restaurants listed with North Berwick and Muirfield, it is as accessible from one as the other. Open March to October.

Glasgow and the South-West

Although Ayrshire is the only county in the British Isles which can claim three venues for the oldest golf tournament, the Open Championship, golf was comparatively late in arriving on the west coast of Scotland from the land of its origins in the east. The first golf club in the west was founded in Glasgow in 1787 and Prestwick, the first of the Ayrshire clubs, was not formed until 1851 but obviously the game was known on the west coast as well as the east much earlier. There is a reference to golf in one of Robert Burns's political ballads published in 1788 (significantly, perhaps, after the poet's visits to Edinburgh).
When golf was taken up in Ayrshire it was with enthusiasm and the competitive spirit of the west of Scotland was not slow in asserting itself. The members of Prestwick Golf Club invented the Open Championship when they subscribed to a Challenge Belt for annual competition in 1860, inspired, it was said, by a desire to show that golfers in the west were every bit as good as anyone who played the game on the shores of Fife or Lothian. Unfortunately for this worthy ambition the first Championship was won by Willie Park of Musselburgh and for the first twelve years, when the

Championship continued to be played at Prestwick, it was always won by an east-coast player—although Tom Morris senior did play under the banner of the Prestwick Club where he was the professional. The Morrises, Tom senior and junior, dominated the tournament until 1872, winning eight out of the first twelve.

Glasgow golf clubs tend to be rather clannish about visitors and you should enquire well in advance if you want to play. There are several municipal courses in and around the city but none of them are as good nor as interesting as those in Edinburgh—to say nothing of the town courses at St Andrews, Carnoustie and Troon.

GLASGOW

COURSES
Glasgow Golf Club, Killermont: 5970 yards SSS 69
Glasgow Golf Club, Gailes: 6432 yards SSS 71
Pollok: 6257 yards SSS 70
Buchanan Castle: 6032 yards SSS 69
Clober: 5068 yards SSS 65
Dougalston: 6683 yards SSS 72
Hilton Park: 6002 yards SSS 70

RESTAURANTS

The Ubiquitous Chip ***	Rogano ***
Café Gandolfi **	Triangle **
October **	Braeval Old Mill, Aberfoyle ***

COURSES

GLASGOW GOLF CLUB,
Killermont, Bearsden G61 2TW tel: (041) 942 2340
Gailes, by Irvine Ayrshire tel: (0294) 311347

Before the Glasgow Club was formed in 1787, golf had been played on Glasgow Green for hundreds of years. Like most early clubs the members played in various other places before they moved to the wooded estate of Killermont to the north-west of Glasgow, where Old Tom Morris laid out his last course for them in 1904.

The club is unique in having two courses, 35 miles apart and very different in character. Killermont is a fairly short parkland course set among magnificent ancient oak, chestnut and beech trees. It begins with a par 4, which at 278 yards is barely longer than the par 3 following it. Then there is a substantial par 4 of 402 uphill yards, strategically bunkered, followed by another short hole and the longest hole on the course the 5th, 525 yards with two changes of direction, needing a drive to the right and a long iron to the left to have a chance of reaching the green in regulation. Three short par 4s end the first nine but the 10th requires well-placed shotmaking because of the trees and there is a similar hole at the 12th with a humped green which is difficult to catch.

After the par 5 15th there is a relatively simple run in to the noble clubhouse, an early nineteenth-century mansion with a superb show of silverware, including the Tennant Cup, the oldest amateur trophy in the world, still played for annually over thirty-six holes at Glasgow Gailes and thirty-six at Killermont.

Glasgow Gailes is an entirely different kind of course, a links measuring 6432 yards, originally laid out by Willie Park junior in the 1890s and situated on the Ayrshire coast near Irvine.

It is a more rigorous test than Killermont and has been used as a qualifying course for the Open when it is held on the west coast of Scotland. There are not so many trees as at Killermont, the main problems come from the heather and gorse which line the fairways and make keeping the ball straight imperative. The 3rd, a heather-bordered dog-leg, is an exacting par 4. The 5th is the longer of the two par 5s, well bunkered and with a saucer-shaped green among the dunes. The direction changes every two holes or so which means that you are not always playing into the wind or down it. The best of the short holes is the 15th where your tee-shot to the raised green can cause problems, particularly into a wind off the sea.

POLLOK GOLF CLUB, 90 Barrhead Road, Glasgow HG43 1BG
tel: (041) 632 1080

A delightful wooded parkland course in the south-west suburbs of the city just 4 miles from the centre, Pollok looks across the River Cart to the gallery which houses the Burrell Collection in Pollok Country Park and to Pollok House which has one of the finest collections of Spanish paintings in Britain. The River Cart comes into play at several holes. There is one par 5 in each half at the 7th and the 15th and a demanding par 4 to end the first nine. Of the three par 3s, the 17th, although only 150 yards requires a shot of great delicacy and accuracy to ensure you can go on to the 18th in the frame of mind to finish off the day with a par 4.

BUCHANAN CASTLE, Drymen, tel: (0360) 60307

Yet another James Braid course laid out in 1936, this site along the Endrick Water which flows into Loch Lomond used to be a private race course. Water can come into play at eight holes, there are no par 5s and only four par 3s but six par 4s measure more than 400 yards.

The 7th is an intriguing hole along the banks of the Endrick then dog-legging left through trees to the green backed by yet another twist of the river. At the 17th you have to carry Jamie's Burn to set up your par on the green below the old castle ruins. Not a fierce course but rewarding and agreeable to play.

CLOBER, Craigton Road, Milngavie G62 7HP tel: (041) 956 1685

A short parkland course 7 miles out of Glasgow on the road to the Trossachs at Milngavie (pronounced 'Millguy') with which the family of Masters and Open Champion Sandy Lyle are associated. Not a difficult course although there is a tricky par 3 at the 5th but a pleasant round of golf to keep your swing in tune.

DOUGALSTON, Strathblane Road, Milngavie tel: (041) 956 5750

This tough John Harris-designed course has narrow tree-lined fairways on a moorland setting with water hazards at seven holes. Probably the best test of golf in the immediate Glasgow area and glorious to look at in May when the rhododendrons are in bloom. Dougalston demands straight hitting off the tee, the courage to go for shots across water and the ability to read subtle greens. Located 7 miles north of Glasgow on the A81.

HILTON PARK, Stockiemuir Road, Milngavie G62 7HB
tel: (041) 956 5124

There are two courses at this Milngavie venue: the Hilton (6043 yards SSS 70) and the Allander (5374 yards SSS 67), 4 miles north-east of Bearsden on the A809. Windswept moorland for the most part and quite hilly, playing at Hilton Park is exhilarating rather than demanding of great golf shots. One of Glasgow's most sociable clubs it makes visitors welcome provided they book in advance and play before 5pm on weekdays.

RESTAURANTS

The Ubiquitous Chip, 12 Ashton Lane, Glasgow G12 8SJ
tel: (041) 334 5007 ∗∗∗
The Chip, in a lane just off Byres Road in Glasgow's West End, is one of the most agreeable restaurants in Scotland. It is relaxed, the ambience in the converted white-washed mews stable plentifully fronded with greenery, is welcoming, the service is good, the food is delicious and the wine list is amazing both in range and price.
Ron Clydesdale's menu is an interesting mixture of French and Scottish—fillets of game with walnut vinaigrette, braised ox-tail, silverside of beef, cod on a bed of clapshot (mashed potatoes and white turnips with chives) with roasted red peppers, duck with apple and cider, venison haggis, Loch Fyne dill-flavoured kipper pâté with yoghurt.
In addition to the astonishing wine list with many good bottles for less than £10, there is Fürstenburg unpasteurised lager and Caledonian 80/- Natural Ale on draught and a mind-spinning choice of malts. House wine is £6.50.

Cafe Gandolfi, 64 Albion Street, Glasgow G1 1NY tel: (041) 552 6813 ∗∗
In this city-centre café the menu is simple but the food is good and not expensive. Smoked venison, gravdlax, pâté, dates and ricotta in Parma ham, avocado salad with warm vinaigrette are some of the starters. There is a hot dish which changes every day as well as gratin dauphinoise with smoked venison, cold baked Cumbrian ham with pease pudding or finnan haddie and potatoes. The list is even shorter than the menu but adequate, with wine available by the glass as well as the bottle and a choice of four beers.

October, 128 Drymen Road, Bearsden G61 3RB tel: (041) 942 7272 * *
Innovation is a way of life in this mirrored restaurant to the north-west
of Glasgow (particularly handy for the Milngavie courses and Killermont). All kinds of contrasting tastes are tried; some succeed better than
others. There can be filling fish soup garnished with a soufflé of herbs
and saffron or game pâté with fruit slices and loganberry sauce to start;
good fish—sole with crayfish mousse, seafood tart, salmon with lobster
mousse—then sautéed liver or kidneys or a vegetarian dish such as carrot
and courgette gâteau.
Also there might be Milanese stew with polenta or teriyaki beef. The list
covers the globe and prices are reasonable. Open all week, except
Sunday dinner.

Rogano, 11 Exchange Place, Glasgow G1 3AN tel: (041) 248 4055 * * *
The Rogano is the oldest restaurant in Glasgow, specialising in top-class
seafood since 1876. In 1935 it was redecorated in art-deco style in
imitation of the original *Queen Mary*, the giant Cunard liner then being
built at Clydebank, and in spite of ups and downs it has maintained its
reputation as one of Glasgow's favourite places to eat. The main
restaurant is on the ground floor and downstairs is the Café Rogano,
where the food and the ambience is bistro style. Fish of any kind is the
main fare here; the style is classical without being over-elaborate. Good
wine list. Open Monday to Saturday.

The Triangle, 37 Queen Street, Glasgow G1 3EF tel: (041) 221 8758 * *
This stylish brasserie and restaurant above Tom Shepherd's Trick Shop,
halfway down Queen Street, has exciting decor by contemporary artists
and exacting standards in the kitchen.
There are table d'hôte and executive lunch menus daily in the Brasserie
and the dining room. Menus change regularly but sample dishes are
guinea fowl and pheasant terrine, poached Loch Fyne oysters with
spinach, cream and Parmesan, bresaola, crab in pastry parcels, mousse-
terrine of duck: Tay salmon marinière, beef with wild mushrooms,
saddle of venison, west-coast lobster, Islay scallops and langoustines
cooked in court bouillon and flavoured with herbs. The wine list is
strong on Burgundy, California, Alsace, Italy and Spain. Open all year.

Braeval Old Mill, by Aberfoyle, FK8 3UY tel: (087-72) 711 * * *
This beautifully restored old watermill is just 10 miles north of Buchanan
Castle golf course on the A81 and is a charmingly peaceful place to have
a quiet evening meal. Starters can include seafood cocktail, sweet-cured
fillet of Orkney herrings, terrine of chicken and woodpigeon or a filo
pastry basket of mussels and clams or game terrine with onion
marmalade.
As a main course you might have fillet of turbot in sorrel sauce,
marinated lamb on lentil and apricot purée, roast breast of duck with
cranberry and orange sauce or seafood fricassee with saffron and chives.
There are inventive and delicate sweets and an excellent cheeseboard.

The list offers a catholic balance between Europe and the New World with a good range of half-bottles. Open Tuesday to Sunday, dinner only and Sunday lunch.

ROYAL TROON, tel: (0292) 311555 *6641 yards SSS 73*

RESTAURANTS
Chapeltoun House ∗∗∗   Marine Highland Hotel ∗∗∗

The great west-coast golf courses begin in Ayrshire. At Irvine, in addition to Glasgow Gailes, there is the lovely Western Gailes (6833 yards SSS 72), on the other side of the railway, a beautiful links with springy seaside turf, superb greens and wonderful views over the Firth of Clyde. The excellent Barassie (6460 yards SSS 71) is officially the Kilmarnock Golf Club but is in fact just on the north edge of Troon. It is also used as an Open qualifying course when the championship is being played in Ayrshire.

Early golf history in Troon is somewhat bedevilled by a dispute which came to a head in the 1930s about whether the townsfolk of Troon who were not members of Troon Golf Club were allowed to play over the Old Course. Such rights existed—and still do—on certain courses in the east of Scotland, but in Troon's case it was maintained that it had always been a private club and that golf had not been played at Troon prior to the formation of the Troon club in 1878. (In view of the founding in 1851 of Prestwick, just across the Pow Burn, this is a dubious contention in my view.) However, that put tradition firmly in its chosen place: obscurity.

Troon founded its club just when the game began to boom. The introduction of the gutta-percha ball, made of moulded rubber gum, in 1848, had made the game less expensive and golf clubs were mushrooming all over the world. Troon soon established a reputation for its testing links and glossy greens and in 1904 it was the venue for the Ladies' British Open. It hosted its first Open Championship in 1923 and it changed its name from Old Troon to Royal Troon in 1978 when Her Majesty the Queen granted the club the right to use the royal prefix on the occasion of its centenary. One venerable Troon member is reputed to have said, 'the prevailing idea at Troon is to make the first holes easy enough not to discourage a good score in anticipation and the last sufficiently easy not to smash a good score at the end'.

Just when this pronouncement was made is uncertain but I suspect that quite a number of architects from James Braid to Frank Pennink have been at the course since. Braid added forty new bunkers in 1923 and the famous Postage Stamp got two of them.

What is true about the Oldest Member's dictum is that the opening holes are easier than the rest but he would find it difficult to get Greg Norman to agree with him about the last after his heartbreaking Open Championship finish there in 1989 when he lost the play-off for the title to Mark Calcavecchia.

The 1st and 2nd are straightforward par 4s with nothing to worry about except staying on the fairway. At the 3rd this is complicated by the Gyaws Burn which crosses the hole about 250 yards out. The 4th is the first of

Troon's big par 5s, 556 yards, slightly dog-legged right with the drive played from a tee set above the beach and very exposed to the elements. There is a 150-yard carry to the fairway and a bunker around 240 yards on the right so you do not want to be too clever about cutting angles. The second shot is simple if you avoid a left-hand bunker and should leave you a classic high approach to the two-level green.

The 210-yard short 5th is an easy hole on a calm day but at the 577-yard 6th you face the longest hole in British championship golf.

After the opening holes the terrain gets wilder and more menacing and to do well at this punishing hole you must hit a long, straight drive to the distant fairway, positioning it carefully between two bunkers. The second fairway wood or long iron must be aimed with great exactitude, right to avoid the first fairway bunker below the green and not far enough to carry into the second. The approach into the long narrow green is difficult and a ridge across the green does not make putting any easier after you get there. A dangerous hole. It was here that the wheels came off for American Bobby Clampett in the 1982 Open in the third round when, after shooting 67 and 66 he was leading the tournament by 5 shots from Nick Price, and took 8 at this hole and slumped to a 78. From the high tee at the 7th you seem to be aiming only at bunkers but in fact there are only five of them. The 8th is one of the most notorious holes in the world.

The shortest hole anywhere in championship golf, The Postage Stamp is played in a totally different direction from the earlier holes, often straight into the south-west wind. Only 126 yards long it makes club choice very difficult.

You must pitch the ball from a high tee to a small, raised green set into the side of a large sand dune and ringed by five bunkers, two set into the dune on the left, one yawning in front of the green and two more round the right-hand edge. There is no safe way to play this hole so perhaps the best thing is to think of Gene Sarazen who, at the age of seventy-one, had a hole in one here in the 1973 Open and not of Herman Tissies who took 15 at The Postage Stamp in the Open of 1950.

After the turn it is red flags for danger all the way home. At the 437-yard 10th, you drive blind over a gorse-covered ridge and then there is a demanding second shot to a gorse-hedged plateau green. The 481-yard 11th has the Glasgow–Ayr railway running all along its right edge; there is another gorse-covered ridge to fly from the tee; a large bunker in front of the green threatens the birdie-seeking second shot to the green tucked into the railway fence and the long narrow green is difficult to hold. Jack Nicklaus took 10 at this hole in his first attempt at the Open in 1962. Palmer, who won, had a par, two birdies and an eagle!

The tight finish is made by the 17th, a very unyielding short hole of 223 yards to a raised, sloping and punishingly bunkered green.

From the back tee, the 18th is a severe test with menacing fairway bunkers and a narrow entrance to the green, and an out-of-bounds path below the clubhouse behind it.

There are four other golf courses at Troon, Portland (6274 yards SSS 71), adjoining Royal Troon and the fine municipal courses near the station,

Lochgreen (6765 yards SSS 72), Darley (6326 yards SSS 70) and Fullarton (5064 yards SSS 65).

Chapeltoun House, Stewarton KA3 3ED tel: (0560) 82696 ***
Chapeltoun is about 12 miles from Troon just off the B769 from Irvine to Stewarton. A solid house built at the beginning of the century, it is now a fine restaurant with an accomplished chef, Kevin McGillivray, formerly at Craigendarroch in Ballater. The menu reflects the character of the house, classically constructed from local ingredients richly presented with style and panache: smoked woodpigeon terrine; loin of lamb with parsley and corn-seed mousse, glazed with red-currants; salmon layered with sole and scampi, and a coulis of yellow peppers; fine local fish with inventive sauces; beautifully cooked game; and an exotic choice of desserts. The list is heavily French orientated with a good range of respectably aged clarets but there are also well-chosen wines from Italy, California and Australia.

Marine Highland Hotel, Troon KA10 6HE tel: (0292) 314444 ***
The Marine overlooks the 17th and 18th holes of Royal Troon on the landward side of the course and the Firth of Clyde with the peaks of Arran on the horizon. Crosbie's Brasserie serves snacks and meals all day, and in the dining room there is a good menu of exotic and local fare, cooked with imagination and flair.
Wild boar, locally caught wild salmon, scallops, lobster and other crustaceans fresh from the sea, Scotch lamb from the hills and beef from Galloway are the staples. Open all year.

PRESTWICK, Links Road, Prestwick KA9 1 QG tel: (0292) 77404
6544 yards SSS 72

RESTAURANTS
Fouters Bistro, Ayr ** Pickwick Hotel, Ayr **

Prestwick was the course on which the Open Championship and all world-wide tournament golf began in 1860 when the members of the club, founded in 1851, put up a Challenge Belt for annual competition. The first Open was by invitation and there were only eight contestants.
Boldly, the following year Prestwick declared the championship to be 'open to all the world', a status it has held ever since. Something like justice was done that year when the Challenge Belt was won by Tom Morris senior, who, although a St Andrews man, was also the professional to the Prestwick Club, the first golfer ever to hold such an appointment.
There was a hiatus in the championship in 1870 when young Tom Morris, son of the 1861 champion, won the Challenge Belt for the third time in succession, thus winning it outright. There was no prize to play for in 1871 and no competition, but that was soon put to rights. In 1872 the present cup was subscribed for by Prestwick, the Royal and Ancient Club of St Andrews and The Honourable Company of Edinburgh Golfers.

Although Prestwick was taken off the Open Championship rota in 1925 when the tight contours of the course proved too much for crowd control, only the Old Course at St Andrews has hosted the Open as many times. The Amateur Championship and other major tournaments are regularly played at Prestwick.

Although it may be considered on the short side for modern professionals, lesser mortals still find it quite tough enough and it is a memorable and truly enjoyable experience to play here.

The 1st, a 346-yard par 4, runs along the railway line and there is a carry of about 150 yards to the fairway. A slice here can put your ball on the next train to Glasgow. Two bunkers guard the green which has a right-to-left slope. The 2nd is a short hole with the Pow Burn at the back and bunkers all round the green.

The Burn runs all the way along the right hand side of the rugged 3rd, a 482 yard par 5 with the massive Cardinal bunkers faced with railway sleepers all the way across the fairway at around the 220-yard mark—and another hidden behind the hump on the left. Your second has to be played across the Cardinal bunkers and the corner of the right-hand dog-leg to a bumpy fairway short of the small green. Disaster looms everywhere on this hole and if you get it right, you can feel justifiably pleased.

But don't get over-confident. Another dog-leg along the burn follows and you do not have the cushion of the extra shot because, although 100 yards shorter, this par 4 has bunkers on the corner and the second shot to the green needs every ounce of precision you can muster. Then there is the Himalayas. A blind tee-shot over a high ridge to a green beset by bunkers. Aim left of the disc on the ridge for the best line but nothing is safe at this hole. There are four long par 4s from the 7th to the 10th and then another bunker-spattered par 3; the 12th is a long par 5 bunkered all the way up the left; there is a narrow rolling green to catch at the 13th, a pond to carry at the 14th; very tight shooting to a sloping green at the 15th. Two short par 4s in the last three holes bring some relief but at the 17th, Alps there is just about everything the course can throw at you. Ridges, a blind second shot with a bunker behind the hummock and a narrow green.

A wonderful course to play, with just the right elements of skill and fortune in its make-up. If you don't enjoy Prestwick, you are playing the wrong game.

There are two other courses at Prestwick, the excellent Prestwick St Nicholas (5926 SSS 70) with no par 5s and some shortish par 4s but, as the Old Course at Prestwick conclusively proves, length is not everything. Prestwick St Cuthbert (6470 yards SSS 71) is flat parkland, completely different is character from the other two courses.

Fouters Bistro, 2a Academy Street, Ayr KA7 1HS tel: (0292) 261391 **
Laurie and Fran Black have been waving the gastronomic banner for years in the vaults of an old bank on the corner of Academy Street and Sandgate, just south of the bridge over the River Ayr which brings you the 2 miles down the road from Prestwick. Very good food in an amiable and unfussy atmosphere. Ayrshire pheasant with game sauce; venison

with Glayva butter; guinea fowl with red-currants and green pepper-corns; smoked chicken and venison and always a choice of fresh seafood. Also organically grown fruit and vegetables. The list is full of good bottles at fair prices. Open Tuesday to Saturday, and Sunday for dinner.

Pickwick Hotel, 19 Racecourse Road, Ayr KA7 2TD
tel: (0292) 260111 **
The restaurant at this comely hotel set in its own gardens on the A719 specialises in seafood with local poached salmon and prawns, sole fillet stuffed with prawns and similar marine dishes but it also offers chicken breasts stuffed with smoked salmon and goat cheese, Aberdeen Angus steak stuffed with haggis, good starters and interesting puds. There is a reasonable wine list and some good beers. Open all year.

TURNBERRY, Ayrshire KA26 9LT tel: (0655) 31000
Ailsa: 6927 yards SSS 73   Arran: 6350 yards SSS 69

RESTAURANTS
Turnberry Hotel **** Malin Court Hotel **

Turnberry hosted the Open Championship in 1977 and 1986 and it is the most scenically stunning of the Open venues. From the red-roofed hotel on the hill and the two courses below, the Ailsa and the Arran, the eye sweeps over one of the finest views in the world.

To the south-west the great volcanic hump of Ailsa Craig rears out of the sea and the faint purple smudge behind it is the coast of Ireland. To the west the long finger of the Mull of Kintyre probes south towards Ulster and just across the sparkling waters of the Firth of Clyde, the jagged and dramatic outline of the island of Arran gives an almost theatrical air to the land and seascape.

The Ailsa Course, on which the championships are played, opens quietly with a short par 4 and abruptly gets tougher with two holes going in opposite directions. Then you reach the magnificent run of five holes along the shore with two really tantalising par 3s, two exacting par 4s and a long and difficult 5.

To set off the first half on a literal pinnacle you hit your drive at the dramatic 9th from a high rock thrusting into the sea. Steer it carefully across the rocky wave-swept bay and keep it well to the right of the light-house and the ruins of Bruce's Castle to get a good look at the invisible green for your second shot.

And on it goes, one demanding hole after another, pitted with heavily fringed bunkers, across streams, down gullies and over glens filled with nothing but tangled herbal disaster until the long up-and-down par 5 17th takes you within range of the small clubhouse and the 18th's relatively kindly run home.

As a golf course, Turnberry is something of a recurring miracle, not only because of its magnificent setting and the challenge it presents, but because it has gone through the death and resurrection process not once but twice. In 1914 and 1939 it was a war casualty, but on both occasions it was restored to life and rose from the ashes like a phoenix to live and be played on again.

The second time Turnberry was requisitioned (in 1914 it was taken over by the newly-created Royal Flying Corps), before the course was bulldozed into oblivion to serve the needs of the planes of Coastal Command, models were made. When peace came, these were available to help the new Turnberry architect, Mackenzie Ross, to rebuild.

The great dunes which guard the outward holes on the Ailsa Course from the sea had been left untouched and within them, Turnberry was rebuilt with the aid of machinery developed during the war which had obliterated the golf courses. There are still parts of the wartime runways to the left of the 12th fairway where they provide handy car-parking for spectators when tournaments are played on the Ailsa.

The Arran Course, although it lacks the drama of the Ailsa, is a good test with its whin-lined fairways and well-guarded greens.

Turnberry Hotel, Turnberry KA26 9LT tel: (0655) 31000 ****
Turnberry is rather isolated but its situation is splendid. The best eating place after golf is undoubtedly at the luxury hotel above the golf courses, where the restaurant, in addition to good food, offers spectacular views over the courses and the sea. There is ingenious use of local produce presented in an elegant and impressive manner. Scotch beef, wild salmon, scallops, crayfish and lobster, sole, turbot, halibut, monkfish and skate all feature on the menu and the cooking skills to back up the first-rate fresh ingredients are exemplified by game dishes such as collops of venison with hazelnut stuffing and two sauces and gâteau of venison with cabbage and apple compôte. The menu is ornamented by a superb, wide-ranging and rather expensive wine list. Down on the course, bar meals are served in the clubhouse all day. Open all year.

Malin Court, Turnberry KA26 9PB tel: (0655) 31457 **
This hotel on the north side of the golf courses, just south of the village of Maidens, has a charming and well-appointed restaurant where good meals, featuring local beef and lamb, pork, salmon and seafood, are gracefully presented in *table d'hôte* or full *à la carte* menus at very reasonable prices. There is a short but carefully selected wine list. Open all year.

SOUTHERNESS, Dumfries and Galloway DG2 8AZ tel: (038788) 677
6548 yards SSS 72

RESTAURANTS
Clonyard House Hotel, Colvend **   Cairndale Hotel, Dumfries ***

Southerness is the most southerly and the least known of Scotland's great golf courses and although it has a highly traditional and even old-fashioned look, it is the creation of Mackenzie Ross, the architect of Turnberry. It is the only course I know in Scotland from which you can see England, in the shape of the purple hills of Cumbria, across the Solway Firth. It opened in 1947, when it proved so difficult that it had to be remodelled.

Even in the revised version there is nothing mealy-mouthed about Southerness. It states its challenge from the start. Outside the modern clubhouse you begin your round on one of those tees which looks like a tiny green island in the middle of a great malachite sea of heather, setting off westwards into the prevailing wind.

The struggle against the wind continues at the long par 4 2nd (453 yards), with a treacherous bunker just on the left of the fairway directly on the line to the flag and heather and whins menacing the wayward shot.

For the first eight holes the course circles a meadow with grazing cows. At the 3rd it turns towards the sea. The 4th is a tricky short hole in a cross-wind and it seems a respite when you find the 5th turning back downwind until you read the length on the tee-box—494 yards with a brute of hog's back run-up to the green and a bit of terror out at the knee of the dog-leg when you spot a couple of black and white posts marking a stream.

Although the first nine is longer by 130 yards, the second half seems to call for more precise and skilful golf. After the short heather-enshrouded 10th, the 11th has a stream across the fairway, cunningly hidden just 30 yards short of the green.

The 12th is the best and most spectacular hole on the course. It turns back southwards towards the Solway Firth and you stand on the tee and peer into the linksland rolling flatness which makes distances so deceptive. Once you have accepted that the flag is on the land's edge, starkly outlined against the bright water, you look at the card again and refuse to accept its measurement of only 419 yards, par 4.

It is not even as if you could get there directly. The 12th is a right-hand dog-leg calling for a drive carefully placed between fairway bunkers and a powerfully accurate shot into a saddle green between two tussocky humps with the beach immediately behind. The only vestige of compassion in the design of this hole is that, from where you play your second shot, you cannot see the pond that creeps into the left of the green and into which the south-westerly wind threatens to blow your ball. A rare hole.

There are two long par 4s at the 13th and 14th. The 15th is another of Southerness's dangerous short holes. The 16th is a long dog-leg of 433 yards which requires two powerful straight shots to get home, the 17th is another deceptive short hole and you turn thankfully downwind for the 18th, only to find that it goes on for all of 485 yards.

The wind makes a great deal of difference at Southerness, but in this sheltered part of Scotland, it does not blow all the time. However, its absence can make judgement as tricky as its presence. This is a superb course, the kind of links on which the game was born and only a short turn off the road from Carlisle to Glasgow, 35 miles westwards from Gretna Green via Dumfries. A most diverting diversion.

Clonyard House Hotel, Colvend, Dalbeattie DG5 4QW
tel: (055-663) 372 **
This handsome Victorian house in six acres of wooded grounds is about

6 miles along the A710 Solway coast road towards Dalbeattie. In its big nineteenth-century dining room there are succulent scallops from Kirk-cudbright, tender Galloway beef and lamb, Solway salmon, venison and Scottish goat cheeses on the menu as well as a mouth-watering range of home-made desserts. There is a sound wine list and informal meals are served in the cocktail bar. Open all year.

Cairndale Hotel, English Street, Dumfries DG1 2DF
tel: (0387) 54111 ***
A large and comfortable hotel in the middle of Dumfries converted from three Victorian town houses, the Cairndale is 14 miles from Southerness on the A75 Dumfries–Carlisle road. The restaurant serves excellent food made from local products: smoked salmon mousse with tayberry cream sauce; noisettes of Border lamb with apricots and a brandy sauce; scampi in chef Hoefken's own style; sirloin of Galloway beef; and good puds like hot butterscotch pancake with pear. The wine list offers a choice of half-bottles. Open all year.

ENGLAND

North

The north of England has some of the best and most renowned links anywhere in the world at Royal Birkdale, Royal Liverpool and Royal Lytham St Annes, but also at Silloth, Southport and Ainsdale, Hillside and Formby and many fine inland courses of different character, on fell and moor and parkland like Brampton and Windermere, Ganton, Moor Allerton, Fairhaven and Clitheroe. Except for the big names, the pressure of play on these courses is not as intense as it can be in the south of England and the Midlands but with interest in golf growing all the time and not enough new courses being created to meet the demand, it is always best to book. You should carry your golf-club membership card and a handicap certificate, as many clubs ask for them before allowing you to play.

SILLOTH-ON-SOLWAY, CA5 4AD tel: (06973) 31304   *6343 yards SSS 70*
RESTAURANT
Quince and Medlar, Cockermouth **

The club was founded in 1892 and was part of the expansion of the railway age when many golf courses were built to encourage people to travel by train. Turnberry, Gleneagles and Royal St Georges are other examples. Silloth became famous through the prowess of Cecil Leitch, who was the greatest woman golfer of her day. She won the British Ladies' title four times and also the French and Canadian titles; in 1921 setting an unsurpassed record in winning the Canadian final 17 and 15!
Just across the Solway from Southerness, Silloth is remarkable for its superb seaside turf and undulating fairways and sand, gorse, whins and heather all play their part.
The 1st is not long at 380 yards but it is difficult because the second shot is blind and the greens at Silloth are never large. There is another blind shot over a gulley at the 4th and you need a good straight drive at the 486-yard 5th along the seashore because there is a long carry to the fairway and the out-of-bounds beach threatens all the way. There are beautiful views over the Solway to the Galloway hills at the 8th and the 9th looks easy, just a flick of 127 yards from elevated tee down to a green ringed with six pot bunkers, but like most things at Silloth, it is not as simple as it appears.
The inward half begins with a right-angled dog-leg where it is very tempting to try to cut the corner but only if you are prepared to find—or not find—your ball in the deep rough and there is a splendidly testing hole at the 13th. This par 5, played down a valley with heathery hills on each side, has a very perilous approach to the green, a humped fairway which can throw your ball off-line into trouble if you don't hit it absolutely right. Off-line shots are punished without remission at Silloth but it is an exhilarating course to play, especially when the wind is off the sea.

Quince and Medlar, 13 Castlegate, Cockermouth CA13 9EU
tel: (0900) 823579 **
Cockermouth is just 14 miles down the B5301 and the A595 from the
golf course at Silloth, and, as its fruity name might suggest to the discerning traveller, this is a vegetarian restaurant. However, if it might, don't let
that put you off. The dishes served in the chintzy dining room are inventive, tasty and substantial—even if you have just played Silloth in a gusty
south-westerly. Roasted aubergine soup, Stilton soufflé, terrine of young
vegetables with chives, cream and spinach in a red pepper sauce, soya
flour pancake with mushrooms, cashews, poppyseeds and spinach with a
basil and tomato sauce, mushroom and watercress roulade with asparagus.
There is plenty on your plate and side salads are substantial. Not many
wines but some organic German house wine, elderflower and sparkling
gooseberry and organic Greek.

BRAMPTON, Talkin Tarn, Brampton, Cumbria tel: (06977) 2255
6420 yards SSS 71

RESTAURANTS
Farlam Hall, Brampton *** Fantails, Wetheral ***

Brampton lies about 8 miles east of Carlisle on the A69 cross-country
Newcastle road or you can reach it from exit 43 on the M6. Its other name,
Talkin Tarn, comes from the lake near the 9th and 10th holes. A real fell
course, 400 feet above sea level and surrounded by hills, it was laid out by
James Braid in 1907 with his usual exacting ingenuity and no-one has ever
broken 70 over it in a competition. Wayward tee-shots are swallowed up
by whins, trees, heather or rushes or carried away down the steep slopes
which often border the fairways.
At the 3rd your drive has to carry dense rough to reach the playing surface
more than 150 yards away and there is out-of-bounds along the railway line
and a green tucked in near the tracks. The 4th is the longest hole (550
yards), and the elevated green makes even the most ambitious and talented
play it as a three-shotter. At the 5th there is a long drop away to the right,
bunkers left and usually the wind in your face. After that it gets more
merciful, with a few relaxing par 4s, but the 11th poses problems of club
selection because it is a dog-leg par 5, not excessively long, where the main
dilemma is choosing which club to use in order to get to the elbow without
running out of fairway.
The finish is tough with another par 5 which leaves you a blind second shot
at the 16th and the 18th is the longest par 4 on the course. Straight hitting
rather than length is the recipe for this invigorating hilly course.

Farlam Hall, Brampton CA8 2NG tel: (069-76) 234 ***
On the A689 road south to Alston, 2 miles from Brampton (not at
Farlam village) in a house above a duck pond, the Quinions serve a one-
sitting dinner in a comfortable family atmosphere. There are three
choices to each course with a sorbet in-between, cheese is served after
the main course à la française and sweets follow from the sideboard.

Duck with kumquats could be the main offering or chicken stuffed with mushrooms, preceded by seafood pancake, pear with walnut and tarragon salad, smoked chicken salad or a seafood terrine. After the English cheeses, non-diet puds in good helpings arrive, like nut fudge cake or almond and strawberry meringue. Not a stunning list but plenty of half-bottles. Open all week, dinner only.

Fantails, The Green, Wetheral CA4 8ET tel: (0228) 60329 ***
About 3 miles back towards Carlisle on the A69, turn off down the B6253 to reach Wetheral. There is a dovecote next to this converted barn which accounts for its name, but there are no doves on the menu. Instead you may be offered chicken mousseline filled with Dunsyre blue cheese from Lanark, with orange hollandaise; three marinated fishes or duck with tagliatelle and a peach sauce. Sliced chicken with wild mushrooms and spinach and asparagus soufflé are other possibilities. The list is wide-ranging with a strong Australian element. The house wine is, however, French and reasonably priced at £6.95. Open Monday to Saturday.

HEXHAM, Spital Park, Hexham NE46 3RZ tel: (0434) 603072
6272 yards SSS 70

RESTAURANTS
Manor House Inn, Kiln Pit Hill ** Laburnum House, Wylam ***

Farther along the A69, just 21 miles from Newcastle, this pretty rolling parkland course has good views through the numerous imposing trees over the Tyne valley and offers quite a different game from the windy slopes of the fell courses.
It opens with a stiff par 5 dog-leg round a copse of trees, followed by a very short but testing par 3 in the opposite direction. Then a long par 4 takes you back towards the woodland and another short well-bunkered par 3. The next three holes go up and down the course in contrasting directions, with the 6th a lengthy and difficult par 4. At the 7th and 8th holes you are at the limits of the lay-out and the 9th sets you back on the homeward track towards the handsome clubhouse, with a dog-leg round a stand of trees down to a green close by the cemetery wall.
Two more long par 4s take you to the 502-yard 15th along the boundary fence, the 16th is a well-protected par 3 with trees and bunkers, the 17th takes you out again towards the road running through the course and the final hole leads you back uphill to the angled green in front of the clubhouse. One of the best parkland courses in the north of England.

Manor House Inn, Kiln Pit Hill DH8 9LX tel: (0207) 55268 **
On the A68 southbound from Scotland about 10 miles from Hexham, this stone-built coaching inn with fine views over the Derwent valley and its picturesque reservoir, serves dinner only, except by special arrangement. Kebabs and yoghurt from Turkey, Italian cannelloni with spinach and ricotta and French-inspired pork with prunes and brandy are on the

international menu and there is a short list with some good Spanish as well as French wines and a house wine for £5.95. Open Tuesday to Saturday.

Laburnum House, Wylam NE41 8AJ tel: (0661) 852 185   ✱✱✱
In an eighteenth-century house between Hadrian's Wall and the River Tyne, just 7 miles towards Newcastle from the Hexham course, this pretty restaurant in an attractive village gives its customers good local produce with a French accent. Smoked pheasant with nut and honey dressing, fillet of wild salmon with asparagus and lime, king prawns with garlic butter, turbot with crab sauce, peppered duck breast with raspberries, plus a wide choice of ice creams and sorbets and Normandy crêpes with calvados and hot strudel as desserts. Fair wine list and reasonable prices. House wine £6.25. Open Tuesday to Saturday, dinner only.

THE NORTHUMBERLAND, High Gosforth Park, NE3 5HT
tel: (091) 2362009   *6629 yards SSS 72*

RESTAURANTS
Fisherman's Lodge, Jesmond Dene   ✱✱✱✱   21 Queen Street   ✱✱✱✱

Charles I played golf at Newcastle on the Town Moor when he was a prisoner of the Scots in 1646 but The Northumberland Club was not founded until 1898 and the course as it is now was laid out after the First World War by Harry Holt and the inescapable James Braid, mostly inside the Gosforth Park race course. Numerous championships have been played here, including the Dunlop Masters.
As it shares the site with the race-track, naturally the terrain is flat. After a quiet opening hole, there is sterner stuff at the 2nd, a long par 4 with a stream and out-of-bounds down one side.
Two par 5s running along the inside rails of the race track serve to concentrate the mind for the very tricky par 3 of 186 yards where, amazingly, no birdies were recorded the last time the Masters was played here. The 13th is a daunting hole with a carry over the race course for the bold and a difficult shot into an elevated green, guarded by trees and the course rails. The rails come into play again at the 14th, the 16th and the 18th, where your second shot must be played uphill towards a well-protected green just below the splendidly old-fashioned clubhouse. Not an easy course because in addition to the ever-present invitation to go racing out-of-bounds, there are heather, bushes and trees to contend with.

Fisherman's Lodge, Jesmond Dene NE7 7BQ tel: (091) 3281   ✱✱✱✱
At this smart restaurant in one of Newcastle's top suburbs, north of the city centre and not far from the golf course, the long menu at the luxuriously furnished Fisherman's Lodge concentrates on fish, mostly sole, turbot or halibut but shellfish and lobster too, which you can also have surf 'n' turf—a half lobster with a garlicked fillet steak.
Non-fishy dishes include fillet of beef in Parma ham with mushroom fricassee, guinea fowl and duck breast with artichokes or wild mushrooms

and asparagus. The wine list is lengthy but not expensive (except for rather pricey house wine) with an unusually large choice from Germany as well as white burgundies and well-selected Italian reds. Open Monday to Saturday, excluding Saturday lunch.

21 Queen Street, 21 Queen Street, Princes Wharf NE1 3UG
tel: (091) 222 0755 ★★★★
In the redeveloped quayside area, this polished restaurant offers a short à la carte menu, strong on market availability, particularly for fish with a reasonably priced set menu for lunch.
Fish is not by any means the only thing on offer, although when it is there you can depend on the dish having an intriguing modernistic presentation—terrine of red mullet with grilled peppers and a sharp sauce, scallops with a Thai dressing, monkfish with potatoes and artichokes and a Beaujolais sauce.
Wild-mushroom soup with truffle and foie gras ravioli, panaché of lamb with its offal, venison with sweet and sour sauce and fresh pasta, veal cutlet with pistachio stuffing and chicory and original puds are the style of other good things on offer. The list is quite comprehensive but expensive and good half-bottles are scarce. Open Monday to Saturday, excluding Saturday lunch.

WINDERMERE, Cleabarrow LA23 3NB tel: (096-62) 3123
5006 yards SSS 65

RESTAURANTS
Miller Howe ★★★★ Porthole, Bowness ★★★

Although Windermere is not exactly a savage test of golf at a length of just over 5000 yards, this invigorating hilly course just 1½ miles east of Bowness-on-Windermere sets its own problems. There is only one par 5, the 480-yard 16th, but it comes at a crucial part of the round, which is full of blind holes across the fine moorland turf, the hillocks, heather, gorse and rocks with wonderful views over the Langdale Pikes and quite often no view at all of the hole you are playing to.
Here, 500 feet up in the fells in the middle of the Lake District, you feel on top of the world. The opening holes are not difficult even if one of them is blind but there is a threatening pond at the 2nd and the 4th is a tough par 4 and the 7th is no pushover either.
A stream at the 12th can make life difficult if you are off-line but for the most part this is not a course on which to prove you have missed your vocation as a master golfer, but simply one on which to enjoy yourself, have a good sporting round with friends and delight in the wonderful air and the scenery.

Miller Howe, Rayrigg Road, Windermere LA23 1EY
tel: (096-62) 2536 ★★★★
John Tovey's hotel and restaurant, in an Edwardian house above gardens falling away to Lake Windermere and the view across the water of Claife Heights and the Grizedale Forest, lies on the A592 between Windermere

and Bowness. His fame as a TV cook and writer brings lots of people to the restaurant, so you have to book, but the menu order is quite strict and simple, even if the food is not.

The set menu has a fruit or vegetable starter, a subtly flavoured soup, then fish such as escalope of salmon with a chive and vermouth cream. The main dish is sometimes a roast or something more complex like lamb with mushroom pâté and greengage purée. After the plat du jour you get a choice of puddings, often fruit pies or tarts, sticky toffee or trifle.

There is an eclectic wine list, enthusiastic about Australia, New Zealand and America. Naturally in such a celebrated place nothing is cheap, particularly the house wine, but eating here is an agreeable and satisfying experience. Closed December to March, otherwise open all week for dinner only.

Porthole Eating House, 3 Ash Street, Bowness on Windermere LA23 3EB
tel: (096-62) 2793 ***
This Italian-run restaurant is big on service and welcome and, surprisingly, very good on interesting and original food and wine too.

Gianni Berton claims that he has culled many of his recipes from his mother's Venetian memories and established family Tuscan dishes but there has been a sea change en voyage.

The specialities' part of the menu, changed regularly, propose such unItalianate dishes as thinly sliced Scotch salmon with a shallot, tomato, vermouth and mushroom garnish, deep-fried mushrooms marinated in sherry, honey, soya and ginger. There is also Dover sole with parma ham, and a cream sauce, bresaola and other dishes nearer the north Italian heart and stomach. The wine list is magnificent, well researched and informative, and if it is especially strong on fine Italians, there is almost nothing else from the world's vineyards worth drinking that is missing and there are plenty of tempting half-bottles. House wine is £8 a litre. Closed mid-December to mid-February; otherwise open all week for dinner except Tuesday.

GANTON, Station Road, Ganton, Scarborough YO12 4PA
tel: (0944) 70329 *6693 yards SSS 73*

RESTAURANT
Lanterna, Scarborough **

The man who put Ganton on the golfing map was Harry Vardon from Jersey who won the first of his record six Open Championships when he was the professional at the Yorkshire club in 1896. During his seven years here Vardon won the Open on another two occasions and in 1900 he became the first British professional to win the American Open.

Justly famed as one of the best inland courses in Britain, Ganton has hosted many major tournaments and international matches, including the first Ryder Cup to be played in Britain after the war, the Dunlop Masters, the Amateur Championship and the PGA.

A tree-lined moorland course built on the sandy soil of the Vale of Pickering 10 miles west of Scarborough on the A64, it begins with reassuring calm with three easy-looking par 4s but there is plenty of sand and gorse around to trap the straying shot, and the green at the 2nd with its backward slope is hard to find and even more difficult to hold.

There is a testing second shot at the 397-yard 4th over a gully to a raised green with wilderness at the back. The pond to the left of the first of Ganton's two par 3s, played over the gorse to the tightly bunkered short 5th, makes further demands on precision and the 6th is a really tough par 4, needing two long and solid shots over dangerous bunkers to reach the rolling green. The second nine features two very short par 4s, but they are not as simple as their yardage may make them appear. At the 280-yard 14th you must carry a huge bunker more than 200 yards from the tee to take advantage of the shortness and at the 17th you have to hit a really bold drive across the road, avoiding the gorse and the bunkers round the green, to set up a birdie. The 16th is the toughest hole on the course with a large cross-bunker threatening the underhit drive, whins and trees all the way down the fairway edges and a very difficult approach into the high green. The 18th demands a long carry from the tee over gorse and sand to the fairway and a difficult second even from the ideal spot, avoiding the pines on the left, to the five bunker green with its cunning and deceptive borrows. In the friendly clubhouse you can only look in wonder at the card of Michael Bonnalack, the current R & A secretary, who went round in 61 when he won the English Amateur here in 1968.

Lanterna, 33 Queen Street, Scarborough YO11 1HQ
tel: (0723) 363616 ∗∗
This Italian restaurant in central Scarborough off Castle Road is a small and crowded trattoria where Gianluigi Arecco serves good pasta, polpette with tomato sauce, osso buco, cannelloni, bistecca Barolo, chicken pizzaiola with saffron rice, beautiful mussels in wine and garlic sauce, good, fresh-landed sole and lobster and delicious zabaglione. The wine list is not long but not pricey either, with good choices from Italy and there is house wine for £8 a litre. Open Tuesday to Saturday, dinner only.

ROYAL LYTHAM ST ANNE'S, Links Gate, Lytham St Anne's FY8 3LQ
tel: (0253) 724206 *6673 yards SSS 73*

RESTAURANTS
River House, Thornton-le-Fylde ∗∗∗∗ Cromwellian, Kirkham ∗∗∗

Royal Lytham St Anne's is the least picturesque of the venues for the Open Championship. Surrounded by the houses of the seaside resort of St Anne's, it is a links course without a view of the sea. It lacks the magnificent sweep of water and islands of Turnberry, the wide skies and rolling dunes of Royal St Georges and Royal Birkdale, the great vista of beach and bay at the Old Course and Troon and the steely wildness of Muirfield. Even its most fervent admirers—and they are many—could not call it pretty or impressive to the eye. But on championship days it takes its toll.

Royal Lytham has hosted the Open eight times, the first in 1926, the only year in which it has been won over these links by an American, a result which tends to rankle with golf scribes from the USA who have been downright abusive about Lytham when their stars have yet again been striped with failure on this formidable golf course.

The tally of Open winners so far has been one American, Bobby Jones, two South Africans, Bobby Locke and Gary Player, one Australian, Peter Thomson, one New Zealander, Bob Charles, one Englishman, Tony Jacklin and one Spaniard, Seve Ballesteros, twice. None of them have found it easy. Uniquely for a major tournament course in Britain, it opens with a par 3, 206 yards to a small green protected by seven bunkers with two others short to trap the under-struck shot. There are trees to the left of the tee and all the way along on the right by the railway line. It is a good test of nerve and skill to get a 3 at the opening of the round. At the 2nd and the 3rd, both long par 4s, the railway line, thinly bordered by trees, threatens all along the right and there are plenty of bunkers, a warning of what is to come.

At the 4th you turn back towards the clubhouse, threading a dog-legged route through a wilderness of tussocky hummocks to turn left-handed towards the five-bunker green. The second of Lytham's par 3s runs across the course, so you have a choice of three wind directions in the first five holes. At the first of the par 5s you turn east, back into the prevailing wind and the second shot is made more complex by a series of cross bunkers in the swale in front of the green.

One par 5 follows another at the 7th, considerably longer at 551 yards, and you are back with the railway to the right and the trees and bunkers to the left make the fairway very narrow. The railway continues as a menace down the 8th but departs at the 9th, a short hole where you have the feeling of playing straight down the shopping street behind the flag, necklaced by bunkers.

At the 10th there is a bumpy fairway amid the humps and hollows and a difficult drive to be steered between two hillocks; the 11th is a long par 5 with a narrow drive area between bunkered mounds and the short 12th looks easy but is dangerous with its green close to the boundary fence.

Lytham is notorious for bunkers with 191 in all. At the 13th you could think this the most bunkered hole on the course with ten down the right and six on the left but, in fact, the 7th with seventeen and the 17th with eighteen exceed it. From here in you had better get used to looking at sand for eighty-two of Lytham's bunkers are on the final six holes.

In fact the 13th and 14th are relatively simple holes if you hit the ball straight and stay away from the fairway edges, unlike the 15th which is cross-bunkered to inhibit the long approach to the deviously contoured green. The six finishing holes are all par 4s but only two of them play in roughly the same direction, so that the wind changes at every hole.

The 453-yard 17th is a monster, a left-hand dog-leg which looks rather as if it had barely survived an air raid. There are bunkers all along the left, they sweep across the angle about 300 yards out and there are seven more around the oval green. Unless your drive is on the right, you cannot see the green, hidden by trees and a large mound from the left side. Beside one of the left bunkers is a plaque commemorating Bobby Jones's famous 173-yard shot out of it to the green with which he clinched the 1926 Open. There are also a lot of bunkers at the 18th, two sets across the fairway and eight round the subtly rolling green. 'A fine, fierce, searching test of golf' Bernard Darwin called it and no-one who has played Royal Lytham is likely to disagree with him.

Nearby there are two other fine golf courses, St Anne's Old Links (6601 SSS 72), Highbury Road, St Anne's: tel: (0253) 21826, the site of the original Lytham and St Anne's course and still an intriguing and challenging inland links and Fairhaven (6808 yards SSS 73), Lytham Hall Park, Ansdell: tel: (0253) 736976, a long, multi-bunkered parkland course which has five holes over 500 yards with two of them in the first three.

The River House, Skippool Creek, Thornton-le-Fylde FY5 5LF
tel: (0253) 883497 * * * *
Nine miles north of Royal Lytham on the estuary of the River Wyre, a boat and bird-haunted creek is overlooked by The River House, a small hotel and restaurant of great character and its own individual style. You can forget the fashionable cult of *cuisine minceur*, Bill Scott's cooking leans towards generosity even lavishness. The menu is not long and it can change daily because of his insistence on fresh produce so that the availability and choice of fish from Fleetwood and seasonal vegetables and game are influences.

There are usually about ten dishes to each course. Salmon in several manners, cured according to The River House's own recipe then cold-smoked at Fleetwood; with sauce bordelaise or en papillote with a sauce of chives. Meat is often roasted, prime cuts of lamb with mint sauce; hare and pigeon; venison in game sauce; veal with tomato and basil. For dessert there is chocolate mousse in three colours; crème brûlée with orange compôte. Bread and biscuits for the cheese are home-made; there are three kinds of coffee and a dozen choices of tea. A happy browsing list in which there are bargains to be found among the Italians and mature clarets. Unusually, there are Swiss wines. Open Monday to Saturday, excluding Saturday lunch.

Cromwellian, 16 Poulton Street, Kirkham PR4 2AE
tel: (0772) 685680 * * *
Kirkham is about 6 miles from Royal Lytham on the A583 to Preston. Peter and Josie Fawcett's restaurant, with the somewhat austere name, is more cavalier than roundhead in style, offering a three-course menu changed monthly with five main dishes, one usually steak and another vegetarian, plus such things as sole with prawn mousse, guinea fowl stuffed with wild rice or pork with a sage and apple purée and burgundy sauce.

For starters there are smoked trout, filo parcels of chicken and garlic cheese, soup, pâté or fruit. For dessert there are substantial old favourites like treacle tart, apple and almond crumble or rhubarb Brown Betty. There is a lengthy, largely French list with a grading system for sweetness in white wines and robustness for reds. Open Tuesday to Saturday dinner, Sunday lunch.

ROYAL BIRKDALE, Waterloo Road, Birkdale, Southport PR8 2LX
tel: (0704) 69903   *6711 yards SSS 73*

RESTAURANTS
High Moor ✱✱✱   Bold Hotel ✱✱

It took fifty years after Scotsmen trading with Manchester had founded Old Manchester, England's second golf club in 1818, for the game to move in the north of England to the kind of territory on which golf had been created, with the founding of the Royal Liverpool Club at Hoylake in 1869. In the 1880s courses were opened at Formby, Hesketh and Royal Lytham St Anne's and in 1889, the most testing of the Lancashire courses was created at Birkdale.

Although Royal Birkdale is now recognised as the most demanding of the north-western links courses in England, it took sixty-five years for the Open Championship to be played there. Since 1954, however, the Open has come to Birkdale seven times and has provided some of the most exciting finishes in its history.

As with all seaside courses, playing Royal Birkdale and meeting the challenges it presents is primarily affected by your ability to play in wind. The prevailing winds here are westerly and when it blows hard from this point of the compass, reaching the fairways off the back tees at some holes can become a tough problem. However, Royal Birkdale is not one of those courses which sink back into nonentity if the wind does *not* blow. Come sun, rain, wind or calm this course sets a scale and quality of golfing problems not encountered often elsewhere.

The supreme virtue at Royal Birkdale is straightness, because off the fairway the rough can be literally impenetrable, not just long tough grass, such as you find on most seaside courses, but willow scrub and thick, thorny tangles of wild blackberries, which are almost impossible to get a club through. At several holes the rough comes very close to the green so the approach has to be played with great accuracy to avoid trouble just off the putting surfaces.

The 1st sets off northwards. A double dog-leg par 4 of 450 yards where the green is difficult to see for the second shot because unless you are virtually (or actually) in the rough on the left, it is hidden by a large mound with bunkers beyond. The 2nd is a similar par 4 where if you do not get the drive in the middle of the fairway, carrying the projecting left hand mound, the green is difficult to attack, especially as it slopes from back to front. At the 3rd being on the wrong side of the fairway can again ensure no view or an incomplete sight of the green. It is generally downwind but your tee-shot has to finish on the left to get a clear shot at the green. The wind is difficult to judge at the short 4th, for you are sheltered at the tee but exposed approaching the narrow and tightly bunkered green.

There is a pond, the home of the rare natterjack toad, on the right as you come into the well-guarded green of the 5th but if you are that far off-line with your approach, you are in real trouble, which is likely to increase when you get on to the roly-poly green.

Jack Nicklaus reckons that the 6th, even with the fairway widened at the right-hand dog-leg, still plays 4½ and certainly a long and accurate tee-shot is needed to get a sight of the green or you must lay up short of the cross-bunker on the knee and play the second blind. The short 7th was toughened up for the 1991 Open by the tee being moved, so that you must play more directly into the wind, and by putting in two new bunkers below the mounds, scrub and other sand surrounding the green.

The 8th, an otherwise relatively simple par 4, is renowned for the subtle borrows of its dune-shielded green. At the 9th, the tee is 30 feet below the fairway and the tee-shot is completely blind; at the left-hand dog-leg 10th you have another blind shot to the green if you are on the left (and not in any of the bunkers on the angle, when you have no shot).

The 11th is not a problem hole if you keep straight and stay out of the bunkers on the right and the dunes on the left. But the 12th, a new hole created for the 1965 Open, has been claimed to be the best short hole in Britain. Certainly it asks for a very difficult tee-shot, 184 yards into the half-right prevailing wind with steep tangled banks all round the green, four bunkers in front and a crowned putting surface.

The 13th used to be an easy 5 but for the 1991 Open it was reduced to a much more testing 4. However, it is still not too much of a problem if you keep straight and don't stray off the fairway. The green slopes from the back and can provide some tricky putts, depending on the pin position. The large green is wide open at the 199-yard 14th and although it slopes front and left, only the wind makes it a difficult hole.

The 15th is the longest hole on the course, needing a powerful and tight drive between three bunkers on the left and the encroaching rough and a stand of trees on the right to get into the ideal position for the second shot, played over the eight bunkers spattered across the fairway between 160 and 110 yards from the green. On no hole on the course is it more important to choose exactly where you must place the ball for each shot. Any error of distance or direction can be very costly. Even when the second shot has found an unpenalised haven between or beyond the minefield of bunkers short of the green, the approach must be played with skill and care—for there are two bunkers at the front edge of the green, which slopes gently from back to front, making putts difficult to judge.

The 16th is known as Palmer's hole, although it was the 15th when he played it in 1961. From the scrub and rough to the right of the fairway he hit the miraculous shot from behind a bush which almost certainly won him the Open that year. A plaque commemorates the shot and it is a good spot to stay away from because Palmer's great par-saving, earth-moving 5 iron is unlikely to be repeated.

The hole dog-legs right and the drive should be aimed at keeping away from Palmer territory and should be struck towards the rolling hummocks on the left to give a clear view into the plateau green. A crowned approach to the green means that the second shot must be hit on to the putting surface to prevent the ball being thrown off into the greenside bunkers waiting to gobble it up. A bunker on the left, halfway up the green and a bank falling away to the right complicate still further this dangerous hole.

For the 1991 Open the 17th was lengthened and adjusted to return it to being a par 5 of 543 yards, enough to stifle anyone's temerity one would think, yet Seve Ballesteros reached it with a drive and an 8 iron—and then holed the eagle putt!

However, it still presents plenty of problems for the less talented and more timid. The drive has to carry one large sand dune on the right and get past another on the left and stay on line down a fairway bordered by high banks tangled with severe rough and enveloping bushes. The entrance to the green has been made narrower by new bunkers in front, the green slopes towards you and there is dense willow scrub at the back. Most people will be grateful for a par 5.

The final hole back towards the white 1930s-style clubhouse is a 472-yard par 4 with a central fairway bunker demanding that you make an early decision on where you want to play your second from. With the hole dog-legging half-right you are probably best aiming left of the bunker, but don't be too long—for there is another bunker farther on and the punishing rough swings right just about where you can run out of fairway. From the left side of the fairway the entrance to the green, although not wide, is not as intimidating, and the green, once you are on it, is not too tortuous.

This part of Lancashire is rich in fine courses. Hillside (6858 yards SSS 73: tel: (0704) 69902) and Southport & Ainsdale (6612 yards SSS 73: tel: (0704) 78092) are near neighbours to Royal Birkdale and similar in terrain and Formby (6700 yards SSS 73: tel: (070-48) 74273), just a couple of miles down the road, is another great links course with its own character, in this case including pine trees.

High Moor, Highmoor Lane, Wrightington WN6 9PS
tel: (025-75) 2364 ***
In the middle of the Lancashire moorland on the B5250, about 16 miles from Southport via Burscough and the A5209, High Moor offers, in compensation for a complex journey, genuinely classical cooking and an atmosphere of splendid isolation.

As starters there can be duck-liver terrine; melon with red fruits in elderflower jelly; scallops in a ginger and oyster sauce or fruit soup followed by quail with mushroom stuffing, foie gras and orange; loin of lamb with onion and chive purée and red-currant sauce; honey-coated duck with apple pancakes and cider vinegar sauce or fillet of veal wrapped in bacon with calves' liver and tarragon gravy. The list has some good wines from Spain, decent clarets and a fair selection from elsewhere but not enough half-bottles. Open Tuesday to Sunday, except Saturday lunch and Sunday dinner.

Bold Hotel, Lord Street, Southport tel: (0704) 532578 **
This white-painted coaching inn, right on Southport's main street, has a very well-run restaurant with an imaginative menu which makes good use of fresh ingredients, particularly local fish. Scampi, scallops, crab,

lobster and mussels, salmon and seafish are all cooked well in traditional styles aided by a touch of originality. There are good steaks and chops and a reasonably-priced wine list.

ROYAL LIVERPOOL, Meols Drive, Hoylake L47 4AL tel: (051) 632 3101
6821 yards SSS 74

RESTAURANTS
Beadles, Birkenhead ** Rondelle, Birkenhead **

'At Hoylake', Bernard Darwin said, 'the golfing pilgrim is emphatically on classical ground.' Here in 1897, almost thirty years after the founding of the Royal Liverpool Club, the Open Championship was played in the north of England for the first time. The first Open in England had been just two years before, when the great John Henry Taylor, a Devon man, had won the first of his five Opens on Royal St Georges at Sandwich. He was not, however, the first Englishman to win the Open.

That honour belongs to one of the two great amateurs produced by the Royal Liverpool Club, John Ball. The other was Harold Hilton.

John Ball was born at Hoylake on Christmas Eve, 1861 and his father owned the Royal Hotel there before the race course was transformed into a golf links in 1869. When it opened, the golf course became young John's playground and his prodigious talent was soon evident. In 1876 when he was fifteen, he competed in the Open at St Andrews and finished sixth, just eight strokes behind the winner, Bob Martin, and ahead of many of the leading professionals of the day. He won the Amateur Championship eight times between 1888 and 1912, and in 1890 at St Andrews he became the first amateur to win the Open.

The record books sometimes attribute the first English victory to Jack Burns of Warwick in 1888 but Jack Burns hailed from St Andrews and did not go to Warwick as a professional until after his Open Championship victory—and almost certainly because of it. So the honour remains firmly with the north of England.

Appropriately enough, when the Open did take place at Hoylake in 1897, it was won by an amateur of the host club, the only occasion in the history of the tournament on which this has ever happened.

His name was Harold Horsfall Hilton and he had the remarkable distinction of having won the Championship once before, at Muirfield in 1892, the first time it was played over seventy-two holes instead of thirty-six, when Hilton established a record aggregate score of 305 which was to last for eleven years. He won the Open twice and the Amateur Championship four times and became the first golfer ever to hold the US and the British Amateur titles simultaneously. A powerful man of small build—he was just 5 feet 7 inches in height—in addition to being a great player, he was one of the earliest golf journalists, the first editor of *Golf Monthly*, still a universally respected golf magazine.

Like John Ball, who lived to the ripe old age of seventy-nine, Harold Hilton, who died in March 1942 in his seventy-fourth year, proved conclusively that golf on the north-west coast of England is good for you!

The Open has been played at Hoylake ten times, among them the memorable occasion on which Arnaud Massy, a Basque from south-western France, became the first overseas player to win the Championship in 1907 and the only European to do so until Severiano Ballesteros won the first of his three Open titles at Royal Lytham and St Annes in 1979.

Hoylake was also the scene of the last of J H Taylor's five Open victories in 1913. It was part of the never-again-to-be-achieved triumph of Bobby Jones in 1930 when he made the Grand Slam, winning the Open Championships of Britain and the United States and the Amateur Championships of both countries, all in the same year.

In 1956 it saw the third in succession of the Open wins by the remarkable Australian, Peter Thomson, who was to go on to add two more to his list of Open victories and, in 1967, on the last occasion the Open was played at Hoylake, it was the setting for one of the most popular Open victories of modern times, when the Argentinian, Roberto de Vicenzo, at the age of forty-five, in the tournament in which he had so often been the bridesmaid but—until that year—never the bride, won by two shots from Jack Nicklaus. It also provided the venue for the last time there was any serious challenge by an amateur for the Open title.

In 1947 Fred Daly, the only Irishman ever to win the Open, was in the clubhouse at Hoylake with a total of 293 when he heard that the American amateur, Frank Stranahan, was on the 17th tee needing a 4 and 3 to equal his score.

The last two holes at Hoylake are par 4s, the 17th 418 yards long and the 18th 395 yards, one into the prevailing wind and one with it. At the 17th the wind defeated Stranahan and he took 5 but at the 18th, needing a 2 to tie, he hit a magnificent 3-iron shot downwind straight at the flag; towards which it rolled, seemingly inexorably, accompanied by a huge roar from the dense crowd lining the fairway, only to pull up three inches from the hole.

Hoylake, despite its title Royal Liverpool, is not in the city but on the Wirral peninsula between the Rivers Mersey and Dee which is joined to Liverpool by two tunnels. It was dropped from the championship rota for the Open because there was not enough room for all the ancillary activities that go on at such a tournament—the tented village, car-parking and local accommodation for players and spectators—but like Carnoustie rumours persist about its return.

As a golf course the initial emotion which it inspires is one of terror. In addition to the course boundaries, there are several areas of out-of-bounds within the course and this is a problem which faces you immediately at the 428-yard 1st.

The practice ground between the 1st, 15th and 16th holes is surrounded by a low turf wall known as a 'cop' beyond which is out-of-bounds. Along the right-hand dog-leg of the 1st, this threatens all the way for the cop is too low to contain a shot which bounces right, and plenty of players have been out-of-bounds twice before reaching the green at this hole.

The 3rd is a tough par 5, bunkered right at the angle of the dog-leg and with a massive bunker in front of the green. At the 6th, there is another out-of-bounds area in the orchard at around drive length. At the short 7th there is another cop and the 200-yard 11th, right along the shore is also a tough one-shot hole.

The finish is very long and demanding, 2318 yards from the 14th tee to the 18th green, include two petrifying flirtations with the practice ground cop at the 15th and 16th. In fact by the time you get to the 16th, just in front of the clubhouse, you may well feel you have done enough to complete your round but there are still another 818 yards to go. Not a course for the strayers from the straight and narrow.

Beadles, 15 Rose Mount, Oxton L43 5SG tel: (051) 653 9010 **
The Gotts' restaurant in a revamped Victorian shop has good Anglo-French food in a menu offering several choices on each course, generally classically cooked but offering also such personalised specialities as gravdlax cured in vodka; grilled langoustines with garlic mayonnaise; veal with mango sauce; beef with pickled walnuts; duck with calvados and apple; fennel à la grecque; venison and other game in season. Interesting and fairly priced list. House wine: £5.50. Open Tuesday to Saturday, dinner only. Closed August.

Rondelle, 11 Rose Mount, Oxton L43 5SG tel: (051) 652 8264 **
The dishes on the Wilkinsons' menu are pretty smart and avant-garde for Birkenhead but it fulfils its innovative promise with such fare as venison and hare terrine with bramble sauce, marinated scallops with herbs, gingered mussels and more substantial nurture like pigeon with home-made pasta and chocolate sauce, salmon with a rhubarb sauce; poached lamb with leeks; and interesting and imaginatively exotic puds. You get a glass of sweet wine with dessert and there are five kinds of bread. There is a good if rather muddled list and house wine for £5.65. Open Monday to Saturday, dinner only and Sunday lunch.

MANCHESTER, Hopwood Cottage, Rochdale Road,
Middleton M24 4LY tel: (061) 643 2718 *6450 yards SSS 72*

RESTAURANTS
Blinkers French *** Quan Ju De **

Manchester can boast the second oldest golf club in England after Blackheath, for golf was played there in 1818 on Kersal Moor but that course disappeared under the expansion of Greater Manchester and there is no clear line of inheritance. However, Manchester Golf Club was founded in 1882 and plays over a rolling moorland course, 7 miles north of the city, an agreeable rather than testing place to play golf within sight of the Pennines, with invitingly broad fairways and generous greens. A stream comes into play at the 4th on the outward half and at three holes coming home, and there are some other little local difficulties which require nerve as well as skill.

At the 5th you must carry deep rough to reach the fairway and then play a hard-to-estimate shot to a green on the brow of the hill. At the 12th there is a threatening gully on the right and the par-3 13th is one of those on-the-green-or-else holes. Another substantial carry across a valley is demanded at the 16th. At the 17th you must aim carefully to stay out of the encroaching bunkers and a solid tee-shot to a humped fairway at the final hole rounds off a good tight finish.

Blinkers French, 16 Princess Street M1 4NB tel: (061) 228 2503 ***
It is possible to get the impression that there are only Chinese, Indian and Middle Eastern restaurants in Manchester; certainly it has some of the best and least expensive oriental eating places in the country but Blinkers French, in a basement near the Town Hall, is a European outpost. Here good fish and lobster, presented in various combinations, are a speciality. Diverting starters such as Stilton with red peppers, smoked halibut and smoked salmon with wild rice give a raffish air to the menu but there can also be good stuffed mushrooms, chicken supremes with herbs and grilled sea trout.
The wine list is pricey at the connoisseur's end but quite reasonable for those who do not feel life is empty without a bottle of Montrachet with a lobster fantasy. House wine is £7.50. Open Monday to Saturday, except for Saturday lunch.

Quan Ju De, 44 Princess Street M1 6DE tel: (061) 236 5236 **
This tastefully decorated restaurant is about as unlike the standard Chinese eating house concept as can be imagined. There is sculpture, fine porcelain vases and abstract paintings on the walls of the glass-screened dining room. The cooking is Pekinese and offers rarities such as marinated sea anemones, grilled dumplings with vinaigrette, fried smoked chicken and marinated duck breast in bean paste as starters and a wide and unusual choice of main dishes, such as deep-fried Pekin-chicken with aubergines and green peppers and shredded fried beef with chilli. There is a separate vegetarian menu. The French house wine is £7.25. Open all week.

MOOR ALLERTON, Coal Road, Wike, Leeds LS17 9NH
tel: (0532) 661 1154 *6542 yards SSS 72*

RESTAURANTS
Paris, Leeds **   Pool Court, Pool in Wharfedale **

Moor Allerton is the only course in Britain designed by the most celebrated (even notorious) golf architect of the post-war years, the American Robert Trent Jones. The twenty-seven holes on this rolling parkland course bear many of his distinctive hallmarks: weirdly shaped bunkers, lakes and streams, contoured greens and length.
The 1st is a long par 4 with a stream to pitch over to the uphill green. The 4th is a tricky par 3 played from a high tee to a low green, always one of the most difficult shots to judge.
Next comes a par 5 where only the bold will think of trying to get up in two, because of the lake in front of the green. There is a longer par 5 at the 8th, 550 yards with a blind tee-shot and out-of-bounds along the right.

On the back nine there is another difficult par 5 at the 14th where, with water all over the place, it demands very accurately struck and well-estimated shots and when you have escaped that, a pond awaits you at the short 15th, snuggling up against the right-hand edge of the green. The dog-legged 17th has a valley guarding the flag and there is more water at the 18th, coming into play for the approach. Worth a detour. There is nothing else quite like it in Britain.

Paris, 36a Town Street, Horsforth, Leeds LS18 4RJ
tel: (0532) 581885 **
This upstairs restaurant has a menu which combines the kind of sound French country cooking you get in bistros with more fantastical dishes created not from tradition but by the chef's imagination. Alongside the daily fish chalked on a blackboard and the choucroûte garni, beef bourguignon, cassoulet and stuffed pig's trotter with madeira sauce there is seafood en papillote with tarragon, scallops in pastry with Gruyère sauce, chicken breasts stuffed with cream cheese, calf's liver with spring onions, mushrooms, bacon and sage and lamb with apricot purée. Puds oscillate from the solid steamed ginger to the more ethereal crème brûlée and the list offers a good selection of Australian and French wines and a few others. House French is £6.50. Open all week, dinner only.

Pool Court, Pool Bank, Pool in Wharfedale LS21 1EH
tel: (0532) 842288 **
Pool is about 7 miles west of Moor Allerton, just off the A659 and Pool Court is a very well-run restaurant. There is an undeviating set three-course meal and a four-course dinner priced by the cost of the main dish which allows a lot more choice. Such things as mussels and scallops with smoked bacon, home-made pasta and saffron sauce; char-grilled sea trout; oysters with salmon roe and spinach; chicken terrine or pea and mint soup are offered as starters. Later, roasted calf's liver in herb sauce; chicken with stir-fry vegetables; pigeon and rabbit terrine with herbs and truffles; osso buco; stuffed breast of guinea-fowl or duck with cal-vados could follow. Then succulent desserts like passion fruit parfait or white chocolate mousse to finish. The list is rather expensive although well chosen but there is a page for 'Everyday Wines', all priced at £8.95, which rather begs the question of what you drink daily but offers some bargains. Open Tuesday to Saturday, dinner only.

LINDRICK, Lindrick Common, near Worksop S81 8BH
tel: (0909) 485802 *6615 yards SSS 72*

RESTAURANT
Old Vicarage, Ridgeway ***

Lindrick sprang to fame when Great Britain and Ireland, as it was then, won a rare Ryder Cup victory over the Americans there in 1957. Straddling the A57 from Worksop to Sheffield, it is a testing and fascinating heathland course founded in 1891 by a group of Sheffield enthusiasts who were prepared to travel 14 miles out of town for their golf, an arduous journey in those days.

The most famous (or infamous) hole on the course is the 4th, 480 yards long with a blind second shot down a steep bank into a hollow where the counties of Yorkshire, Nottinghamshire and Derby were said to meet. This used to be a favourite spot for prize-fighting and cock-fighting because the participants and spectators when challenged by the law could instantly flee into another county where their pursuers had no jurisdiction.

However, what is more likely to concern the golfer than this historical vignette is that the green is backed by the River Ryton and a fine stand of trees. Bernard Darwin considered the 4th 'the worst hole on the course. But it must never, on any account, be altered.' The 10th has a very narrow area in which to place your drive and more craft than power is needed for the second shot to steer the ball over the cross-bunker which protects the green. There is only one par 5 and two 3s in the outward half but there are two 5s, the 14th much the longest at 557 yards, on the way home to the intractable 18th, a mere par 3 but one on which it is perfectly possible to ruin a good score. The tee-shot must be flown the full distance to the green 206 yards away underneath the clubhouse windows, for there is a treacherous bunker just 12 yards short of the putting surface, to penalise anyone who does not make the carry.

The Old Vicarage, Ridgeway Moor, Ridgeway S12 3XW
tel: (0742) 475814 * * *

If you cut across country south-west to the A616, Ridgeway is just off the B6054 about 5 miles from Sheffield city centre. The Old Vicarage is just opposite the village church. Mrs Bramley's cooking is a skilled amalgam of English tradition and modern innovation and much is made of local supply strengths and the large and well-organised family garden. So fillet of lamb comes with fresh mint and garlic and chicken terrine is accompanied by apple and geranium jelly. Wild rabbit—the menu is strong on game at the appropriate times of year—is served as either a herby roast saddle or a pie.

There are also signs of European influence in dishes like devilled lamb's kidneys with bruschetta or smoked rosemary-flavoured beef fillet with polenta. Desserts show the same inventive touches, although the traditional favourites like baked chocolate pudding still have their place. The list is excellent, with knowledgeable choices made from Spain as well as France. House wine is £12. Open Tuesday to Saturday.

SHERINGHAM, Weybourne Road, Sheringham NR26 8HG
tel: (0263) 823488   *6430 yards SSS 71*

RESTAURANTS
Yetman's, Holt * * *   Moorings, Wells-next-the-Sea * *

Sheringham's part in history is claimed by Joyce Wethered, who recorded her first championship victory here in 1920 at the age of nineteen when she had joined the competitors in the English Ladies' Championship 'just to keep a friend company.' What happened to the friend is not recorded but the young Miss Wethered went on to beat the great Cecil Leitch from Silloth in the final round.

It is also one source of the story about her putting for victory at the 17th when a train went by. She holed the putt and when asked afterwards how she concentrated with the noisy train clanging and huffing past, she said: 'What train?' Mark you, I've always thought that was at the 16th at the Old Course at St Andrews in 1929—but you know what legends are.

This splendid East Anglian links is set on a cliff top and the holes vary a good deal, some have open and generous fairways, some are strung along the edge of the cliffs with fine views up the coast and over the sea, some are pure heathland with lots of gorse and some have rolling fairways and difficult greens.

The 1st is a short par 4, with bunkers where it angles left and a two-level green. The 2nd is a good 5 and at the 3rd you start on the first of the cliff-top holes, 424 yards but the line for the tee-shot takes you away from the plunge to the beach.

But the perils of the sea come fully into play at the next hole where, after a shot from a high tee to the fairway below, the second demands a nerve-tingling blow over a shallow valley to a green on the cliff edge. The par-3 6th is also played from a high tee down to the green 217 yards below, with threats from both bunker and beach.

After the 7th you leave the cliffs and strike inland through (or preferably alongside) the gorse. The 12th is a tough hole where you have to dog-leg round a bunkered gorse slope with a difficult second into a well-guarded green. Joyce Wethered's railway still haunts the 17th, although the green has been moved away from the tracks, but they return at the final hole to make the drive intimidating.

Very enjoyable golf with the variety in the nature of the holes providing additional interest.

Yetman's, 37 Norwich Road, Holt NR25 6SA tel: (0263) 713320 ✳✳✳
This yellow-washed restaurant about 7 miles from Sheringham has a daily menu offering three or four dishes at each course, which include Norfolk delicacies such as lobster, crab, asparagus and artichokes, cooked plainly to preserve their intrinsic flavours.

There are home-made pickles to go with the roast pork as well as dishes like cassoulet; chicken with curry and mint sauce; ham with beetroot or the more traditional skate with black butter. Despite the limited menu, there is always a vegetarian dish. The list from a Colchester wine merchant is fairly priced and there is wine by the glass and some half-bottles. There are ten house wines from £7. Open Wednesday to Sunday.

Moorings, 6 Freeman Street, Wells-next-the-Sea NR23 1BA
tel: (0328) 710949 ✳✳
Wells-next-the-Sea is 17 miles from Sheringham along the A149 but it would be worth going much farther to eat at Moorings, the kind of fish restaurant which concentrates on the fish and not the decor nor the

verbiage on the menu. There are other things to eat and vegetarians are catered for with more exotic dishes like kofta with creamed tahini or aubergine purée. You can also have pigeon with red wine, port and cream, pork brawn or keftédes.

The glory of the menu however is the harvest of the sea—crab, oysters, sole, skate, sea trout, mullet, salmon, dabs, smoked cod's roe and three kinds of smoked fish can be on the menu at one time. Spicy fish soup; cockle pie (casseroled cockles and cream with a breadcrumb crust); taramasalata; stockfish marmite; smoked fish Russian salad with beetroot, apple and potatoes; gravdlax with mustard sauce: shrimp and anchovy sauce with dabs; tomato, garlic and capers with mullet.

Puddings are solidly traditional, apple tart or trifle and there are good British cheeses. The list shows careful buying, good French from well-researched regions but some classics as well and an interesting sweet wine, intriguingly named Ovid's Tears (he was banished after writing *The Arts of Love* to the Black Sea by Augustus in AD 8), from Romania. Eight French house wines are priced at £6.25 a bottle. Open all week, except for Tuesday, Wednesday and Thursday lunch.

ALDEBURGH, Saxmundham Road, Aldeburgh IP15 5PE
tel: (0728) 452890   *6630 yards SSS 71*

RESTAURANTS
Regatta, Aldeburgh ∗∗∗   Old Rectory, Campsea Ash ∗∗∗

Aldeburgh is a mixture of seaside links and heathland with a few trees thrown in for good measure. It is one of the oldest courses in England dating from 1884 and the tale has it that it was here the doyen of golf writers, Bernard Darwin, hit his last shots shortly before he died in 1961 and muttered 'Now I can retire gracefully from this unspeakable game.'

A few others have muttered gracelessly on the swards of Aldeburgh for it is a very difficult course on which to score well, judging by both the amateur and professional records of 65 and 68. Nine of the par 4 holes measure more than 400 yards, most of them considerably more. Indeed there is only one short 4 and that is a definite two-shotter for most people at 324 yards.

There are deep bunkers, trees and humps and hollows to contend with. At the par-3 4th you have to carry a Scottish-type bunker faced with railway sleepers on the edge of the green to be putting for your next shot. The second nine is partly links in character with undulating fairways. However at the 14th the drive path is flanked by trees and there is a ridge to be carried to the dog-leg before you play your second shot to a raised green. Perhaps a musical rhythm acquired from the famous Aldeburgh Festival and an equable temperament are the qualities most required to get round this course in a good score.

Regatta, 171–173 High Street, Aldeburgh IP15 5AN
tel: (0728) 452011 ∗∗∗
A restaurant with a wine bar in Aldeburgh's main street. You can eat in the wine bar, which is less expensive and more informal, but the restaurant

offers good value, more comfort, a bigger variety of dishes and eager service. There is always fresh fish cooked to emphasise its recent emergence from the North Sea.

But there are also good soups like courgette and mushroom; starters such as smoked haddock with Parmegianoed mushrooms or trout fillet terrine with sour cream and chives: main courses could be steak and kidney pie; grilled sole; duck with soya and sherry sauce or onion and cream tart with tomato coulis; desserts like chocolate and brandy mousse or passion fruit bavarois. The list by a Colchester wine merchant is fair in price and reasonably comprehensive in range. House wine is £6.25. Open all week.

Old Rectory, Campsea Ash IP13 0PU tel: (0728) 746524 ＊＊＊
About 10 miles from Aldeburgh just off the A12 going south to Ipswich, on the B1078, the restaurant in this seventeenth-century rectory is very much the individual creation of chef-patron Stewart Basset. There is no menu choice, meals are planned from the kitchen and there may also be an imposed wine.

However, this somewhat dictatorial attitude is ameliorated by the good food when it produces dishes like poussin in honey and ginger sauce; ragoût of lamb garnished with pickled quinces or monkfish with a sauce of watercress and tomato. Poached pears stuffed with glacé fruits and crème brûlée suggest the style of desserts on offer. Not a conforming eating place but any gripes against authoritarianism can be stilled by the list, which contains a large number of wines of high quality and distinction at prices which permit enthusiasm and might almost be said to encourage over-indulgence. Open Monday to Saturday, dinner only.

THE BELFRY, Litchfield Road, Wishaw B76 9PR tel: (0675) 70301
Brabazon 6975 yards SSS 73   Derby 6127 yards SSS 70

RESTAURANTS
Marston Farm Hotel, Bodymoor Heath ＊＊   Franzl's, Birmingham ＊＊

The Belfry has become famous as the venue on which Europe won and then retained the Ryder Cup. Opened in 1977 it was always intended to be a major championship course and was laid out by Dave Thomas with emphasis on length and target golf, a system of design which was supposed to give an advantage to the Americans but so far it has not proved to be so.

A number of important holes involve water. There is a stream across the fairway of the 340-yard 2nd which reappears just in front of the green at the par-5 4th and at the 5th where you must keep your drive right to stay out of the lake and the stream which flows from it.

The 6th is a really terrifying hole with a dangerous drive which has to find the 30-yard width of the fairway between two lakes and then needs a very accurate second shot to the green very close to the water on the left. Water is still there along the left side at the fine par-5 8th and it lurks on the approach to the green at the dog-leg 9th as well.

The 310 yard 10th is a par 4 but much more difficult than its modest length would make it appear because the stream which runs all the way down the right becomes a pond as the hole angles right-handed in front of the tree-shaded green. It was made famous by Severiano Ballesteros in 1978 when he faded an immense drive on to the green, a feat repeated by Greg Norman a few years later.

The 12th at 225 yards is a difficult par 3 for even the better than average player because of water in front of the green. There are two par 5s of 540 and 555 yards in the final four holes and at the end is the par-4 18th. This 455-yard scene of many dramas demands two carries over water, where you have to bite off as much of the first part of the lake as you dare with your drive. Without a long tee-shot it becomes almost impossible to reach the awkwardly sloping, three-level green over the second half of the lake in two. Most people play it as a 5 which rather takes the sting out but it is a wonderful tournament finishing hole.

There is no club at The Belfry. Its place is taken by a 120-bedroom hotel, conference and leisure centre with squash, tennis, swimming, snooker, sauna and a gymnasium as added attractions.

The Derby, 6127 yards SSS 70, is a less rigorous course with no lakes but a stream in play at two holes, long enough and entertaining enough for the average player.

La Galerie, Marston Farm Hotel, Dog Lane, Bodymoor Heath B76 9JD tel: (0827) 872133 **
Tucked away up a farm road just five minutes from The Belfry, the restaurant of the charming Marston Farm Hotel offers simple, uncomplicated food, well cooked and amiably served in a peaceful setting, in the middle of the Warwickshire countryside. Devilled whitebait; king prawns with garlic sauce; scallops with lobster and brandy sauce; pigeon breast with orange and walnut salad are among the starters. You get a grapefruit or lemon sorbet before the main course, which can be tournedos in curry sauce, lamb noisettes with rosemary and thyme or veal with onions, mushrooms and calvados. Short but adequate wine list.

Franzl's, 151 Milcote Road, Bearwood B67 5BN tel: (021) 429 7920 **
In the midst of all the flurry of exotica of Birmingham's Chinese and Indian restaurants, the Geireggers provide a welcome haven of Austrian *gemütlichkeit*. There is jolly *lederhosen*-type music, picturesque plates embossed with onion-tower churches and timbered *gasthausen* and brightly braided cowbells on the walls. Good *Wiener schnitzel*, venison; deep-fried pâté in bread; ham and cheese pancake; fillets of herring marinated in sour cream; red cabbage and strudel; white cabbage with carroway; haricot beans in thyme vinaigrette and massive portions of pork, beef and veal with a thick tomato, onion and paprika sauce through which you could hardly drag a violin string called *zigeuner goulasch*. Other than champagne, all the wines on the list are Austrian and most are inexpensive; House Austrian is £8. Open Tuesday to Saturday, dinner only.

LITTLE ASTON, Streetly, Sutton Coldfield B74 3AN tel: (021) 353 2942
6724 yards SSS 73

RESTAURANT
Jonathans, Oldbury ***

This is one of those peaceful gems tucked away in the roaring industrial
landscape of the Midlands which you might well have believed impossible
of existence until you found it. One of the finest inland tests of golf in
Britain, Little Aston, set in a former deer park, is an enticing blend of parkland and moorland with holes of every kind in that geographical range. One
of the few courses ever laid out by the great Harry Vardon, it was altered
slightly two years after Vardon designed it by Harry Colt, because some
members found the carries from the tees too demanding.
It opens quietly enough with a modest par 4, just a drive and a pitch but
things soon get more difficult at the uphill 437-yard, cunningly bunkered
2nd, where the misdirected shot will be in sand and a fence at the back of
the green can make the over-hit approach unplayable. The 5th is a par 3
with a testing tee-shot to an elevated green with trouble everywhere else
around. From the 4th to the 8th offers the best chance to build a good
score because that stretch contains some makeable holes where even
birdies are possible. However, the short 9th is deceptive because the tee-
shot is played from the shelter of trees and the wind over the exposed
green can be something quite different from what is felt on the tee.
The 10th is a double dog-leg, first left then right, flanked by silver birches,
where it is almost impossible to get home in two if you get your drive in
anything but the right place—over the trees on the left, missing the bunker
to the right and short of the heather cross the fairway. There is still a tight
line into the green even from this position A, skirting the trees on the right.
To get a par 4 here feels like a birdie.
At the 12th, a 491-yard par 5, the average player should abandon any idea
of going for the green in two, even off a very good drive, because the pond
which borders the green puts too much pressure on a long iron or a fairway
wood. The 14th at 313 yards seems a short 4 but the huge cross-bunker on
the fairway is difficult to carry from the tee. The 17th demands a drive up
the left half of the fairway if you are to reach the green with your second
shot and because of the treacherous slope of the green, you must be near
the pin to be sure of a par.
The 18th makes a good stimulating uphill finish. On the right, a tree
threatens the drive and crescent-shaped bunker guards the green. A
demanding kind of pleasure.

Jonathans, 16–20 Wolverhampton Road, Oldbury B68 0LH
tel: (021) 429 3757 ****

This elaborate Victorian pastiche restaurant purports to present all the
virtues attributed to the reign of the great Queen by blue-rinsed
members of the Tory Party while managing to sneak in a few deft, more
contemporary touches but certainly there is nothing even faintly
minceur about the size of the portions.

To begin with perhaps a mackerel and apple gratin; oatmeal cake made with cheese and hazelnuts; a salad of duck and chicken served with pickled raspberries; or asparagus enveloped in smoked salmon with prawns. As the main courses there can be steak stuffed with Stilton and Cheddar mousse: fillet steak in Yorkshire-pudding batter with carrack sauce; boned trout stuffed with two different kinds of mousse or duck with fruit sauce. Tasty herb bread and substantial puds like spotted dick and chocolate pot with cinnamon cream. A good world-ranging list with some bargains outside the clarets. House Duboeuf is £6.90. Open all week.

MOSELEY, Springfield Road, King's Heath, Birmingham B14 7DX
tel: (021) 444 2115 *6227 yards SSS 70*

RESTAURANTS
Nuthurst Grange, Hockley Heath ✳✳✳✳
Brockencote Hall, Chaddesley Corbett ✳✳✳✳

This parkland course in the southern suburbs of Birmingham offers, for your attentive consideration, water in the form of streams and a lake, and tall mature trees in getting round. One very long par 4 at the 4th and three par 3s and one 5 on the first nine need concentration and the 6th demands boldness as well as skill but although the inward half is longer and has two lengthy 4s as well as only one 3 and one 5, it never seems quite as troublesome, once you have negotiated the first few holes.

The 5th is a 208-yard par 3 played through a narrow woodland gap over a stream to a saucer-shaped green tight with trees and the gardens of bordering houses. Unless you hit your tee-shot absolutely straight through the forest tunnel you are nowhere—except possibly off the course via a tree or in the damp hollow in front of the green.

The 6th is even more alarming, a remarkable really challenging man-or-mouse hole. To begin with, its 396 yards are somewhat illusory. From the tee you have to carry a lake of about 130 yards to a steeply rising fairway which disappears round a high wood towards an invisible green.

Played strictly around the dog-leg the length would be more like 440 yards and you must hit a very good straight drive of more than 200 uphill yards to get a sight of the green for your second shot.

Virtually the only route to par is to carry the wood as well as the lake off the tee, which needs a drive of more than 200 yards clearing 40-foot trees with its dying fall. Then you still have a tricky shot to a platform green tucked into the side of the hill with a sharp fall away to the left. The big boys aim even nearer the green which needs a carry of around 240 yards, clearing some gigantic beeches as you come in to land.

If you make it this way, then you have a comparatively simple 9 iron to the green but any way you play it, there are few more satisfying par 4s anywhere.

Nuthurst Grange, Hockley Heath B94 5NL tel: (0564) 783972 ✳✳✳✳
Hockley Heath is about 5 miles down the A34 from the Moseley course and this cheerful and welcoming hotel restaurant has set price menus for lunch and dinner offering a wide spectrum of choice.

As starters you could have turkey brioche; cockles, prawns, lobster and mussels in white-wine jelly; avocado with pine nuts, toasted goat cheese and bean sprouts; tomato and basil soup or pasta with curried crab. Then brill with beetroot and garlic sauce; braised ox-tail with sage; duck with armagnac and prunes or veal escalope with lemon sauce as a main course and such desserts as bread and butter pudding; apricot sorbet with mango coulis or orange soufflé.

The list shows a good deal of care and knowledge in its compilation, Australian wines from Brown Brothers, Californian from Robert Mondavi, southern burgundies from Delorme and equally eclectic choices from Alsace and Bordeaux. House wines from £9.55. Open all week, except Saturday lunch.

Brockencote Hall, Chaddesley Corbett DY10 4PH
tel: (0562) 777876 ****
This beautiful country-house hotel overlooking a private lake and within sight of the Malvern hills, 12 miles west of Moseley on the A448 to Kidderminster, offers eight dishes to choose from on each course of its *prix fixe* dinner menu. Fish and other daily extras are displayed on a separate page. You might begin with a terrine of duck and foie gras or of monkfish and lobster or gravdlax with scrambled eggs. Main courses can include guinea-fowl with a truffled sausage made from the thighs and a filo purse of chopped vegetables; quail roasted with game livers with home-made pasta and roasted garlic cloves; steaks with various sauces or escalope of veal with oyster mushrooms. Lemon tart or slices of rum-soaked pineapple in deep-fried filo pastry with caramel sauce are among the desserts and there is a largely French list with a few Australians and some bargains although bordeauxs and burgundies are rather pricey. House wine from £10.50. Open all week, except Saturday lunch and Sunday dinner.

THE WORCESTERSHIRE, Wood Farm, Malvern Wells WR14 4PP
tel: (0684) 573905 *6449 yards SSS 71*

RESTAURANTS
Hope End, Ledbury ***   Croque-en-Bouche, Malvern Wells ****

The Worcestershire is the oldest club in the Midlands, founded in 1880 but it has not always been at its present site at the foot of the Malvern Hills. For the first forty years the game was played by Worcestershire members over common land with all the problems that has always caused and, in 1927, the course was moved to Malvern Wells. There were more problems during the war when part of the course was requisitioned for agriculture and an emergency hospital was built on the rest. For a while there were only nine holes.

Now the course is back to full length and a fine open and enjoyable place to play golf it is, with views up to the Malverns and across the Vale of Evesham to the Cotswolds. After a tranquil start, the ditches and streams which criss-cross this course start to come into play at the 2nd, where you must keep your drive right to stay out of the water and there is then a testing approach to a high green. The drive is blind at the par-5 4th and unless you hit it solidly, the green can still be invisible—and there is plenty of trouble round it.

Another ditch-avoiding tee-shot is demanded at the 10th and at the 14th, where both shots must stay away from out-of-bounds on the left and at the 17th, you have to carry a pond with your approach to the green.

Hope End, Ledbury HR8 1JQ tel: (0531) 3613 ∗∗∗
This country hotel just a mile north of Ledbury and about 5 miles from The Worcestershire was once the home of Elizabeth Barrett Browning, before the Barretts moved to Wimpole Street. It now belongs to John and Patricia Hegarty, enthusiastic restorers and organic gardeners and highly able restaurateurs. However, although vegetarians are amply catered for, the menu is not all from the garden. There is an emphatic use of herbs in the excellent soups, such as sorrell and potato, mushroom and marjoram and broad bean and lemon and in other dishes as well.

Kidneys with tarragon might be a main course or wild salmon in chervil aspic; cardoon and lobster hot-pot; scallops with saffron sauce and tomatoes; fillets of whiting in cider and lovage or lamb casserole. This is English traditional cooking at its best, simple and straightforward, living off the land and not dismissive of modern techniques but with a mission to preserve freshness and flavour.

Desserts follow the same philosophical pattern, fresh fruits in season; ice creams made with yoghurt; chocolate marble tart; curd tarts and quince ice cream. There are good, sometimes unpasteurised British cheeses served with home-baked biscuits and an excellent list, over-whelmingly French with good Côtes du Rhône and very good clarets and plenty of half-bottles. House wine is £6. Open Wednesday to Sunday dinner only (Monday and Tuesday dinner residents only). Closed mid-December to mid-February.

Croque-en-Bouche, 221 Wells Road, Malvern Wells WR14 4HF
tel: (0684) 565612 ∗∗∗∗
A small restaurant with just seven tables run by just two people, Marion Jones in the kitchen and her husband, Robin, everywhere else. The short menu has a fixed price and is changed every week but there are three choices on the fish and meat courses and five on desserts. The cooking is British but not old-fashioned and influences from Japan, the Middle East and Italy creep in.

You might, for example be offered sushi as an appetiser or a globe artichoke with crab mousse; lamb smoked with applewood and rosemary or vegetable broth with pesto then monkfish with mizuna greens and hijiki seaweed with soy, chervil and sherry vinegar sauce; a Turkish borek with spinach and shiitake mushrooms or venison chops with a port and fruit sauce or honeyed roast duck served with brown lentils. The cheeses are all impeccably British and the puddings such as toffee rice with passion-fruit ice cream are inventive.

The list is simply amazing and of such dimensions that it comes in two volumes, one for whites and one for reds. The range is global and even includes Chinese. On many wines there are several choices of vintages from the same domaine. The prices are very fair and there is a wonderful list of liqueurs. House wine from £6.80. Open Wednesday to Sunday dinner only. Closed from the Sunday before Christmas to the Wednesday after New Year and for a week in July and September.

South

WOBURN, Bow Brickhall, Milton Keynes MK17 9LJ tel: (0908) 370656
Duke's: 6940 yards SSS 74   Duchess: 6641 yards SSS 72

RESTAURANTS
Paris House, Woburn **** Swan Hotel, Leighton Buzzard ***

The senior of these two courses is the Duke's. Since it opened in 1976, it has had an unequalled rise to fame as a televisual golf course on which Peter Alliss takes his guests and, in more serious vein, the Dunhill Masters is played every year. The two nines of the Duke's are somewhat out of kilter because the back nine is over 500 yards longer than the front. However, there are some picturesque and dangerous holes on the outward half.

The much-photographed 3rd, a downhill par 3, through trees and over bushes to a green ringed by rhododendrons, can leave you strokeless if your tee-shot strays off the green. The par-5 5th, a left-hand dog-leg, is reachable for the mighty with the second shot but it has to be played with care as well as power, for a ravine lurks in front of the flag. The 7th is a tough par 4, again a left-hand dog-leg, with a tight second shot to a green which is stepped and can all too easily be three-putted.

You are back with the long gully-carry for your second shot at the 419-yard 13th and the 14th plays straight through the narrow channel of the pine forest from which the course is carved. Being on the edge of the fairway means that your next shot is blocked by trees and at this 565-yard hole you need to get on in three and your pitch must stop on the right level of the double-tier green to have the hope of a par.

The Duchess, although about 300 yards shorter, is not as narrow and demanding, with a few shorter par 4s than on the main course but it is just as rewarding to play for most people and, as is right proper for a Duchess, prettier.

Paris House, Woburn MK17 9QP tel: (0525) 290692 ****
This must be one of the best restaurants, close by a golf course any-where. The charming half-timbered building which looks vaguely Tudor but was in fact built for a nineteenth-century International Exhibition and transported here, sits very naturally in the parkland of Woburn Abbey and it is the roe deer and pheasants from the woods which look like stage props.
Peter Chandler, the chef-patron, trained with the Roux brothers and the cooking is mostly *classique* with a few touches imported from the less

and less mysterious East, as in brochette of marinated chicken with peanut sauce; stir-fried beef with ginger and chives; and smoked haddock with a red pepper sauce. Mainstream classical may be represented by leg of lamb with tarragon and tomato sauce; ragoût of salmon and monkfish; creamed leeks; confit of duck with a sharp blackcurrant and lettuce salad or breast of chicken with oyster mushrooms. Desserts are tart and flavourful generally, apart from some over-indulgence in spun sugar. Good on original ice creams and delicious raspberry soufflé. The list is comprehensive but over-priced, although there is house wine for £9.50. Open Tuesday to Sunday, except Sunday dinner. Closed February.

Swan Hotel, High Street, Leighton Buzzard LU7 7EA
tel: (0525) 372148 ***
This well-maintained Georgian post house in the centre of Leighton Buzzard just 6 miles from Woburn, offers a wide choice from a seasonally amended menu and cooking of high quality and imagination. A scallop and spinach pasty is cooked in walnut oil and served in a lime butter sauce, for example. You can have lamb and lentils in pastry; Stilton and celery fritters with port sauce, medallions of monkfish with cucumber and ginger, braised kidneys with shallots and mushrooms. Delectably crisped duck; wild mushrooms with shredded bacon; black pudding with cinnamon apple sauce and gravy. There is a big, mostly European list, reasonably priced. House wines are from £8.25. Open all week.

ASHRIDGE, Little Gaddesden, Berkhampsted HP4 1LY
tel: (044-284) 2244   *6508 yards SSS 71*

RESTAURANTS
The Bell, Aston Clinton *** Pebbles, Aylesbury ****

Ashridge was founded virtually in the middle of the Depression in the 1930s and might well have struggled to stay in business had not their new 1937 professional gone off to Carnoustie that summer and, in the teeth of all the top Americans who were over for the Ryder Cup, brought home to Ashridge the Open Championship trophy. The members must have been additionally impressed by the course's credentials as a spawning ground for talent by the fact that there were two golfers from Ashridge in the top ten at Carnoustie, Henry Cotton's assistant, Willie Laidlaw being seventh, ahead of Horton Smith, Sam Snead and Ralph Guldhal.
The course is set in beautiful parkland and is one of those which have the grace and tact only to be hard on the powerful and ambitious. Most of the bunkers on the fairway are more than 200 yards from the tees and on the lines favoured by those to whom the idea of not being set up for a birdie on every hole is anathema. For the rest of us, this is a most agreeable and most pleasurable place to play.
The most famous hole is the 9th, named after Ashridge's most famous player, because the great Henry could conjure up a shot which would go round the corner and reach the green 350 yards away.

For anyone else the best advice is to keep left and try not to get on to the downhill slope for your pitch to the plateau green. At the short 11th you must go for the green and not be short as there is room at the back to chip up but the shot is much more difficult from the front. The 14th has a green set diagonally across the approach line with a bunker on the left and a road behind, rather like the 17th at St Andrews. But you do not have to drive over the corner of an hotel, and, at 376 yards, it is 90 yards shorter than the northerly Road Hole. The 18th makes a good finish because, although the tee-shot is downhill, the long approach has to be played across a gully. There are two levels on the green, so you must be on the same tier as the flag to get down in two.

The Bell Inn, Aston Clinton HP22 5HP tel: (0296) 630252 ∗∗∗
The Harris family have been running The Bell for more than half a century and naturally, down the years, things have changed. The menu prose has got more herbaceous and convoluted, dishes have become more elaborate but the wine list still has some of the best bargains in the country and if you take a particular fancy to something you can pop next door to the wine shop and take home half-a-dozen bottles.
There are various set menus and a long and over-written *carte* but despite all this gilding, the lilies remain very edible and in some cases a good deal more than that. You can have cauliflower soup with caviare; a truffled seafood pastry; morels with salmon and asparagus; or a warm salad of quail and duck with raspberry vinaigrette to begin with, and go on via the sorbets to something substantial like Irish stew with red cabbage; pig's trotters stuffed with herby chicken; risotto of langoustines with foie gras or medallions of pork in a paprika sauce.
The list is extensive rather than expensive with German, New Zealand, Australian, Californian, Spanish and Italian as well as French wines. There is a proper respect for winemaking skills and longevity, as well as a 'Wines of the Week' selection offering cheaper choices. House wine from £9. Open all week.

Pebbles, Pebble Lane, Aylesbury HP20 2JH tel: (0296) 86622 ∗∗∗∗
The personality of chef-patron Jeremy Blake O'Connor is stamped on this cottage restaurant in a lane leading from Kingsbury Square to the parish church and the food on the set menus reflects his tastes and the skill and refinement of his cooking.
The main dinner menu offers five or six courses with extras. Soup or a cold appetiser may be followed by a warm salad of salmon in coriander hollandaise or a seafood cassoulet cooked in Noilly Prat court-bouillon. Then perhaps fricassee of game; boned leg of chicken with port and wild mushrooms; lamb with spinach and cherry tomatoes; woodpigeon with pheasant ravioli and chanterelles or fallow deer with shallots, morels and a pepper sauce.
There is home-made bread and petits fours with the coffee as well as delicately-wrought puds like chocolate marquise with lemon sorbet or nougat glacé with red-currant coulis. The list ranges wide but is

especially strong on clarets, sound on burgundies with a nod to the New World which even includes a Canadian wine from Niagara. Open Tuesday to Sunday, except Sunday dinner.

THE BERKSHIRE, Swinley Road, Ascot SL5 8AY tel: (0990) 21495
Red: 6369 yards SSS 70   Blue: 6260 yards SSS 70

SUNNINGDALE, Ridgemount Road Sunningdale SL5 9RW
tel: (0344) 21681   *Old: 6586 yards SSS 71   New: 6676 yards SSS 71*

WENTWORTH, Wentworth Drive, Virginia Water GU25 4LS
tel: (0344) 842201   *West: 6945 yards SSS 74   East: 6176 yards SSS 70
Edinburgh: 6979 yards SSS 73*

RESTAURANTS
Waterside Inn, Bray **** Latymer, Bagshot ****
La Malmaison, Hersham *** L'Ortolan, Shinfield ****

Seven magnificent golf courses, very different in character in a small area 20 miles or so west of London near Ascot. The Berkshire's two courses were built together and are similar only in that most of the holes are on their own, isolated from others by woodland or heathland heather. The Red is the longer by 100 yards but it is distinguished from its neighbour largely because of its peculiar structure of six of everything, par 5s, par 3s and par 4s. It begins with a 518-yard par 5, a par 3 and another par 5 of 481 yards. The most intimidating 3 is the 10th where you have a long tee-shot of almost 200 yards to a green with a severe drop to the right threatening all the way. The 11th seems a simple enough 4 but reaching and staying on the small plateau green in two needs a meticulously struck pitch. A narrow tree-lined fairway at the par-3 16th puts a premium on the straight drive and catching the punishingly-bunkered green 221 yards away is real target golf.

The 17th at 529 yards is not only the longest but the most testing of the par 5s. Even after two full-blooded shots there is an exacting pitch to the double-tier green. The final hole on the Red is a par 3 and the 1st on the Blue is also a 3.

The green is set on a hummock and there is nothing but heather all the way there, so it is a formidable shot with which to open your round—especially with the tee just outside the clubhouse windows!

The Blue has a more conventional lay-out with four 3s and three 5s, none of them as much as 500 yards. There is a ditch to be carried at the par-5 6th and also at the 11th where a wandering stream menaces the second shot to within 100 yards of the green and there is also danger from water at the cunningly bunkered 16th. Two fine courses whose wonderful springy heathland turf positively encourages you to play thirty-six holes in a day.

Sunningdale, just down the road, also has two courses; the Old and the New and both have their advocates for supremacy. The Old was laid out by Willie Park jnr in 1900 and the New twenty-two years later by Harry Colt, who was Sunningdale's first secretary and went on to become one of the greatest of English golf architects. The New is longer and on higher ground and there always seem to be an awful lot of holes where you are hitting shots on to island fairways or greens in a stormy sea of heather, but it is undoubtedly a stiff test of accuracy and skill.

Certainly it is not as comely to look upon as its older sister, even when you are set such devious problems as the two blind shots in one 454-yard par 4 as the Old does at the 2nd. The 5th is a beautiful hole with a long drive over heather to the fairway, steering a steady course between the right-hand bunkers and the trees and then a shot across a lake to the green. Three fine par 4s, two just 400 yards and a testing par 3 to a back-sloping green take you to the turn. On the 10th tee, you have one of the finest golf views in Britain, the long fairway sweeping down between dense woods and then up again to a green on the same level as the high tee, with the splendid prospect of the refreshment hut beyond.

The finish is daunting. Despite its dangerously angled line of bunkers across the fairway, the only par 5 in the back nine, the 14th may lull you into a sense of complacency but you will almost certainly need a wood off the tee at par-3 15th.

For most people 226 yards is a long way to fly the ball and the tangle of heather in front can be intimidating. Then it is three long par 4s to home. The 16th is uphill and a horse-shoe of bunkers in front of the green can trap the second. The 17th is a gentle dog-leg. You must avoid the bunkers on the right but if you go too far left the trees block your view of the green and you can have a hanging lie for your approach. The 18th was bombed during the war and, ever resourceful, the Sunningdale members turned the crater into bunkers and it is these you have to fly with your second shot to be looking at two putts for a 4.

Wentworth now has three full-length courses, of which the most famous is unquestionably the West, the 'Burma Road', so-named by veterans of the Second World War. It has been the venue for many tournaments, including an early Ryder Cup, but it is best known as the course over which the World Matchplay Championship is played in October.

It seems determine to overpower you from the start for the 1st is a par 4 right on the limit at 471 yards and with a dip in front of the green, although it has been made easier of late by the fact that the gorse on the left has died back. The par-3 2nd has a bank behind the green, so it is best to be slightly long off the tee because there is always the chance that your ball may roll back off the slope and allow you a putt. The 452-yard 3rd is generally reckoned to be one of the most difficult holes, another lengthy par 4 along a tree-lined valley, perilously bunkered and with a rugged second shot to be played to a two-tier green with more trees at the back.

The 9th is an unyielding hole with a tough drive to a plateau, awkwardly near the out-of-bounds on the left, and a long, highly demanding approach played to a narrow green. At the 12th there is a row of trees across the fairway which have to be carried. Shortly after that you are into the West Course's demonic finish, starting with an uphill par 3 at the 14th and finishing with two long and awesome par 5s, the 17th of 571 yards and the 18th of 502 yards. The

17th dog-legs sharply left and you must hug the trees with the drive to set up the second. The 18th goes the other way but the fairway here is quite wide and it is the bunkers round the green which pose real problems. Although much shorter, the East Course has some excellent holes and it is also claimed that it has two of the best holes at Wentworth in the 4th and the 11th. The new Edinburgh Course opened in 1990. It is a few yards longer than the West Course and when fully matured, should provide another formidable challenge.

Waterside Inn, Ferry Road, Bray SL6 2AT tel: (0628) 20691 * * * *
Appropriately, you can make your way from one of the cathedrals of golf to a temple of gastronomy, just 8 miles to the north across Windsor Great Park. Michel Roux, one of those two jokey French brothers you keep seeing in TV cookery programmes, may site his restaurant in what looks from the outside like a Thames-bank weatherboard pub but, within, the worshipful status is not in doubt.
The food is superb and the service caring and attentive. As you would expect in a temple, the approach is classical, with very few touches—and no wines nor cheeses—which admit to origins outside France. The menu is in French but acolytes translate. There are set menus (minimum £30) for lunch and dinner.
Begin with the stimulating and aphrodisiacal house cocktail of brandied champagne with passion-fruit juice then on to pike dumplings; warm truffled lobster ravioli with lemon and butter sauce; snail vol-au-vent in parsley butter; or dished eggs with truffle and asparagus in madeira sauce. For the fish course perhaps layered salmon and turbot with butter sauce, courgettes and slivers of carrot; lobster in a sauce made with star anise, soya and ginger or shelled langoustines in a fervent tomato coulis. Fillet of veal with madeira sauce; saddle of rabbit with braised parsnips and an armagnac sauce; medallions of beef, pan-cooked with foie gras and truffles or baby lamb with thyme and mint hollandaise could be the main dish. Desserts can be red fruit soup with lemon custard; mirabelle tart or raspberry soufflé; then coffee and petits four in the summerhouse overlooking the gently flowing river to murmur with Spenser; 'Sweet Thames, run softly, till I end my Song.'
Or at least until you get the bill, which, if you have chosen wisely and possibly profligately from the fine French wine list would probably have provided poor Spenser with that pension he was always moaning about in the sixteenth century. But you can always console yourself with the thought that you are not, in the telling phrase of that other Thames-lover Oscar Wilde, someone 'who knows the price of everything and the value of nothing'.

Latymer, Pennyhill Park Hotel, College Ride, Bagshot GU19 5ET
tel: (0276) 71774 * * * *
There is still a bid for temple status at this restaurant in a nineteenth-century country manor transformed to a twentieth-century country club, but it is largely architectural and decorative rather an any quiet veneration of eating as an art form.

In such a place you would expect a menu clamorous with advertisers' hype and some of the prose on the carte is not so much purple as day-glo but you might not perhaps anticipate really good cooking from an inventive chef which manages to combine adventurous ingredients with success and produce first-class dishes from unusual marriages of components.

That however is what David Richards does. If you can take the Roman-style swimming pool and the span-the-ages interior decor, then you will find that such dishes as terrine of crab in lobster jelly; scallops cooked in the oven and served with shrimps and a mango vinaigrette; fried smoked salmon on crab ragoût or a tart of wild mushrooms glazed with goat's cheese sabayon can be delicious. There are also comparatively straightforward offerings like three pink noisettes of lamb in spinach leaves and steamed monkfish and salmon with a sauce of cucumber and dill and venison fillet stuffed with chestnuts and apricots with a pepper sauce. Desserts are elaborate but beautifully made. The service is good and enthusiastic. Mostly French wines on the list with some classic names and vintages. House wine is £12.95. Open all week, except Sunday lunch.

La Malmaison, 17 Queen's Road, Hersham KT12 5ND
tel: (0932) 227412 ∗∗∗
If the Waterside Inn is a temple to French cuisine, this charming small restaurant near Walton-on-Thames station could be the vicarage. But it is a vicarage with a pedigree because Jacques Troquet was once chef to a French ambassador and standards are high in the dining rooms over-looking a small courtyard.

Monsieur Troquet has a penchant for fish—fish soup with rouille and garlic croutons; scallop mousse with sea-urchin sauce; thin slices of grilled salmon on walnut oil-dressed salad; red mullet in lime and fennel; grilled sea bass on fennel or turbot roasted with shallots in full-flavoured mushroom sauce.

For less aqueous tastes there is beef in three peppercorns, rabbit stew, sweetbread with nettles and veal in sea urchin sauce as a kind of surf 'n' turf compromise. There are good classical French desserts like nougat glacé and chocolate mousse and a few dozen reasonably priced French wines on the list. The house wine is £8.20. Open Monday to Saturday, except for Sunday lunch.

L'Ortolan, The Old Vicarage, Church Lane, Shinfield TG2 9BY
tel: (0734) 883783 ∗∗∗∗
This vicarage, 15 miles west of Sunningdale on the A327, more than makes up for any marine tendencies offered by Monsieur Troquet. John Burton-Race's menu is a carnivore's delight. It offers eight dishes on each course of the menu and although fish is not eschewed, it is often an extra and the emphasis is heavily on meat, game and poultry.

Guinea-fowl breast comes with a sausage from the leg meat in a pig's trotter; lamb with a ham, sweetbread and foie gras mousse; veal kidney is stuffed with sweetbreads and wrapped in an escalope; squab with a mousse of its liver and foie gras; pig's trotter stuffed with pheasant and chestnuts; duck with ginger, sauternes and peach juice with the leg served separately on a salad with a slice of foie gras.

It all sounds very rich but the blending of flavours is handled subtly to give a harmony of taste and the cooking and preparation is very exact to achieve this. Fish dishes include scallops on a salad of mixed leaves with roasted hazelnuts and Jerusalem artichoke slices; John Dory with truffled cream sauce and wild mushrooms and a salad of crayfish and duck liver pâté. An excellent choice of unpasteurised cheeses is available and there are rich and splendid desserts like orange nougat with mango, hot chocolate soufflé, chocolate and cherries in kirsch sauce and wild strawberries with passion-fruit. An interesting but high-priced list. Open Tuesday to Sunday, except Sunday dinner.

WALTON HEATH, Tadworth KT20 7TP tel: (0737) 812060
Old: 6883 yards SSS 73   New: 6659 yards SSS 72

RESTAURANTS
Partners West Street, Dorking ✳✳✳ Michels', Ripley ✳✳✳

The two courses of Walton Heath lie 700 feet up on the exposed hills between Redhill and Leatherhead. They were created in a basin of soft sand among the chalk hills, of little use to farmers but marvellous territory on which to build a golf course, combining the virtues of quick drainage and the wind influence of seaside links with the characteristics of a heathland course.

Walton Heath is imperishably associated with James Braid, the first man ever to win the Open Championship five times and the most prolific golf architect of his day, who has left his mark on more courses in Britain than anyone else. He was there from the start in 1904 and remained at Walton Heath until he died in his eightieth year in 1950 but, oddly in view of his subsequent career, he had no hand in the designing of Walton Heath.

This was done by property developer Herbert Fowler, who went on to design other courses at Cruden Bay, Yelverton, Saunton and Westward Ho! in a unique way. He looked over the territory first for good par 3s, marked out their sites and designed the rest of the course around them.

Since these days, Walton Heath has been invaded by motorways and various other factors but it retains its character as one of the finest inland courses in Britain, an intriguing mix of short par 4s, long 3s and tough 5s, none of them easy.

The 4th, for example, is a mere 391 yards but it requires a downhill drive to a fairway sloping towards bunkers on the left. Aim too far right and you can be in heather or more sand. The shot to the raised green, subtly folded with borrows, has to avoid the bordering bunkers. Quite a thought-provoking hole.

At the 395-yard dog-leg 9th the green slopes towards you and is difficult to hold. The 12th bends right and the fairway is banked like a motor race-track which can lead to all kinds of strange places. The last six holes include three par 5s, the most menacing the 16th, with heather to right of you heather to left of you, and a crested green with a yawning bunker and one of Walton's lightning-fast putting surfaces to follow. The par-3 17th may seem a relief but a very precise shot is needed to carry its 181 yards to a green ringed with sand. At the 18th there is a long carry from the tee and a set of ferocious cross-bunkers guarding the green. The New Course is less exposed and of a more usual inland character, but there are many testing holes particularly the fiendishly bunkered par-4 3rd and the heather-threatened 12th with a long, tough approach to its narrow green. When tournaments are held here, such as the European Open and the 1981 Ryder Cup, the courses are often combined using three holes of the New Course to prevent players and spectators crossing the busy road which runs through the heath.

Partners West Street, 2–4 West Street, Dorking RH4 1BL
tel: (0306) 882286 ***
This recently-opened restaurant in a luxuriously refurbished Tudor house offers set menus with a choice of five or six dishes on each course. There is good fish and such refined peasant offerings as guinea-fowl with foie-gras sauce and saddle of rabbit with a rabbit liver mousse to follow modish starters such as ratatouille soup with mullet and scallops in various guises.
Salmon, bass and scallops with chive hollandaise; sea bass with aubergines, peppers and garlic and a generous white-fish stew are other items. The desserts are classic and delicate, like marquise and lemon tart.
The list is adequate, although unenterprising, but fairly priced. Open Tuesday to Sunday, except for Saturday dinner and Sunday lunch.

Michels', 13 High Street, Ripley GU23 6AQ tel: (0483) 224777 ***
This attractive pink restaurant, in a brick house on the old Portsmouth Road off the A3, south-west of Cobham, is essentially French in tone but is not above borrowing a few ideas from other cuisines. Thus, you may have gnocchi with the goat's cheese, polenta with the coq au vin and a pastry filled with creamed rhubarb (a plant most French people still think of as a purgative).
For the purists however, there can also be asparagus soup; aubergine and pimento mousse in lemon and basil sauce; poached salmon with chanterelles; chicken stuffed with langoustines; partridge with lentils and leeks; lamb with tarragon and your rhubarb cream tart does at least come with a strawberry coulis.
The list is not long but the wines are chosen with discrimination from distinguished growers mostly French but not too chauvinistically so, with a good selection of half-bottles. Open Tuesday to Sunday, except for Saturday lunch and Sunday dinner.

ROYAL ST GEORGE'S, Sandwich CT13 9PB tel: (0304) 613090
6534 yards SSS 72

PRINCE'S, Sandwich CT13 9QB tel: (0304) 612000
27 holes 6238–6947 yards SSS 70–73

ROYAL CINQUE PORTS, Golf Road, Deal CT14 6RF tel: (0304) 374007
6407 yards SSS 71

RESTAURANTS
George's Brasserie, Canterbury **
Wallett's Court, St Margaret's at Cliffe ***

These three great golf courses on about four miles of the Kentish coast in the extreme south-east of England have all been venues for the Open Championship, Princes once in 1932 when it was won by Gene Sarazen, Royal Cinque Ports twice in 1909 (won by J H Taylor) and 1920 (won by George Duncan). In 1894 Royal St George's became the first English course to stage the Open and it is still the English course on which the championship has been played most often. In 1993 it will host the world's oldest international golf tournament for the 12th time.

The founding of Royal St George's in 1887 arose from a dispute among the members of the London Scottish club and the Wimbledon club, both of whom played over Wimbledon Common. Things on the common got over-crowded, with disputatious groups of golfers and members of the public who used the common, nurtured by the golfers for golf, for other purposes such as walking, picnicking, playing football and courting and loudly dis-puting and resisting all attempts by the golfers to shoo them away. Greens were cut up and flags stolen and there were terse encounters on fairway and tee.

At this point one of the Wimbledon members, Dr Laidlaw Purves, and the club secretary, Henry Lamb, decided to look farther afield. There are various stories about how the plotting eye of Dr Purves first lighted on the cluster of dunes overlooking Sandwich Bay which was to become Royal St George's. One says that Purves and Lamb were travelling by train from Canterbury to Dover when they first saw the coast along the Channel. There was a strong tradition that golf was truly a seaside game—still maintained in the choice of courses on which the Open is played—and Dr Purves, who came from Edinburgh and had been a member of the Bruntsfield Club, would have been brought up in that discipline and could instantly recognise good golfing territory when he saw it.

He is said to have walked the entire coastline from Rye to Ramsgate looking for a suitable site, and that his search for golfing land on the Kent coast was fuelled by his wish to play golf on Sundays—a most iconoclastic reason for a Scotsman in the nineteenth century. Certainly Dr Purves was no ordinary man. The scope of his activities had an almost Renaissance quality. A specialist at Guy's Hospital, he was also a writer not only of medical books but the editor of an edition of Defoe's *Robinson Crusoe* and the translator of Alain René Lesage's *Gil Blas*, the archetype of the picaresque novel. It could well be that Sunday was the only day he had time to play golf.

With his friends, he leased 320 acres of land from the Earl of Guildford and with the help of a skilled caddymaster/greenkeeper he laid out what is now Royal St George's. It was a typical and tough links course of its time. There were lots of blind holes using the sand dunes both as shelter and markers for the greens. Nineteenth-century golfers liked what they called 'sporty' courses, convinced that one of the great joys of the game was taking a mighty swipe at the ball and propelling it over a distant sand dune with all the mysterious thrill of seeing where it finished up on the other side (an attitude still reflected in some of the holes at Prestwick).

The farmhouse on the site was the nucleus of the present Royal St George's clubhouse. Originally the facilities offered there were primitive indeed and the club had a suite of rooms in the Bell Hotel in Sandwich, thus continuing the Scottish tradition of golf clubs beginning their social lives in inns. Most of the members came from London and were professional men like Dr Purves, prosperous businessmen and gentry. They came to Sandwich by train which took about the same time for travel as the modern railway—2 hours. The fare was 12 shillings return.

Like all places and bodies which become institutions, Royal St George's had its critics. In time, not everyone agreed with Dr Purves's original design. Nor was he the only man of letters to be a member of the club. Two of the most celebrated golf writers of our time, Bernard Darwin and Henry Longhurst, were members, as was the novelist and creator of James Bond, Ian Fleming. Indeed Darwin was at one time club president.

Darwin has been accused of disliking the course because, although he was a good enough golfer to have played for England and to be recruited into the Walker Cup team in America in 1922 when the captain fell ill, he never did well in club competitions. He was a grandson of the even more illustrious Charles Darwin (who wrote *The Origin of Species*) and as the most famous golf writer of the first fifty years of this century and a man of wit and erudition, he could certainly barb his pen when he wanted to. He had this to say of Laidlaw Purves's course in 1910:

> Royal St George's was heralded with much blowing of trumpets and burst full-fledged into fame. For some time it would have ranked only a degree below blasphemy to have hinted at any imperfection. Then came a time when impious wretches, who had the temerity to think for themselves, began to whisper that there were faults at Sandwich, that it was nothing but a driver's course, that the whole art of golf did not consist of hitting a ball over a sandhill and then running up to the top to see what happened on the other side. Gradually the multitude caught up the cry of the few, till nobody who wished to put forward a claim to a critical faculty 'had a good word to say for the course.'
>
> Then the club began to set its house in order, lengthening here and bunkering there, not without a somewhat bitter controversy between the moderates and the progressives, until the pendulum has begun to swing back and poor Sandwich is coming to its own again.

Although Frank Pennink's amendments to the course, which came into play in 1975, did much to eliminate the blind shots at Sandwich, because of the nature of the terrain, they do so often only when you put your drive in the elusive position A.

Deviate only slightly from the perfect line (only too easy in one of Royal St George's two prevailing winds) and you cannot see the flag for your second shot to the long par 4s.

Modern St George's opens with a long but fairly innocuous par 4, but at the 2nd you must carry the cross-bunkers on the left-hand dog-leg to a long lateral ridge, from which the approach to the unbunkered green is simple if you avoid the undulations and hollows in front of it. The 3rd is the first of Royal St George's famous short holes, a long carry over pretty fearsome dune country to a green hemmed in by hummocks with a thorn bush on the right and two bunkers on the left.

At the 4th you begin to see what all the trumpeting is about. It demands a mighty blow off the tee over very wild country, avoiding the huge bunkers in the dunes and finding the fairway in a narrow gap. Then you need a bravely struck second shot over a whorling fairway and two demon putts on a two-tier green to make par.

The 5th is another big drive from a tee high in the dunes, probably into the north-east wind, to a patch of fairway between sandhills. If you have hit the perfect drive—over 230 yards and bang in the centre of the fairway patch— then you can see the little square white flag with the red St George's cross, waving in the breeze by the shore some 200 yards away through a cleft in the dunes. From anywhere else the second shot is blind. This is a hole at which, no matter what you think about its yardage, you take the biggest practicable club for you second shot. 'No-one' said a very experienced member 'is ever through the green in two at this hole.'

The 6th is a short hole whose difficulty depends very much on wind direction. The 529-yard 7th demands another huge drive over fierce duneland to reach the fairway and the cross-bunkers which line its front edge.

Your second shot must avoid three bunkers guarding the right-hand side of the narrow green and land on the plateau ridge approaching it. Birdies other than seagulls or larks at this hole are not common.

After the turn the problems start at the 10th where the green is set on a plateau surrounded by deep and terrible bunkers and the approach shot must be played with a dangerous mixture of boldness and delicacy to hold. The 11th is a par 3 of no great complexity, created in 1975; the 361-yard 12th is a tough multi-bunkered dog-leg. At the 13th you head out towards the red roof and white walls of Prince's clubhouse next door, driving towards a gnarled fairway from which there is a long and difficult shot into the closely-bunkered stepped green.

The second par 5, the 14th, has Prince's course as out-of-bounds on the right, a long carry over yellow wilderness to a hummocky fairway and a stream to be flown with the second shot to the bumpy fairway in front of the green. At the 467-yard 15th you have to carry a ridge with your drive to have a clear shot into the heavily fortified two-level green. The 16th is a par 3, 165 yards to a green ringed with sandhills and eight bunkers.

Undoubtedly the simplest way to play it is to emulate Tony Jacklin in the 1967 Dunlop Masters, when he holed his tee-shot here in the last round, providing TV viewers with their first-ever hole in one.

At the 17th you turn south on a fairly simple par 4 if you are striking the ball well and the wind is with you as it often is in summer. But the 458-yard 18th reminds you that Royal St George's still has teeth. The drive is over rough to a fairly flat fairway but the second has to be a powerful and accurate blow carrying the cross-bunkers to the right-to-left sloping green, where holing the final putts is a real trial of nerve and technique.

A marvellous place to play golf, as even that old curmudgeon Bernard Darwin was compelled to admit:

> Sandwich has a charm that belongs to itself and I frankly own myself under that spell. The long strip of turf on the way to the 7th hole that stretches between the sandhills and the sea, a fine spring day, with the larks singing as they seem to sing nowhere else, the sun shining on the waters of Pegwell Bay and lighting up the white cliffs in the distance: this is as nearly my idea of Heaven as is to be attained on any earthly links.

No wonder he never won any club championships if he was dreaming up prose like this.

Prince's, just north of Royal St George's across the fence at the 14th, was first played on in 1907 but during two wars it was used as a training ground, and in the Second World War that included minefields and tank-traps. After the war it was redesigned by Sir Guy Campbell and it is now a lay-out of twenty-seven holes, three loops of nine each, the Dunes, the Himalayas and the Shore.

Most of the fairways run between sand dunes and, despite the ominous name of one of the nines, Prince's is much flatter than Royal St George's. If you are on the fairway, you are less likely to have a stance where the ball is below or above your feet.

It has many fewer bunkers than its neighbour and there are no long carries off the tee over rough ground, although you may have to clear a cross-bunker or two but almost all the greens are raised and despite the lack of bunkers, they make approach shots very difficult to judge. Indeed, it is a course like this that makes you realise the value of bunkers as markers for the length of shot.

The 6th on the Himalayas is a tough par 5 of 596 yards which imposes a straight as well as long drive between bunkers and rough and there are more bunkers on the left to trap the second shot and three more round the green. At the 7th the tee is almost on the beach and club choice to carry the 195 yards to the small and sloping green can swing between a 5 wood and 5 iron, depending on the wind.

There really is not a poor hole in the twenty-seven and as you contemplate the ground here being used for all that battle training in the Second World War, you may well sympathise with the graphically indignant comment of one of Royal St George's captains, Lord Brabazon of Tara, on Prince's being used for artillery practice, 'like throwing darts at a Rembrandt'.

Royal Cinque Ports at Deal to the south of Royal St George's was twice host to the Open but it seems now to have been dropped. On two other occasions when it was scheduled to be the Open venue, in 1938 and 1949, high tides swept inland and the salt burnt the fairways and greens.

It is a very tough course in the wind and in a stiff south-westerly, by no means an uncommon occurrence in these parts, you must make the most of the first eleven holes because the way back to the clubhouse is going to be a real slog.

It begins with deceptive placidity with a modest par 4 of 328 yards with a ditch in front of the green and the 3rd looks easy enough with its broad fairway but, in fact, it is a very demanding par 4 of 449 yards, needing a very straight drive with absolutely no hint of fade to set up a long iron shot over a bunkered ridge into a punchbowl green. The 6th is a short par 4 down to the sea, but there are bunkers and towsy rough on the right to be evaded and it is a delicate pitch to the plateau green by the beach.

At the 12th you turn back into the usual wind and there is only one 4 under 400 yards on the way in and the par 3 14th is more than 200. At the 15th there are fairway bunkers to be avoided by the tee-shot and even then you have to play a blind second over a sandhill.

The 16th is about as near as you can get to a par 5 and still preserve a sense of decorum and justice in calling it a 4. There are cross-bunkers to catch the drive and a long and powerful shot to be played to a high green to get home in two. The 17th is just 372 yards but the fairway looks like a grassy sculpture of the Channel waves over the Goodwin Sands just off-shore and the 18th has a small, high slippery green which in wind is a real feat to reach and hold.

George's Brasserie, 71–72 Castle Street, Canterbury CT1 2QD
tel: (0227) 765658 **
This is an unpretentious cheerful place with a fixed-price daily menu and a longer and more showy *carte* for the more ambitious eater. Cooking is authentic French Mediterranean style rather than innovative but is good with interesting pasta—tagliatelle with a smoked-salmon sauce, for example—good family soups like lentil, minestrone, mushroom and bouillabaisse; mussels in white wine and garlic; grilled squid with chilli and lemon; pheasant with mushrooms and port gravy; lamb baked with herbs. Short, reasonable list. House wines £6.75. Open all week, except for Sunday dinner.

Wallett's Court, West Cliffe, St Margaret's at Cliffe CT15 6EW
tel: (0304) 852424 ***
West Cliffe is about 5 miles south of Deal going towards the sea off the road to Dover. In keeping with their conversion of this ancient manor farm, Chris and Lea Oakley's restaurant has a menu which could best be described as enlightened English.

But although you can have Cumberland sauce with almost anything and the salmon comes from the Outer Isles, the fish from Folkestone and the lamb from Kent, other imported flavours are not disregarded and the

SCOTLAND

THE BRAIDS, EDINBURGH

CROMLIX HOUSE, KINBUCK, PERTHSHIRE

SCOTLAND

SILVERKNOWES, EDINBURGH

INVERNESS

ENGLAND

ROYAL BIRKDALE, SOUTHPORT

WALES

ST. PIERRE, CHEPSTOW

IRELAND

LITTLE ISLAND, CO CORK, EIRE

MONTE CARLO

LA PALME D'OR, HOTEL MARTINEZ, CANNES

PORTUGAL

VALE DO LOBO, ALGARVE

SARDINES ON THE QUAYSIDE, PORTIMAO

SPAIN

MIJAS, COSTA DEL SOL

TORREQUEBRADA, COSTA DEL SOL

ITALY

PEVERO, SARDINIA

SCANDINAVIA

GOLF IN THE MIDNIGHT SUN, SWEDEN

BENELUX

STEVEN VAN HENGEL WITH HIS COLLECTION OF
ANCIENT DUTCH GOLF EQUIPMENT

cooking is of a high standard. You could start with pork terrine and bacon; mussels with Martini and herbs; game terrine; smoked-goose salad or fettucine with prawns and Pernod.

Then on to smoked duck and game pâté with Cumberland sauce or perhaps a compôte of kumquats; turbot with crab and mustard sauce; roast lamb with mint and nasturtiums; salmon with basil and tomato sauce or pan-fried venison. Meringues with various fruits, raspberry and other syllabubs, and a selection of mousses are among the desserts. Fairly conventional list but well priced. House Bordeaux is £7. Open Tuesday to Saturday, dinner only.

ROYAL NORTH DEVON, Golf Links Road, Westward Ho! Devon EX39 1HD tel: (02372) 73817 *6644 yards SSS 72*

RESTAURANTS
Lynwood House, Barnstaple *** Reeds, Poughill ***

In 1853 when General George Moncrieff from St Andrews visited his brother-in-law, the Reverend I H Gossett, Vicar of Northam in Devon and was taken for a walk over Northam Burrows to Pebble Ridge, he exclaimed with true St Andrews fervour, 'Providence evidently designed this for golf links.' The reverend gentleman, as a man of the cloth and the faith not one to stand in the way of the dictates of Providence, promptly put in hand what subsequently became the Royal North Devon Golf Club, the oldest club in England.

It is rather odd that the same inspirational phrase seems to have crept into the vocabulary of Tom Morris, who said something very like it almost every time he was asked to design a golf course.

A good aphorism, of course, never goes to waste but it would seem more than a coincidence that the man who was summoned down from Prestwick to darkest Devon to convert the makeshift course over which the Reverend Gossett and his fellows were playing, into a proper links was none other than Tom Morris. This was in 1860, the year before he became the second Open Champion, and the club was officially constituted four years later as North Devon and West of England becoming Royal North Devon in 1867 under the patronage of the Prince of Wales.

Tom must have infused the seaside turf of Westward Ho!, the romantically named village nearest the links, with some of his own magic, for it was not long before this remote club began to produce champions. The first was Horace Hutchinson who won the scratch silver medal when he was sixteen and went on to win the Amateur Championship twice and become the first Englishman to captain the Royal and Ancient Golf Club of St Andrews. His caddie on some of these occasions was a young local lad called John Henry Taylor who brought the club even greater renown by winning five Open Championships. When he died at the age of ninety-two in 1965, he was the president of Royal North Devon, where he had once caddied for sixpence a round.

Herbert Fowler from Walton Heath remodelled Westward Ho! in 1908. Today you start out with two fairly simple holes played towards Barnstaple

Bay, but the 3rd, played along the Inland Sea, a lagoon annually replenished by Atlantic storms, is more testing. At the 4th you are out in sandhill country with a huge cross-bunker faced with railway sleepers to be carried from the tee.

From the 8th green at the north end of the course overlooking the Taw-Torridge estuary, you face an additional hazard over the next four holes in the huge sharp-pointed Great Sea Rushes, over which the ball has sometimes to be flown and which press in upon the fairways.

You escape from the rushes at the 13th back into more usual undulating links country. There is a tricky par 3 at the 16th where the tee-shot must find the plateau green and stay there to have any prospect of par and, at the 18th, the burn over which you drove with such insouciance at the 1st, comes into play again, this time dangerously near the green.

Lynwood House, Bishops Tawton Road, Barnstaple EX32 9DZ
tel: (0271) 43695 ***
The Roberts family have been running this restaurant overlooking the River Taw for more than twenty years and it maintains its high reputation as a fine fish restaurant with a few side-lines. Most of the fish is local but the salmon is Scottish and comes from Loch Fyne. There is the famous Lynwood Pot, a selection from the day's catch, served on a bed of rice with a cream and wine sauce; prawns in pastry; fish stew; prawn omelette with salad; lobster with garlic butter; mussels marinière, brill with langoustine sauce; skate with capers and brown butter or pan-fried sea bass. Also crispy duck and various steaks. Desserts can be flummery, praline ice cream with butterscotch sauce or double-cream crème caramel. Good list, predominantly French but including bottles from Germany, Greece, Italy, Spain and Australia. House wine is £6.75. Devonshire cider. Open all week.

Reeds, Poughill EX23 9EL tel: (0288) 352841 ***
This quiet and restful guest house, set in a fine garden with views of the sea and good original paintings on the walls, is just off the A39, 20 miles down the road from Bideford to Bude but, if you can make a booking in the small restaurant, it is well worth the journey. The menu offers no choice but you are consulted beforehand as to your preferences and prejudices, and Mrs Margaret Jackson is a fine and skilful cook.

The menu is seasonal, affected by the local availability of fish and game and the vegetables in the garden. Soup or perhaps tomato ice cream with prawns and avocado to begin with, followed by sole wrapped round smoked salmon in mushrooms and cream; salmon cutlet poached in Pineau de Charentes then quail pie stuffed with herbs and sausage with red wine; poached salmon in lime juice with chives and tarragon; chicken parcelled in bacon with a red-wine sauce and a choice of puds—rich chocolate mousse; pears in lemon syrup; chocolate brandy cake; a tart of plums in red wine with red-currant jelly and Japanese almond meringue or Grand Marnier soufflé. Splendid local and foreign cheeseboard. Good and interesting list for a small place. House Duboeuf is £6.50. Open Friday to Monday, dinner only.

ST ENODOC, Rock, Wadebridge, Cornwall PS27 6LB tel: (020-886) 3216
6207 yards SSS 70

RESTAURANT
Seafood Restaurant, Padstow * * * *

> *How straight it flew, how long it flew*
> *It cleared the rutty track*
> *And soaring, disappeared from view*
> *Beyond the bunker's back—*
> *A glorious sailing, bounding drive*
> *That made me glad I was alive*
>> John Betjeman, 'Seaside Golf'
>> *John Betjeman's Collected Poems*

Thus John Betjeman at St Enodoc, the very spirit of holiday seaside golf. And that is exactly what St Enodoc is, a marvellous holiday golf course. This description is sometimes taken as a disparagement but there is nothing to disparage about St Enodoc, it is a perfect place to enjoy playing golf and what makes a better holiday?

Although golf was played here earlier, in the late nineteenth century, the course was laid out by James Braid in 1907 and he revised it in the 1930s. Its curious territory is part of its charm, for it has more water hazards and more hills than most seaside courses; yet it is distinctively a links course. It opens with the longest hole, down a valley where the ground rolls and surges like the sea to the green 504 yards away. At the 2nd you have to drive over a ridge and play up to a high green. The 3rd is another long par 4 and with a bold second shot needed to carry the road and a wall to the green; the 4th is a short 4 but the tee-shot is tricky and a trap for the over-ambitious.

The 5th, a simple par 3, leads to the notorious 6th where you are faced by the Himalayas, a huge sandhill which has to be carried by a high second shot which, if the monster dune was not there, would never give you a second thought. Head still and swing through the ball and you could find it on the green. You play back over the dune at the next hole but from the elevated tee of the 7th it does not seem so menacing.

More truly difficult is the 10th, which has a stream all the way down the left side and a massive slope on the right, a tough 449 yards for your 4. Then there is a loop of three holes round St Enodoc Church, the last of which is the 13th where

> *The very turf rejoiced to see*
> *That quite unprecedented three*

when the Poet Laureate got his birdie . . .

The 16th has the shore of the estuary to the River Camel all along the right, a fairway of green waves with a hollow like St Andrews Valley of Sin in front of the green. The 17th is a tough par 3 of 206 yards from a high tee over wilderness to a raised green; at the last there is a big bunker to carry off the tee and a good shot to get to the green from the rolling fairway for the last two putts.

> Ah! seaweed smells from sandy caves
> And thyme and mist in whiffs
> Incoming tide, Atlantic waves
> Slapping the sunny cliffs,
> Lark song and sea sounds in the air
> And splendour, splendour everywhere.

Seafood Restaurant, Riverside, Padstow PS28 8BY
tel: (0841) 532485 ∗∗∗
This basically-named restaurant opposite the car park overlooking the estuary of the River Camel is not merely one of the finest fish restaurants in the country but a one-family, fish-related enterprise. Richard Stein has already produced a much-praised cookbook, he runs a delicatessen and a bakery and is the chef-patron in the kitchen. Padstow is directly across the water from the St Enodoc golf course and to eat fish in this greenery bedecked, white-painted, bright-postered eating house is a rewarding experience.
There is a set-price menu with three choices on each course and quite a number of supplementary extras like lobster, crayfish, turbot and salmon. There is a charcoal grill and blessedly no music. You could begin with ravioli of lobster with spinach; mussels stuffed with celery, tomatoes and courgettes or coriander and hazelnut butter; sliced cured duck with ginger; scallops with pesto, whitebait with persillade. As a main course there could be lobster with herb butter, hake with tomatoes and parsley; salmon with champagne and chives; sea bass steamed with clams and scallops or monkfish baked with garlic and fennel.
British cheeses come with home-made walnut bread. Sweets feature chocolate marquise with coffee sauce; crème brûlée ice cream with toffee sauce; fruit tarts, raspberry vacherin with blackcurrant coulis. The list is mainly white and mainly French but there are also Australian, New Zealand, Californian and Italian wines from good growers. House white is £8.90. Open Monday to Saturday, dinner only.

WALES

ROYAL PORTHCAWL, Porthcawl CF36 34W tel: (0656) 712251
6691 yards SSS 74

RESTAURANTS
Egerton Grey Country House Hotel, Porthkerry ***
Bardells, St Bride's super Ely ***

This senior Welsh course is an exception among most British links courses. You can see the sea all the way round. The first holes start along the rocky coast of the Bristol Channel, all quite difficult with the big cross-bunker at the 2nd a real decision-maker in determining from where you play your approach to the hollowed green. Another cross-bunker at the 3rd defies the drive and there is a dip in front of the green, which is perilously near the beach.

After that the course turns inland and more or less abandons its links character for a moorland guise with lots of bracken, heather and gorse to entangle the off-line shot. The par-3 4th at 193 yards is the toughest of the short holes. A long and determined tee-shot to fly the two bunkers guarding the flag is made more complicated by the tilted double-tier green. The 5th is a fine testing par 5. A boundary wall runs all the way along the left, there are bunkers on the right around drive length and the approach is uphill to a narrow sloping green with a very deep bunker on its right edge. At the 6th you are still going uphill and the 7th is a real curiosity, one of the shortest holes in the British Isles, 116 yards. It should be simple but there are five bunkers round the green and lots of bumps and humps on it to throw you off into them.

The drive is blind as you turn downhill at the 8th, and the 9th although only 371 yards, turns back across the course, usually into the wind, towards a green on the crest of a ridge with heavy gorse flanking the fairway. The par-5 12th demands a long carry over gorse and heather and sand to reach the fairway but, that accomplished, it is not too difficult. The 13th, if back into the wind, is however another matter. Choosing the club for your second shot, downhill to a bunker-ridden green, is a tricky business.

The 508-yard 17th is not a simple hole, unless you can hit the ball long and straight, for there are bunkers strategically placed to catch the second shot which strays even slightly off target. The 18th rolls downhill, all bumps and hummocks on its route towards the clubhouse and the sea, with a gully crossing the fairway about 200 yards out and a very difficult green to read when you get there. A very beautiful course to play on with splendid turf and fascinating holes and the wind off the sea just adds zest.

Egerton Grey Country House Hotel, Porthkerry CF6 9BZ
tel: (0446) 7166 ***
Porthkerry is not far from Cardiff's Rhoose airport, on the coast over-looking the Bristol Channel. Egerton Grey is beautifully furnished and

although the dining room has a somewhat ecclesiastical air, the food served there reflects modern rather than ancient cooking styles.

The menu is *table d'hôte* but there is a good choice of dishes. You might have a salad of smoked duck breast with orange and raspberry coulis; mushroom and walnut soup or a puff pastry with leeks, quail breast and gazpacho to begin. Home-made lamb sausage with lentils, broad beans and a red-pepper salad or salmon mousse with shellfish and tarragon sauce to follow: then sea bass with braised endive; salmon with hazelnuts, prawns and a saffron and ginger sauce or fillet steak with wild mushrooms, brandy and horseradish could be the main course.

Good and well-made desserts like poached pear in two sauces and glazed strawberries with shortcake are also on offer. The list is well chosen and sensibly priced. House wine is £8.50. Open all week.

Bardells, St Bride's super Ely CF5 6EZ tel: (0446) 760534 ✳✳✳
Just off the M4 to the right on the way back from Royal Porthcawl to Cardiff, this village with a medieval name is home to a restaurant in an up-dated version of a Lutyens house in a family-run business. Jane Budgen and her daughters do the cooking and son-in-law Panikos Antoni runs the front of the house.

Sensibly the set menu is short with just three choices on each course. As starters there can be moules à la marinière; smoked pigeon salad with balsamic vinegar dressing; quail and duck-liver parfait; chicken-liver timbale or gazpacho mousse with red-pepper coulis. Main courses could be lamb with port and herbs; salmon in saffron sauce; guinea-fowl on lentils with lime and lemon or lamb with lemon and herb stuffing and mint sauce; then sweets like apple tart; chocolate mousse; coffee and praline ice or chocolate and rum charlotte. More than thirty well-selected wines adorn the list. House wine is £6.25. Open Tuesday to Saturday, dinner only; Sunday lunch.

ROYAL ST DAVID'S, Harlech LL46 2UB tel: (0766) 780857
6427 yards SSS 71

RESTAURANTS
Cemlyn, Harlech ✳✳✳   Llew Glas, Harlech ✳✳

Not many golf courses enjoy such a splendid setting as Royal St David's, with the ancient castle of Harlech standing in ruined splendour on its steep rock overlooking the links.

You can see it from every hole on the course and on a clear day the mountain range of Snowdonia fills the northern horizon.

Eyri, 'the eagle's nest', is the Welsh name for Snowdon but there are no eagles to be found there now and not many on the links of Harlech by the shore, 3500 feet below. Despite its beautiful setting, the 1st can be rather discouraging, a long slog for a par 4 against the prevailing wind, trying to hold your ball up to the left to avoid the bunkers but still remain on the tight-cropped springy turf of the fairway. The 463-yard 3rd needs pin-point accuracy from the tee and a strong second shot to miss all of the three bunkers around the green.

The 4th is a good one-shotter to a plateau green. It is generally a good idea to hit one club more than you first thought of, because not to be on here is to be in all sorts of trouble. The 6th is the only hole flanked by gorse and for its 371 yards you need to be straight to avoid the undergrowth and the bunkers narrowing the line into the green. The 7th and 8th are both 5s, played in opposite directions, and the 9th is a tight short hole, closely bunkered round the green.

The 10th is a long 4 with a second shot played over a ditch which can be troublesome into the wind. At the short 11th you turn for home via the heavily bunkered 451-yard 13th and the final loop which begins and finishes with long par 3s. At the 218-yard 14th in former days you could not see the flag behind the huge sandhill masking the green. Now a slice has been cut out of the hill to give you just a glimpse of it.

A good drive down the hummocks of the 15th sets you up for a needle-threading shot through the narrow gap to the low green dominated by a high mound. On the tee at the 16th you have your only view of the sea but you would be better to concentrate on getting your ball to a spot on the rolling fairway where you can pitch comfortably on to the green, hemmed in by six bunkers.

At the 421-yard 17th you must be resolute in decision. After you have driven and stayed out of the ladder of bunkers on the right, you must then decide whether you can carry the cross-bunkers in front of the green. Into the wind you should make the 'mouse' decision and play short.

The last, 202 yards par 3, should provide a triumphal finish but beware the two bunkers in front of the flag. If you are going to miss the green, miss it long.

Cemlyn, High Street, Harlech LL46 2YA tel: (0766) 7804425 ∗∗∗
You can continue to look at the majestic old stones of Harlech Castle from this comfortable and welcoming restaurant on the High Street. Ken Goody offers an attractive menu with between five and eight choices on every course, each set-priced by the number of courses you take. Soups are substantial and delicious: chicken and vegetable full of both ingredients, pea with tarragon, tangy gazpacho. The fish course could be a gratin of shellfish with avocado or salmon with saffron and champagne. Main dishes might include chicken with cumin, cardamom and coriander; pork with Roquefort and almond sauce; duck with sage and sultanas and peach purée; Yunnan-style ham braised with soy sauce, sherry and spices or chicken and hare terrine with onion marmalade. Good local cheeses of which there are plenty in Wales; pecan pie, pavlova, fruit tarts and roulade all feature on the dessert menu. A comprehensive and excellent list at generous prices includes half-bottles. House wines are from £6.50. Open all week, dinner only. Closed November to Easter.

Llew Glas, Plas y Goits, High Street, Harlech LL46 2YA
tel: (0766) 780700 ∗∗
This is another all-out family food enterprise which includes a tea-room, delicatessen and bakery on one level and a restaurant upstairs. Trevor

Pharoah's food, announced on a blackboard, changes by the day but it has a strong leaning towards the worthily egalitarian and unpretentious. Thus on offer are red mullet and ratatouille; quail on turnip sauerkraut; salmon and monkfish with a kind of Alsatian gnocchi; black pudding and peas as well as traditional roast beef and Yorkshire pudding; pasta with pesto but also fish terrine with quails' eggs and caviare and calf's liver in a wine, onion and mushroom sauce and good sweets like lemon tarts with strawberry sauce and pistachio ice cream with plum soup. The wine list is short but has some good bottles. House wine is £6.95. Open all week, except for Sunday dinner. Closed November to February.

ST PIERRE GOLF AND COUNTRY CLUB, Chepstow NP6 6YA
tel: (0291) 625261   *6748 yards SSS 73*

RESTAURANTS
Thornbury Castle **** Crown at Whitebrook ***

This course just 5 miles from the Severn Bridge, has become well known on television by the important tournaments played there. Long and tough parkland with lots of towering mature trees, the Old Course (1962) makes its mark straight away with the opening hole of 576 yards which says emphatically 'wha daur meddle wi' me' or whatever its equivalent is in Welsh. And indeed except on a few holes where the fairways are broader, St Pierre is very intolerant of the loose shot and demands the most precise shot making talents to build a good score.

The first is the only 5 in the outward half but there are two in the back nine, the shortest of which is 521 yards. Obviously this is a course which puts a premium on hitting the ball a substantial distance but that is far from being the only problem. At the 12th, as if being 545 yards long was not enough, there is a massive oak tree blocking the most profitable line for the drive. The short holes also present difficulties. At the 219-yard 13th, from a tee high up on a bank, you are playing down to a fiercely beringed green, where there seems almost as much sand as undulating putting surface.

At the par-4 15th there is water immediately behind the green and swans and ducks who regard with cynical yellow eyes your attempt to reach and stay on it. The dog-leg 16th has a big chestnut tree on the corner, which is a serious impediment to getting your drive into position for the demanding second shot. At the 17th the water at the green is even more perilous because not only do you have to play a longer approach, but the flag is usually out on the spur of the green thrusting into the lake. This means you have to carry water to reach the putting surface as well as hitting an exact shot to stop there and stay out of the broad lake on the other side.

The last hole is a long par 3, 228 yards right across the lake to a banked green which is higher than the tee. Pretty to look at but this is a rugged course, not for the faint-hearted.

The New Course at 5762 yards, SSS 68, is not as trying, with fewer dangerous hazards, but it makes a fine round for the less ambitious player.

Thornbury Castle, Castle Street, Thornbury BS12 IHH
tel: (0454) 418511   ****

Ten miles away across the Severn Bridge in Gloucestershire, Thornbury is the last crenellated castle built in England, left unfinished by the fall from grace of the Buckingham family in the seventeenth century. An impressive building still, it houses a fine restaurant and is the only one in Britain to have its own vineyard and its own wine, a Müller-Thurgau, on its list.

There is a long dinner menu, priced according to the number of courses you select. Splendid fish soup has long been a tradition of this establishment and there are other starters, including spiced tomato soup, smoked Tay salmon; hot salad of pigeon breasts and devilled crab with Parmesan. Then you can choose from salmon with saffron sauce; rack of lamb with mint and madeira sauce; tournedos with mustard and thyme; paupiette of chicken with an apricot and basil stuffing or a trio of game with a sauce of blueberries and shallots. The pudding *carte* is equally enticing—hot butterscotch; hot orange and passion-fruit soufflé and treacle tart and there is a wonderous choice of matured West Country cheeses.

The list is lengthy and impressive with many distinguished clarets, burgundies and ports and a long selection of half-bottles. House wines are from £9.95. Open all week.

Crown at Whitebrook, Whitebrook NP5 4TX tel: (0600) 860254   ***

This refurbished seventeenth-century inn, up the Wye Valley just on the Welsh side of Offa's Dyke, is about 11 miles from Chepstow off the A466. Roger and Sandra Bates' hotel restaurant is not easy to find but it is worth taking the trouble to locate.

The fixed-price menu offers interesting and delicately cooked food in very agreeable surroundings and quantities generous enough to still the memories of how you got into the lake at whatever hole you chose for aquatic exercise at St Pierre.

Mussels with basil on a bed of mushrooms; smoked-trout pâte enlivened by whisky, hazelnuts and mange-tout can be among the starters. Breast of duck with a sausage made from the leg meat, cooked in honey with apricot sauce; pork tenderloin with pistachio mousse in port sauce or boned quail stuffed with livers and wild rice and an ample choice of vegetables are some of the dishes offered for the main course. There is also a roll-call of mouthwatering puds.

The list is substantial with more than a hundred wines on offer which have obviously been chosen carefully and prices are reasonable. House wine is £7.50. Open all week, except for Monday lunch. Sunday dinner is for residents only. Closed for two–three weeks in January; two weeks in August.

IRELAND

There are more than 250 golf courses in Ireland. Some of them are intimidating monsters like Portmarnock near Dublin, which has two courses of over 7000 yards each, Royal County Down in Ulster beneath the Mountains of Mourne at 6968 yards or the American-style 7194-yard Waterville on the Ring of Kerry on the west coast or Royal Portrush in Ulster, 6809 yards long with ominously-named holes like Giants Grave, Calamity Corner and Purgatory.

Others, like Little Island at Cork, or Tralee, are less demanding, but I have never played on an Irish course which was less than enjoyable, and there are plenty which are much more than that. And it is not just the golf courses, splendid though they are, despite being currently indoctrinated on the Irish as granite-faced gunmen, when you get to the Emerald Isle you have to be a very hard-nosed character not to fall for the local charm.

You may suspect it is turned on to bolster a fluttering tourist industry; that it sells lots of additional pints of the dark creamy Guinness you find nowhere but in Irish pubs; that it encourages you to make wildly optimistic bets on your prowess on the links and prods you towards buying imitation leprechauns, shillelaghs, hand-woven tweed and Connemara marble set into cupro-nickel Celtic crosses, but, in the end, it is impossible to believe that the welcome is anything but genuine.

Playing golf in Ireland is a pleasure made by the people you meet, and the game here is as varied, challenging and unexpectedly well organised as it is anywhere in the world.

I say 'unexpectedly' because there is the other image of the Irish as genial, Guinness-swilling blethers whose idea of time is as liquid as the waters of the Liffey which run through Dublin's fair city.

Some genuine truth lurks in this portrait of the archetypal Irishman—just as the line in the song 'Mollie Malone' where the girls are so pretty . . . is delightfully confirmed by a stroll along O'Connell Street or around St Stephen's Green—but in matters related to tourism, the Irish do not allow legend to get in the way of the practicalities of welcome.

ROYAL DUBLIN, Dollymount, Dublin 3 tel: (01) 336346
6858 yards SSS 73

RESTAURANTS
King Sitric ∗∗∗ Patrick Guilbaud ∗∗∗∗

Dollymount is the second oldest golf club in Ireland and originally played in Phoenix Park and then in Sutton before establishing itself on its permanent base of Bull Island in Dublin Bay in 1889. Like the Old Course at St Andrews, it is an out and back course and as the back 9 is 500 yards longer than the front and contains three long and tough par 5s, playing homewards into the prevailing crosswind can be quite a formidable test of stamina, strokemaking and golf strategy.

There are three par 3s in the first nine and the 2nd is now the only 5. You need to lay the foundations of a good score at the opening holes because things just get more demanding as you go on. The 3rd is a good 4, where you require to hit your drive very accurately to have a go at the heavily-bunkered green. The narrow-fairwayed 440-yard 5th down between ridges is a testing par 4.

When you turn for home, there is a good par 4 to be got at the 10th before the daunting 11th, 525 yards, three shots for almost anyone unless there is absolutely no wind—a very rare occurrence—and three woods for even low handicappers if it blows.

There is a little relief at the 15th where you change direction and play away from the clubhouse for its 432 yards. Then a punishing finish mixes all the skills in the bag with a 251-yard par 4. Here a birdie should be possible, followed by a longer 4 and the par 5 18th dog-legging right, around out-of-bounds on the knee.

In 1966 Christy O'Connor, still the professional at Royal Dublin after more than thirty years, shot 2, 3, 3, five under par on the closing holes to win the Carrolls International. 'Anyone who breaks seventy here' says Christy with becoming modesty 'is playing better than he's really able to.'

King Sitric, East Pier, Harbour Road, Howth tel: (01) 32535 ***
Just a few miles to the north, on the way to Portmarnock is Howth with its pier, where Erskine Childers landed arms for the Irish Volunteers in 1924. Its sixteenth-century castle, ancient abbey and Aidan MacManus's fish restaurant, named after a tenth century Viking king of Dublin, whose troops killed the great Brian Boru after the bloodiest battle in Irish history at Clontarf, are just down the road.

It has long had the reputation of being the finest fish restaurant in Ireland. You might begin with a dish of tender lamb's tongue in madeira sauce or fish soup, before moving on to one of a dozen ways of cooking turbot, lobster, monkfish or John Dory and follow it with the famous fig pudding, washed down by a great Chablis, Alsace or Rhine wine from the splendid list which is also rich in fine clarets and ports. Open Monday to Saturday, dinner only. Closed for ten days at Christmas and on bank holidays.

Patrick Guilbaud, 46 St James's Place, Dublin tel: (01) 764192 ****
This is a temple of modern cooking with only a few nods in the direction of tradition.

Leek and lemon balm soup; ravioli with langoustines and tomato butter; a cucumber coulis with bavarois of basil-flavoured tomatoes; salmon with potato blinis and caviar; sweetbreads with coriander and lemon; duck with wild mushrooms and sweet potatoes.

All these with gravdlax and delicious pink calf's liver vie with black pudding, sweetbreads and crubeens in pepper sauce for your attention on the menu. There is an excellent cheeseboard and a sound, carefully chosen list. Open Tuesday to Saturday: closed on bank holidays.

PORTMARNOCK, County Dublin tel: (01) 332050
27 holes A: 7097 yards SSS 75   B: 7047 yards SSS 75   C: 6596 yards SSS 74

RESTAURANTS
Le Coq Hardi, Dublin **** King Sitric, Howth ***

The discussions about whether Portmarnock, Royal Portrush or Royal County Down is the greatest course in Ireland will never be settled. Rather like the eternal question about claret and burgundy, the only correct answer is 'Yes, please' and keep trying them to further confuse your judgement.

Portmarnock is the youngest of the trinity, celebrating its centenary in 1994. The peninsula on which it is set was originally an island and golfers used to arrive by boat. The first clubhouse was a shack next to the cottage of Maggie Leonard, whose golf-ball-eating cow was considered the worst hazard on the course.

This stubby finger of linksland which points south towards Howth is a splendid if sometimes humiliating place to play golf, an isolated thrust of land into the Irish sea where you are alone among the sandhills with the sky and the waves and the magnificent turf and the constant hassle of the wind. That, tugging and teasing at your game, shifts all the time because the holes change direction constantly, rather like Muirfield, with no more than two in succession playing in the same direction.

The 1st is a gently deceptive introduction, due south, not cruelly bunkered, but at the 2nd you change direction slightly eastward with a long carry to the fairway and a bunkered ridge at drive length and a massive cross-bunker to carry in front of the green.

The 3rd runs east to west with a humped fairway to hold and the marshy fringes of the shoreline on your right; the 4th swings to the north; the 5th turns back to the south-west. There are only three short holes, the 7th played north-east down into a hollow; the 12th played east to the hostility of an eight-bunker green in the dunes and the ferocious 15th, 192 yards due north, where, with a wind off the sea, you may have to hang your tee-shot out over the beach on the right to catch the fiendishly sloping green. The par 5s really ask questions about accuracy as well as power. At the 586-yard 6th there is a huge carry from the tee to a bumpy fairway and bunkers right and left narrow the entrance to a high-set green. The 13th has another long carry from the tee by the shore with bunkers edging the fairway on both sides and sand across and around the green to trouble the approach. The 14th is under 400 yards but the second shot from the crumpled contours of the fairway is difficult, for it must fly a ridge of bunkers in front of the long plateau green. The 16th at 527 yards has a dangerous set of cross-bunkers to ensnare the second shot and six more fringing the green. At the 17th you turn south again to fly over rough to a fairway edged with sand with more bunkers clustered round the tight, ridged entrance to the green. The 18th may look like a welcome relief with the elegant clubhouse to the left of the final green but it needs two good shots to get home to the raised green and avoid the sand along the way and make your closing putts on one of the best greens in Europe.

Le Coq Hardi, 35 Pembroke Road, Ballsbridge, Dublin
tel: (01) 689070 ****
This is a very smart restaurant for well-heeled people, much used by
Dublin financiers and *le beau monde*. Naturally, this means it is expen-
sive but the food is classic, cooked to the highest standards, attentively
served and delicious.
You might start with a herbal duck-liver pâté, a delicate chicken consommé or crab claws, then move on to salmon with crayfish sauce; sea
bass in tomatoes and garlic or steak with beef marrow and Beaujolais.
For dessert perhaps a raspberry mousse, sorbets or a parfait glacé au
Grand Marnier.
There is a loyal and stimulating cheeseboard with a fine selection of
Irish cheeses and a long and distinguished list full of almost lost vintages
and big names with prices to match. House wine is £14. Open Monday
to Saturday, except for Saturday lunch. Closed for two weeks in August
and two weeks at Christmas.

King Sitric, East Pier, Harbour Road, Howth tel: (01) 325235
See entry under ROYAL DUBLIN

BALLYBUNION, County Kerry tel: (068) 27146
Old: 6542 yards SSS 72   New: 6477 yards SSS 71

RESTAURANT
Ambassador Hotel **

Ballybunion has the enviable reputation of being the place where they have
the lowest sale for hangover cures in Western Europe. This is not a tribute
to the sobriety of its inhabitants and their visitors. They say you can drink
all night and never have a hangover. 'For sure' as my friend Tom Clifford
said, 'at Ballybunion ye're breathing air that no-one but yourself ever
breathed before.'
That may be so but perhaps the most impressive thing about Ballybunion
is its eighteen perfect excuses for trying to smash the resort's hangover
record. The course is built among sand dunes with perfect drainage and the
turf is superb. For the most part the greens are high and the rolling dunes
run at angles varying from the horizontal across the line of flight. This
means that unless you play with great accuracy, you get some very funny
kicks—depending on your sense of humour—and are left with second shots
requiring every weapon in the golfer's armoury from thumping brute force
to the soft-flighted skill of genius.
Nor is this all. When you get within what is laughingly called 'striking distance' of the greens, you will find they are all very fast and slope alarmingly
in almost all directions except one—towards the hole.
One of the consolations of having the dunes run across the course instead
of alongside the fairways is that you can actually see the sea—not all that
common a sight at many so-called seaside courses. This, however, can bring
its own particular tremors.

Looking seawards on a calm day you could catch 'The Vision of Killsaheen': a large arch or bridge with people walking about 'as if at a fair', observed for 15 minutes at a time.

The least alarming suggestion is that it is a mirage of the Spanish Arch in Galway, due north of Ballybunion, reflected in some way from cloud formation over the sea. Personally, I think it's what you get at Ballybunion instead of a hangover.

The 1st hole is an innocent-looking par 4 but at the 2nd the course really begins to show its teeth. The drive is uphill and the green is awkwardly set for the approach, then there is a tough par 3 and two 5s, which used to be the finish but were put in earlier in the round when the course was remodelled some years ago. From here on, the precisely struck tee-shot is at a premium, for only by being in the right place will you have a real chance of hitting a scoring approach.

The 7th runs along the Atlantic with nothing between you and Labrador and the 9th is another long and scenically stunning par 4 along the shore. Like the 11th it has a plateau green but the later hole is even more spectacular with huge sandhills on one side and the pounding ocean on your right.

Then it is up into the sandhills to a high green for the testing par-3 12th and the 13th is the first of the inward par 5s with another green up in the dunes. Then comes an unusual sequence of two par 3s, one up and one down and thus homeward along the shore to the hospitable clubhouse. The New Course, designed by Robert Trent Jones, is supposed to be fiendishly difficult and no place for people who know their own limitations only too well. When it matures, it promises to give Ballybunion one of the best 36-hole golf lay-outs anywhere.

Ambassador Hotel, Ballybunion, County Kerry tel: (068) 27111 **
Just a few minutes from the golf courses, the Ambassador offers wonderful panoramic views over the Atlantic and the best of Irish produce in its restaurant—salmon and oysters from Galway, mussels, crabs, lobsters, scallops, prawns, turbot and sole from Kenmare; tender lamb and mutton from Kerry and pale-pink slices of roast ribs of beef, pork, ham and chicken dishes with bacon and leeks, potato cakes and delicious fresh vegetables cooked with skill and flair, and the occasional touch of imported imagination.

As in most good Irish hotels, there is also an unusually varied list which ranges the world for good bottles and reveals a knowledgeable and personal choice, although the Irish preference for good claret is strongly in evidence. Open all week.

KILLARNEY, Mahony's Point tel: (064) 31034 *Mahony's Point: 6727 yards SSS 72   Kileen: 6899 yards SSS 73*

RESTAURANTS
Park Hotel, Kenmare **** Lime Tree, Kenmare ***

Killarney Golf and Fishing Club is on the northern shore of Lough Leane, 3 miles west of Killarney, in one of the loveliest settings in the world. Across the blue waters of the lough, studded with wooded islets, tower the great peaks of MacGillicuddy's Reeks, the highest mountains in Ireland, and on almost every hole of the two courses you are assailed by magnificent views.

The two courses grew out of one, originally laid out by a combination of extraordinary and diverse talents. Viscount Castlerosse, the celebrated *Sunday Express* gossip columnist of the 1930s, owned the land and put his own ideas into the design along with the skills of golf architect Sir Guy Campbell, sprinkled with a few suggestions from Castlerosse's friend and drinking crony Henry Longhurst, plus the professional advice of Fred Hawtree and the counsel of local luminary Dr Billy O'Sullivan, a former Irish Amateur champion and internationalist.

From this potentially explosive and indigestible mixture has emerged two courses both better than the original, which is the kind of miracle you look for in Ireland and certainly you could not have a finer site for such a marvel than the shores of Lough Leane.

Kileen is the longer of the two and begins virtually in the lough itself, from the tee on a spur thrusting into the water and the 1st fairway follows the shore line. The 3rd is a spectacular short hole, straight at the majestic mountain range and with a carry over the curve of the lough shore.

There is an excellent par 5 at the 5th, with the green tucked away round a corner at the end of the fairway. Streams come into play at the 7th and 8th. At the 450-yard 13th you need not only to carry a stream in front of the green but also to thread your second shot through a gap in the trees to get there.

When championships are played at Killarney, the holes on the two courses are scrambled to provide the most testing lay-out. But the original finish, the final three holes of Mahony's Point, is always retained. The 16th sweeps downhill towards Lough Leane, a broad fairway through borders of rough and trees. The slope and the bright water behind the green makes it look shorter than it is, but you must take enough club because this hole plays every foot of its 518 yards and there is a stream across the fairway some 80 yards short of the pin.

The 17th goes back along the lough shore towards the clubhouse but although you need to keep your drive on the left, it must be near enough the centre of the fairway for your second not to be blocked out by a tall pine detached from the forest border on the landward side.

Then comes the splendid finish: a 202-yard par 3 across the shore and rough country to a peninsula green, close-hugged by trees and with a huge bank of rhododendrons beyond the path on the left. You are mercifully shrouded by these flowering bushes from the clubhouse when you play this alarming shot—the most testing and most tactful hole in Irish golf.

Killarney firmly boasts that it has the most beautiful golf course in the world. As you hole your putt for par on the loughside last green, you will find it hard to disagree.

Park Hotel, Kenmare tel: (064) 41200 ＊＊＊＊
At the lacemaking town of Kenmare, 21 miles south of Killarney, 'an amalgam of the prettiest surprises that ever met the eye', Francis

Brennan in the Park maintains the grand hotel tradition: apposite with fine paintings and antique furniture, a captivating setting, friendly and considerate service and imaginative classic food made from Ireland's finest produce. Sole on a bed of spinach with tomato and basil sauce; a parcel of sea trout and turbot filled with shallots; turbot with peach sauce; monkfish with mustard-seed mayonnaise, timbale of smoked salmon stuffed with crab; lobster and scallops represent the harvest of the nearby sea and river. Kerry lamb comes with oysters and a walnut stuffing; an open tart with calf sweetbreads and morels; fine Irish beef and Limerick ham; confit of duck with red cabbage and quail with madeira sauce are other offerings. The list is a good and instructive read, with fine château-bottled clarets and some bargains, including Australian and Californian whites. House French is £14. Open all week. Closed mid-November to 23 December; 2 January till Easter.

Lime Tree, Shelbourne Street, Kenmare tel: (064) 41225 ✱✱✱
This old school house, pleasantly converted into a cottage-style restaurant and decorated with good pictures and pottery, has an interesting and wide-ranging menu, which spans and often unites modern cooking ideas with Irish and classical traditions. Thus you get potato pancakes with the fish soup; delicious brown soda bread with smoked salmon as well as sea bass with red pepper and basil sauce; crab claws with ginger; turbot with mustard sauce and other marine mélanges, dependent on the day's catch. Other dishes feature lamb, pâté and vegetarian meals. There is a short list: House French is £9. Open Monday to Saturday, dinner only. Closed November to Easter.

ROYAL PORTRUSH, Bushmills Road, Portrush, County Antrim
tel: (0265) 823780 *Dunluce: 6772 yards SSS 73   Valley: 6273 yards SSS 70*

RESTAURANTS
Macduff's, Coleraine ✱✱   Ramore, Portrush ✱✱

Portrush, on the northern Antrim coast a few miles from the Giant's Causeway, with the Scottish islands of Islay and Gigha and the Mull of Kintyre in sight to the north, is always listed among the world's top courses.
It is the only one outside the British mainland on which the Open Championships has been played. The Open was played here in 1951 and was won by Max Faulkner. In 1960 the brilliant Irish player Joe Carr defeated the American Robert Cochran by eight and seven here to win the Amateur title for the third time.
The championship course, Dunluce, is laid out among sand dunes on three different levels, mostly on the inland side of the second course, Valley. The narrow fairways and punishing rough of bents grass and heather put a premium on driving accurately, for to be off the fairway here is usually to be in deep trouble.
Only the first and last holes are straight, all the other longer holes curve to a greater or lesser degree. Although there are few bunkers in comparison with most links courses, they are cunningly placed and the hillocks and

hollows, mounds, runnels, swales and gullys protecting the greens make extra sand superfluous.

The first really demanding hole is the 2nd, a par 5 of 503 yards with twin bunkers at drive length and cross-bunkers guarding the flag. There is one of Portrush's most stringent tee-shots to be played at the 4th—with a stream to be crossed, out-of-bounds to the right, bunkers left and a tight humped entrance to the green in the sandhills. Played to a narrow fairway back towards the clubhouse, the 432-yard 7th has a difficult second shot, even after the most perfectly placed drive, for it has to fly over bunkers to an elevated green which falls away dramatically on the right.

The 9th is a par 5 of 479 yards, where anyone going for the green in two must beware of the swale in front and the close-hugging rough round the putting surface. The 11th is one of those charming but deceptive dropping par 3s, where you play from a tee in the dunes down to a small green neck-laced with bunkers. At the 14th you come to the notorious Calamity Corner, a terrifying 213-yard shot, where you must be long enough and straight enough because anywhere else there is just Irish jungle, some of it 50 feet below the flag.

The 15th does not do much to steady the nerves, for although it is downhill the fairway is bumpy. There is a long carry off the tee and you need to judge your pitch very carefully to stay out of the sand which hugs the green.

At the 16th there are cross-bunkers to carry or avoid to the left and there are more bunkers where it hurts as you try to fly your approach into the green at this 432-yarder. They may not be lavish with bunkers at Portrush but they make them all count.

About a third of all the bunkers on the course are on the last two holes, which are long, 520 and 480 yards, and flat. Those on the 17th are in the main around the green but at the 18th they are all over the place; bunkers for pull and fade, cross-bunkers, greenside bunkers, all lurk there to punc-ture any sense of euphoria you might have brought with you on to the last tee. Like all links courses, just how tough Portrush is depends on the wind and wherefrom it blows. But even when it can hardly make up its mind, this course asks questions of us all.

Macduff's, 112 Killeague Road, Blackhill, Coleraine BT51 4HH
tel: (0265) 868433 **
Coleraine is just 6 miles from Portrush at the head of the Bann estuary. This beautifully furnished and decorated one-time Georgian rectory now houses a fine restaurant in its basement. The food skilfully blends the indigenous with the international.

Pork stroganoff: chicken breasts with herb mousseline; rack of lamb with mulled-wine sauce; a delicately flavoured curry; monkfish with garlic and tomato; escalopes of veal or game might be preceded by Stilton puffs with sweet and sour sauce; mushroom and bacon pancakes or asparagus with ham and a cheese sauce.

To follow—carragheen, jellied seaweed dessert with a local whiskey syrup and cream; Atholl brose or hazelnut meringue. Good, well-travelled list, reasonably priced. House French is £6.50. Open Tuesday to Saturday, dinner only.

Ramore, The Harbour, Portrush BT56 8DQ tel: (0265) 824313　∗∗
George McAlpin's splendid restaurant has all the pluses you could wish. Sweeping views over the harbour and West Bay and thoroughly up-to-date cooking, intelligently and imaginatively prepared and presented. Filo purses of scallops with ginger and spring onions; chicken breasts stuffed with prawns and wrapped in caul with leeks and ceps; rack of lamb glazed with ratatouille; timbale of quail with chervil and bacon and madeira sauce; chicken with vin jaune and truffles; salmon and monkfish with saffron sauce; pork with pineapple, coriander and ginger; duck breast in filo with orange sauce.
There is home-made bread to go with the chicken-liver pâté or mushrooms with garlic cream and snail quenelles and excellent fish straight from the quayside. The list is ambitious and well thought out, with lots of good growers' names. House wines are from £6.50. Open for lunch in the wine bar Monday to Saturday; dinner in the restaurant Tuesday to Saturday. Closed last two weeks of January.

ROYAL COUNTY DOWN, Newcastle, County Down tel: (03967) 23314
6968 yards SSS 73

RESTAURANT
Woodlands, Ballynahinch　∗∗∗

This is one of the most admired courses in the world, getting into everyone's top twenty list (*Golf Magazine* in the United States rated it third in 1983). Yet it has never hosted a major golf event, although a few ladies' championships have been played here and Michael Bonallack won his third successive Amateur title at Royal County Down in 1970.
Various reasons have been advanced both for the praise and the ignoring of Royal County Down. Undoubtedly a fair proportion of the acclaim must be for its setting on the shore of Dundrum Bay, with the green hills towards Armagh to the west and the foothills of the purple peaks climbing out of the little town of Newcastle 'where the Mountains of Mourne sweep down to the sea' to the south.
But it also offers a fascinating challenge as a golf course of style, quality and striking originality. Old-fashioned in concept perhaps, but that is what you would expect when it was made by Old Tom Morris in 1889 for a fee of £4 and redone to match the new flying power of the wound ball by Harry Vardon in 1908.
Against it as a championship venue there is the pandering to the modern professional which insists that there should be no blind shots, that the bottom of the pin should be visible from everywhere. Perhaps it is to those of us for whom golf is a pleasure and not a computer-calculated business that courses like Royal County Down make such an appeal.
There are six blind tee-shots and quite a few other places on the course where if you are in anything but the ideal spot, you cannot see much of the

green. It could be, to most golfers playing County Down, that the notion of not being in the ideal spot here seems so ludicrous that it is the reason why it always gets into the charts.

The opening holes head northwards along the shores of Dundrum Bay. The 1st, a long par 5, is screened by a range of dunes from the onshore winds but with a difficult narrow entrance to the green. The 2nd, a par 4, has a long carry over gorse and heather to the fairway and a tightly bunkered plateau green. The 3rd, an even longer 4 of 468 yards, needs a very exact drive to avoid getting entangled with the bunkered ridge which thrusts into the fairway. At the short 4th you head back towards the Mourne mountains, 200 yards over a sea of gorse to a ten-bunker green.

At the 5th the drive is completely blind, for you must head out across wild country to carry the right-hand dog-leg and miss the bunker tucked into its corner, then hit a long approach to the green in the sandhills. The next short hole, the 7th, is just 137 yards, but the green is domed and there is a gully of gorse to fly. There is a fall away to the right also at the 8th green, which you must reach through a tight gap between bunkered sandhills with your second. The 9th goes back to the clubhouse with the dark mass of Slieve Donard, Ulster's highest mountain, looming over the green.

The second half is inland and never returns to the coast. At the 11th there is a long drive over sandhills. The par-5 12th is a comparatively simple hole when it is downwind, although there is a towsy valley to get over to reach the fairway. The boomerang-shaped 13th is a long-thighed dog-leg, well bunkered on the angle. The 14th, heading west, is a combative short hole, requiring a shot of more than 200 yards over gorse, whin and heather to a six-bunker green.

Then you turn back towards the clubhouse. The 15th needs two solid blows if the wind is up, a blind drive and a well-struck second to a shelf green in the dunes. The 16th is a 267-yard par 4, reachable from the tee with an obliging breeze, crag to crag, but there is a pond with an island in the middle in the valley below to encourage you to be long enough.

Another larger pond is a feature of the 420-yard 17th, to be carried with your second shot to the menacingly bunkered green. The 18th at 548 yards is the longest hole on the course with a substantial carry from the tee to a fairway adorned with twenty-one bunkers. Most are down the right-hand side but there is a deep, staggered set of cross-bunkers to threaten the second shot, more in the guardian sandhills on the way to the green and two snuggling into the putting surface itself.

A beautiful place to play and a course which examines the quality of your golf with a very beady eye.

Woodlands, 29 Spa Road, Ballynahinch BT24 8PT tel: (0238) 562650 ∗∗∗

Ballynahinch is 16 miles north of Newcastle on the road to Lisburn and Woodlands is a charming eighteenth-century country house with a restaurant open three nights a week and at other times by arrangement. There is a short set-price menu with a few choices on each course and the cooking combines the best British and French culinary virtues with Irish hospitality in the size of the portions.

Dishes on offer include soup; pancakes with smoked haddock and cheese; gratin of garlic mushrooms; spinach roulade with haddock filling; pigeon breasts with port and juniper; pork with apple and prune stuffing and a calvados sauce; fish from sea and river, according to season, and elegant desserts. There is a short but interesting list, principally French from good growers, very fairly priced. House wines are £7.50.

FRANCE

If you disregard Holland, which, in spite of Steven van Hengel's research, you must do in terms of golf courses, France can claim the oldest European course outside Great Britain. This is at Pau, birthplace of Henry of Navarre, first Bourbon king of France, in the foothills of the Pyrenees between Gascony and the border with Spain. In 1856 the Duke of Hamilton and a group of exiled British aristocrats founded this club, the first in Europe. Thirty years later, Scots professional Willie Dunn, from Musselburgh, the first professional in the United States, designed a course along the cliff tops of Biarritz and so began the clutch of courses in the south-west corner of France which produced the first non-British Open champion, Arnaud Massy in 1907, and sixty years later one of the greatest women golfers, Catherine Lacoste.

Golf has expanded mightily in France in the last decade or so and there are now more than 250 courses between the Pas de Calais and Perpignan. This is a selection of some of the most agreeable to play in some of the most interesting regions of France.

In general, restaurants like golf courses have been chosen for the quality of what they offer, then for the ambience and the service and only lastly for the price. It is impossible to keep up with restaurant prices in France as elsewhere. If you eat *à la carte* it can be very expensive although not always. To give a general guide to cost, I have put stars against restaurants which relate to their lowest priced set menus (many restaurants have set menus at various prices) where these are on offer.

LE TOUQUET, sea course tel: (21) 05-20-22   *6195 yards SSS 71*

RESTAURANTS
Flavio-Club de la Forêt **** Le Café des Arts **

The links lay-out overlooking the Channel, 32 kilometres south of Boulogne and 221 kilometres from Paris is the newer of the two courses here. La Forêt, the inland course next to Le Manoir Hôtel, where the international gamblers worked off their casino losses and hangovers the morning after, is parkland with rolling, manicured fairways set through a pine forest. The Sea Course is longer, a typical seaside links with few trees, hummocky fairways, winds off the sea and sand dunes. Free golf on Le Touquet courses if you stay at Le Manoir, otherwise green fees from FR 240–315, according to season. Le Touquet has been the venue for the French Open and other professional championships.

Flavio-Club de la Forêt, 1 avenue de Verger, Le Touquet tel: (21) 05-10-22 (Menu lunch only) ****
Monsieur Flavio proclaims himself the 'first restaurateur of the Pas-de-Calais' and although this may be adjudged vainglorious, it is not necessarily wrong. An elegant restaurant with correspondingly 'elegant'

prices. Famous for seafood such as duo of salmon (smoked and raw), brill with sea kale, oysters with ginger, lobster from five recipes and similar innovative dishes, it is a rendezvous for casino winners rather than losers but a splendid place to dine.

Le Café des Arts, 80 rue de Paris, Le Touquet tel: (21) 05-21-55 **
Less expensive than Flavio but with a delightful ambience and very original food, particularly seafood dishes such as red mullet in beetroot juice with mushrooms, prawns with tomatoes and unusual fish soups and there is also a mouth-watering list of desserts.

HARDELOT, *Pines Course: 6457 yards SSS 72* tel: (21) 83-73-10
Dunes Course: 6556 yards SSS 72 tel: (21) 91-90-90.

RESTAURANTS
Hostellerie de la Rivière, Pont de Briques **   La Matelote, Boulogne ***

There are two courses at this beach resort, halfway between Boulogne and Le Touquet. The Pines is winding and cut through mixed woodland, the first nine with tight, well-bunkered fairways and two very demanding short holes, the second nine more open and with fewer alleyways through the trees but with two testing long holes in the last three. The new Dunes Course combines the problems of pine forests, seaside links with undulating fairways and water hazards. Green fees range from FR 210–260.

Hostellerie de la Rivière, 17 rue de la Gare, Pont-de-Briques
tel: (21) 32-22-81 **
Pont-de-Briques is 5 kilometres south of Boulogne on the D940 and therefore about 10 kilometres north of Hardelot. As its name suggests, the Hostellerie is primarily a fish restaurant, although in addition to the usual traditionally prepared lobster and sole dishes, there are such novelties as braised salmon with raspberry vinaigrette and quite exceptionally good puds.

La Matelote, 80 boulevard Sainte-Beuve, Boulogne
tel: (21) 30-17-97 ***
Opposite the casino, La Matelote is easy to find and during the week offers a set menu as well as à la carte. As with all restaurants on this coast, there is an extensive and delicious seafood choice but those who do not want to eat fish all the time are also catered for with dishes like filet de boeuf aux morilles and an intriguing choice of desserts such as chocolate fondant with sour cherries.

DEAUVILLE, tel: (31) 88-20-53   *6527 yards SSS 71*

RESTAURANTS
Le Ciro's ***   L'Ambassade d'Auvergne *

There are three nines here on the hills above Deauville and you can pick any two to make up your 18. It is in essence a parkland course, made interesting with lots of dog-legs and trees; enjoyable rather than demanding in its picturesque setting, overlooking the Touques River and the sea. Green fees FR 171–315.

Le Ciro's, boulevard de la Mer tel: (31) 88-18-10 ***
Very much the smart restaurant of Deauville with slightly over-elaborate dishes and particular, wonderfully inventive desserts, it serves the traditional Channel coast seafood in several new guises as well as game, pigeons with truffles and excellent wines.

L'Ambassade d'Auvergne, 109 avenue de la République
tel: (31) 88-74-78 *
A haven of refuge for those fleeing the omnipresent fish menu, this corner of Auvergne has foie gras, duck confit, tripe, Auvernais cheeses at their ripest, delicious apple tarts and characuterie from Aubrac. Although there is good Marcillac on the list, it is always worth remembering in Normandy that the local drink is cider and that it goes well with this kind of menu and, if someone else is driving or you are staying the night, the apple brandy calvados offers a powerful and satisfying finish to a meal.

OMAHA BEACH, *3460 yards SSS 36   3190 yards SSS 36   3440 yards SSS 36*

RESTAURANTS
Le Lion d'Or, Bayeux **
Les Comtes de Normandie, Molay-Littry ***
La Chenevière, Escures ***

The three different nine-hole loops of this course offer diverse types of golfing scenery. The Hedges 9 winds among the apple trees which provide the favoured Norman tipples of cider and calvados; the Pond 9 has views and perils over some inland waters and the lake, and the Sea 9 overlooks the beaches where American troops landed on D-day. Needless to say, it is an American-style course. Green fees FR 144–200.

Le Lion d'Or, 71 avenue St Jean, Bayeux tel: (31) 92-06-90 **
Bayeux, one of the oldest and best-preserved towns in France, famous for its tapestry of the Norman Conquest of England and for being the first town in France to be liberated in the Second World War, is just 12 kilometres or so from Omaha Beach and well worth a visit. Monsieur Jouvin-Bessière's Lion d'Or is picturesquely old-fashioned around its flowered courtyard and, in keeping with its setting, serves classical French dishes like tournedos with garlic mushrooms, delicious terrines and game.

Les Comtes de Normandie, on D5 route d'Isigny, Molay-Littry
tel: (31) 22-90-82 ***
This restaurant in the magnificent eighteenth-century Château du Molay takes a bit of finding via a 15 kilometre minor roads drive to the south

through Trevières and Rubercy, but it is quite definitely worth the effort. There are deer in the grounds but not on the menu, which is classical and seasonal with a light and occasionally inventive touch.

La Chenevière, Escures 2 kilometres south of Port-en-Bessin on D6
tel: (31) 21-47-96 ***
This manor-house restaurant is the nearest of the three to the golf course. It has a young and ambitious chef, François Laurent, whose food has already attracted considerable praise from the touring gastronauts, particularly his filet mignon with honey and black pepper and salmon tartare with a curry sauce. An elegant and agreeable place to eat.

CHATEAU DE CHEVERNY, tel: (54) 79-24-70 *6900 yards SSS 73*

RESTAURANTS
Le Bocca d'Or, Blois ** Grand Hôtel du Lion d'Or, Romorantin ****

The clubhouse here is a cosily converted farmhouse not a château but the Loire Valley is the land of these elegant turreted romantic French castles and the course is built on land belonging to the local baron. Fifteen kilometres south of Blois on the River Loire, site of the most famous royal French château of them all and birthplace of the man who invented the pressure-cooker, it is parkland with lots of trees, some water hazards and even moorland gorse. Green fees FR 150–210.

Le Bocca d'Or, 15 rue Haute, Blois tel: (54) 78-04-74
(Menus weekdays only) **
Despite its Italianate name (perhaps a hangover from Caterina dei Medici who is reputed to have brewed poisons for her political enemies in the great Château de Blois which dominates the town but who also brought *haute cuisine* from Florence to France), the cooking in this stone-arched restaurant is impeccably French, sole with ginger and cucumber fumet, lamb sweetbreads with lemon grass and black radishes, smoked duck breast with lentil purée, pears and walnut oil and spectacular desserts.

Grand Hôtel du Lion d'Or, 60 rue Clemenceau, Romorantin
tel: (54) 76-00-28 ****
Twenty-eight kilometres from Cheverny in Romorantin where François I spent his dissolute youth, is one of the finest restaurants in France, masterminded by chef Didier Clément, one of the great researchers into the *haute cuisine* of the historic past and a collector of antique recipes whose highly original and delicious food is matched by one of the most comprehensive cellars of Loire wines in the world. Zephyr-light vol-au-vents filled with spring onions and morels, duck liver in chilled bouillon, liquorice-flavoured snails and artichokes, prawn risotto with balsamic vinegar, pink rosemary-scented duck followed by a choice from the great goat cheeses of the area and one of Monsieur Clément's paradisal puddings are only a few of the perfections on offer. If the

weather is good, you can dine in the garden, but it is a privilege to eat such food anywhere.

LA BRETESCHE, tel: (40) 88-30-03   *6700 yards SSS 72*

RESTAURANT
Auberge Bretonne, La Roche Bernard **

Not to be confused with Saint-Nom-La-Bretêche, the course near Paris where the Lancôme Trophy is played, this haven of tranquility in the Breton hinterland has a testing and beautiful golf course, with almost every hole isolated by trees, a fourteenth-century château overlooking the lake next to the clubhouse and a delightful hotel. The course is tight with its narrow tree-lined fairways but entertaining to play if you stay out of the trees. A real get-away-from-it-all course.

Auberge Bretonne, 2 place du Guesclin, La Roche Bernard
tel: (99) 90-60-28 **
This is a well-named inn because Jacques Thorel is devoted to the produce of his native Brittany and to preserving old and discovering new ways of cooking it. Not only the seafood for which Bretons are famous but such delicate dishes as tender veal and wild mushrooms and wonderful desserts like his puff-pastry apples and baked peaches. The ingenuity and care naturally extend to fish—sole with hazelnuts or cabbage, capers and winkles, braised lobster, sea urchins with scallops and endive and other dishes enhanced by the herbs which he grows in his courtyard garden. There is also an astonishing list which offers more than 1500 wines. Superb food and good value.

LA BAULE, tel: (40) 60-48-18   *6820 yards SSS 73*

RESTAURANTS
La Marcanderie, La Baule **   La Collégiale, Guérande ***

This intriguing lay-out at Avrillac, 3 kilometres north-east of La Baule was designed in 1976 by Peter Alliss and Dave Thomas. It has nine fairly flat holes through a mixed forest and a second nine set in more hilly country around a 12-acre lake. Water can come into play at twelve of the eighteen holes and the finish with two long holes and two played around the water calls for straight hitting. La Baule is reputed to have the finest beach in France and is a popular holiday resort with a casino and yacht harbour. The golf course has hosted the French Open.

La Marcanderie, 5 avenue d'Agen, La Baule tel: (40) 24-03-12 **
A cheerful, bright and friendly restaurant where chef Jean-Luc Giraud's cooking shows a fondness for the favourite British vegetable, the potato. There is a galette with prawns, jacket potatoes providing a substantial garnish for mixed shellfish but plenty of choice in other types of dishes. Rather a short wine list.

La Collégiale, 63 faubourg Bizienne, Guérande tel: (40) 24-97-29 ∗∗∗
Guérande is about 5 kilometres from the golf course and Christian Port-
ner's charming restaurant in a garden breaks the fish tradition of these
parts with two exceptional veal dishes, one with orange-flavoured
mustard and a delicious veal loin and kidney salad. There is fish, of
course, good fish soup, cod with vanilla and the usual shellfish. Not
cheap but both food and wine are enticing.

HOSSEGOR, tel: (58) 43-56-99   *6566 yards SSS 71*

RESTAURANTS
Les Huîtrières du Lac, Hossegor ∗∗   Cheval Blanc, Bayonne ∗∗

This parkland course 18 kilometres north of Bayonne was made in 1929
through the cork and pine forest just inland from the great dunes of the
Landes coast. Perhaps the proximity of so much sand went to Scots architect John Morrison's head, for this is one of the most cunningly bunkered
courses in France. The importance of placing the tee-shot is underlined at
almost every hole and very particularly at the 9th and the 16th where the
siting of the bunkers as well as the trees makes accuracy paramount.

Les Huîtrères du Lac, 1187 avenue du Touring Club, Hossegor
tel: (58) 43-51-48 ∗∗
This charming lakeside restaurant combines in one of its star dishes two
of the great gastronomic attractions of the region, sea bream and
smoked ham from Bayonne, the bream is stuffed with the ham and
baked and makes a fine substantial dish to follow a plateful of *garbure*,
the local vegetable soup made with bacon and goose fat. Or indeed a
plate of oysters for which the restaurant is renowned. There is a good
selection of wines from the Pyrenees region with complicated names
but excellent flavours like Irouléguy, Jurançon and Madiran.

Cheval Blanc, 68 rue Bourgneuf, Bayonne tel: (59) 59-01-33 ∗∗
Here you are in Basque country and Bayonne has the reputation of
having added finesse to the rather robust cooking of the Pays Basque.
Jean-Claude Tellechea is an enterprising chef who takes the Basque
ingredients—goose, hams, pork, a predeliction for pimentoes and a great
variety of fish and crustaceans—and creates new marvels with them.
Lamb from the foothills of the Pyrenees in a *pot au feu*, goose confit
chipirons, the local squid cooked in a dozen different ways, baked hake
with grilled onions in chicken sauce and langoustines in caviare cream
give some idea of his versatility. A good list of mainly local wines.

CANNES-MANDELIEU, tel: (93) 49-55-39   *6441 yards SSS 71*

RESTAURANTS
La Palme d'Or ∗∗∗∗   La Croisette ∗

Mandelieu, 7 kilometres west of Cannes, is one of the oldest courses in
France and was founded by Lord Brougham and Grand Duke Michael of

Russia in 1891. Bordered by mimosa trees and sea pines and laid out partly along the Mediterranean shore, it also features the River Saigne, between the 2nd and 3rd holes and the 12th and 13th, across which you are ferried by a Charon-like figure in a boat. There are five par 3s and two not very long par 4s but the 13th is a tough par 5, although the two 3s at the 16th and 17th make the finish a little tame. A most agreeable course to play and open all the year round, except on Tuesdays. Green fees FR 240–270.

La Palme d'Or, 73 La Croisette, Cannes tel: (93) 94-30-30 ****
Chef Christian Willer has a brilliant and original talent and in the last few years he has made this gourmet restaurant in the Hôtel Martinez on its terrace overlooking old Cannes, the sea and the Lérin Islands, one of the great restaurants in the world. Herby rabbit compôte with a sabayon of sweet peppers, soup made from lobster and young pigeon flavoured with wild mushrooms, prawns with lettuce braised in passion-fruit juice can be among the starters. Grilled red mullet on a leek remoulade, rabbit pie with olives and Swiss chard, escalope of salmon with thyme, grilled calf's liver with sage and sharp apples, roast baby lamb with herbs, casseroled T-bone of veal, beef fillet with crushed olives and Parma ham and all kinds of wonderful desserts such as wild strawberries, macaronade of wild fennel and crystalized courgette flowers with chocolate are the kinds of dishes making up a dazzling menu, which changes constantly according to the market and the seasons. The menu price includes wine. L'Orangeraie, downstairs overlooking the swimming pool, serves simpler and cheaper but also excellent food.

La Croisette, 15 rue du Commandant André, Cannes tel: (93) 39-86-06 *
This cosy bistro just off the west end of La Croisette serves good homely dishes such as steak, grain-fed chicken, casseroles, cassolette of kidneys and superb apple tart for modest prices. The menu price includes wine.

CANNES-MOUGINS, tel: (93) 75-79-13 *6753 yards SSS 72*

RESTAURANTS
La Colombe d'Or, St Paul de Vence ****
Moulin de Mougins, Mougins **** Le Bistrot de Mougins, Mougins **

At one time the course at Mougins 6 kilometres and 800 feet above Cannes was open only in the winter months because it suffered from the traditional problem of Provence—lack of water. In 1978, however, irrigation was introduced and the course was re-designed by Peter Alliss and David Thomas. Now, on the hills overlooking the resort town, Mougins is one of the best courses in France, a fine testing lay-out with undulating fairways and well-protected greens. The clubhouse retains its rustic charm. Green fees FR 250–290.

La Colombe d'Or, place du Général de Gaulle, St Paul de Vence tel: (93) 32-80-02 ****
St Paul is about 20 kilometres east of the golf course at Mougins, another of the picturesque hill-towns, built as protection against the

slave raids of the Saracens, which carried on along this coast well into the seventeenth century. Its splendid defensive walls, Les Remparts, are well preserved and still to be seen.

Within them is La Colombe d'Or, a rustic inn with excellent food and wines and the most astonishing collection of paintings. Monsieur Roux, the proprietor, befriended many artists who came to paint in Alpes-Maritimes and they paid for his fine food with their work. On the walls of the restaurant there are paintings and sketches which would buy many a meal today (even at Côte d'Azur prices) by Miró, Picasso, Modigliani, Léger, Matisse, Braque, Derain, Buffet and many others. Does sitting under one of Modigliani's pensive elongated girls or a splash of Buffet's sails make the Sisteron lamb, the Côtes de Provence wine and the good local cheeses like Banon, Cachat and Brousse taste better? Lots of people think so, and it is best to book.

Moulin de Mougins, Quartier Notre Dame de Vie, 424 chemin du Moulin, Mougins tel: (93) 75-78-24 ✴✴✴✴
Good Provençal cooking with flair and style: rascasse terrine with lemon; grilled fish with bay leaves; fricassee of mushrooms and asparagus, veal fillet on a purée of basil and tomatoes. Delicious aromatic food reeking of the hills of Provence and the skill of Roger Vergé. Bit heavy on the sauces in some dishes, but a charming place to eat and drink, especially on the garden terrace which almost makes up for the Moulin being rather star-studded and proving it with the wine list and the prices.

Le Bistrot de Mougins, place du Village, Mougins tel: (93) 75-78-34 ✴✴
The Ballatore family offers only one menu but portions are good and the choice is well made in this terraced restaurant, with typical Mediterranean dishes like salt cod and spinach mould, game casserole in season, pigeon with olives, rascasse with olives and anchovies, good local cheeses and a mouthwatering chocolate-cake dessert.

MONTE CARLO, tel: (93) 41-09-11 *6230 yards SSS 71*

RESTAURANTS
Le Louis XV ✴✴✴✴ Polpetta ✴✴

The Mont Agel course is strictly speaking not in Monte Carlo at all but overlooking the tiny Principality of Monaco from a height of 2400 feet above the village of La Turbie in France. Set against the mountain background of the French Alpes-Maritimes, this spectacular and original course was remodelled in 1982 to extend it by 600 yards to full tournament length in order to stage the first Monte-Carlo Open in 1984. Despite its altitude, Mont Agel is not particularly hilly and although not long, it calls for precise shotmaking. The long holes which begin both 9s are demanding but there are still too many short par 4s. However, it is an exhilarating course to play and the views are breathtaking on a clear day. Green fees FR 300–400.

Le Louis XV, place du Casino, Monte Carlo tel: (93) 50-80-80 ★★★★
Alain Ducasse's inspired versions of simple peasant dishes makes this
showy restaurant very popular. The menu is a mixture of the tastes of
Provence with the influence of the Italian Riviera and its hinterland
along the coast in Liguria. Casserole of pork chop and pig's trotter, spit-
roast milk lamb, grilled pigeon with duck liver and a superb nectarine
tart are among the specialities. The list offers a comprehensive selection
of wines from all over France.

Polpetta, 2 rue Paradis tel: (93) 50-67-84 ★★
Good, largely Italian, cooking at moderate prices. Excellent pasta, particularly the various kinds of ravioli, risotto alla marinara and veal dishes
like involtini stuffed with ham. Cheerful and popular.

PORTUGAL

There is a kind of gastronomic parallel between the origins of golf in Scotland and its beginnings in Portugal. In Scotland the game began in taverns and in Portugal it was wine which brought golf to the Atlantic coast of the Iberian peninsula. England's long standing treaty with Portugal dating from the marriage of John of Gaunt's daughter, Phillipa, with King John I of Portugal in 1387, and the lengthy continuous warring with France meant that, for most of the eighteenth century, there was little wine trading with France and much of the wine drunk in England came from Portugal. English and Scots wine merchants who went to Oporto to trade in wine and to improve its quality—a move which resulted in the invention of port—brought golf with them and the game was played on the linksland of the Atlantic coast below the Douro estuary for many years before Oporto, the oldest Portuguese club and the second oldest in Europe, was founded in 1890.

In the 1960s there was an explosion of golf along the south-facing Algarve coast and there are now thirteen courses between Faro and Sagres. More recently new courses have been built in the Lisbon area in addition to the long-established Estoril club and there are now some thirty courses in Portugal.

It is still a game largely for tourists and highly dependent on northern European visitors for its popularity, although more Portuguese have taken it up in the last decade. There are some fine courses and those along the Algarve coast in particular offer ideal conditions for holiday golf in the almost winterless weather enjoyed along Portugal's most southerly shores.

ESTORIL, Avenida da Republica 2765, Estoril tel: (01) 2680176
5726 yards SSS 69

RESTAURANTS
Albatroz, Cascais * * *   João Padeiro, Cascais * * *

There was a time when the balcony of the clubhouse at Estoril at lunch or aperitif time gathered more deposed European royalty than anywhere else. When permanent winter settled on most European thrones, the once crowned heads drifted towards Portugal and a decade or two ago the royal families of Spain, France, Romania, Bulgaria, Italy, Austria and Belgium all had their representatives sipping *vinho verde* on the Estoril terrace. Indeed there was a tale going the rounds in these days that ex-King Umberto of Italy was so popular on the Lisbon coast that he was asked to be the Mayor of Cascais but declined with a modest smile saying 'Thank you, but no. I have given up politics.'

Just why this delightful seaside town, 28 kilometres outside the Portuguese capital, should have been chosen as the ideal spot in which to mourn a throne is not abundantly clear. Perhaps it is the sad music of the *fado*, the traditional songs of Portugal, sung in cellars all over Lisbon and its littoral, which seemed an appropriate requiem to the lost trappings of royalty.

Today the atmosphere is less relentlessly regal but this short but fascinating golf course retains its charm and appeal. In a superb setting above the town between the saw-edge blue peaks of the Sintra mountains and the open sea leading into the Tagus estuary, Estoril's golf course is in splendid condition, offering challenging but not intimidating golf all the year round.

There are some excellent holes on this Mackenzie Ross lay-out, undulating through pine, mimosa and eucalyptus trees, where the demands are generally on skill and accuracy rather than power. Certainly, the par-5 5th, played for 517 yards uphill to a tightly-bunkered raised green, and the 7th, which needs two long shots around a left-hand dog-leg, call for both qualities, but most holes put the accent on sound shotmaking.

The spectacular 9th is just 172 yards long but the tee is 200 feet above the green and the huge bunker in front means you must be straight and just long enough. The 13th is a short par 4 but there is a closely trapped gap with out-of-bounds on both sides at 190 yards which makes the tee-shot more than a little tricky. There is water at the 2nd, the 10th and three of the holes on the back nine and you can be thankful to reach the flower-bordered last green with a score that matches your handicap intact.

Albatroz, 100 Rua Frederico Arouca, 2750 Cascais
tel: (01) 282821 ∗∗∗

This restaurant in a five-star hotel, on a rocky spur on the sea front overlooking the bay of Cascais just 3 kilometres along the coast from Estoril, is a rebuilt nineteenth-century mansion. As Portugal is on the Atlantic coast there is particularly fine sea food to be had in its restaurants. Oysters are served fresh or baked in white wine and butter; sardines simply grilled or baked with olives and tomato in puff pastry; shrimps baked with cream, port and egg yolks; tuna pâté flavoured with *eau de vie* or you can begin with *caldeirada*, the Portuguese fish stew made with sea fish like mullet, cod, bass and hake with shrimps, mussels and clams and coriander and garlic.

The soles round here come in large sizes and a very popular dish in the Lisbon area is sole stuffed with chopped chicken and ham, onions and egg yolks fried in oil and browned in the oven. There are also lobsters, once cheap but now almost as expensive as anywhere else, cooked in various ways. Most typically Portuguese is with *piri-piri*, the hot chilli sauce which the explorers brought back from their voyages.

Although things have improved in recent years, much Portuguese beef still tends to be tough and underhung but game and chickens are good, as is pork. Chicken can come spit-roasted, painted with *piri-piri* or steamed in an earthenware pot with mustard, garlic, tomatoes, smoked ham, port and brandy. Rabbit is cooked in wine and garlic or marinated and fried; and partridge and quail are also cooked in interesting ways, such as stuffed with pâté, marinated and simmered with white wine; or you can have hare with green pepper paste and oranges.

Portuguese wine is excellent and that from the Lisbon area is particularly good. The red Colares from the other side of the Sintra mountains can rival good Rhône wine if kept long enough in bottle. The semi-sparkling extra dry *vinho verde* from the Minho is delicious and both red and white Dão and the white Bucelas (popular with Wellington's officers during the Peninsular War) are worth considered attention.

João Padeiro, Rua Visconde da Luz, Cascais tel: (01) 280232 ✱✱✱
This agreeable and attractive restaurant, decorated with millstones and wooden fittings from old windmills, has excellent seafood from the Atlantic at the foot of the street. The famous *linguado* (sole) of this coast comes freshly grilled or stuffed Portuguese fashion and they can be the size of squash rackets.
Or you can have ocean-fresh lobsters grilled or sauced or baked with bechamel sauce or flambéed in brandy or steamed with Madeira and onions and tomatoes, squid stuffed with minced ham, garlic and herbs, grilled sardines and shrimps.
There are succulent cubes of pork and small clams cooked in a *cataplana*, a kind of double frying pan which acts as an elementary pressure-cooker and the hundred and one things which Portuguese cooks can do with *bacalhau* (dried cod).
This may not seem to you to be a very thrilling dish and it is certainly long in preparation. It looks rather like boiled dried cardboard in its original state (as it was brought back from the Newfoundland banks by Portuguese fishermen in the days before refrigeration) and it has to be soaked in water for at least 24 hours. Then you can cook it slowly with potatoes, olives, garlic, onions and herbs or bake it with cheese or with vegetables or in *vinho verde* or charcoal grill it or make it into something halfway between fish fingers and quennelles. Most ways it tastes very good.
There is a fine selection of Portuguese wines on the list, mostly whites, although there is a school of thought (as in Italy) that you should drink a red wine with a powerful fish stew like *caldeirada*.

Algarve

SAN LORENZO, Quinto do Lago, Almancil 8100, Loulé, Algarve
tel: (089) 396522   *6821 yards SSS 73*

QUINTA DO LAGO, 8135 Almancil, Algarve tel: (089) 394782   *4×9 holes*
A: 3430 yards SSS 36   C: 3568 yards SSS 36
B: 3527 yards SSS 36   D: 3355 yards SSS 36

VALE DO LOBO, Almancil, Algarve tel: (089) 94444   *27 holes SSS 70–72*
Green: 3076 yards SSS 35   Orange: 3253 yards SSS 36
Yellow: 3320 yards SSS 37

RESTAURANTS
Floresta ✱✱   Sergio's, Almancil ✱✱✱   Casa Velha, Quinta do Lago ✱✱✱✱
A Tranca, Almancil ✱✱   Outside-In, Santa Bárbara de Nexe ✱✱✱✱

These courses are all close together, reached from the village of Almancil on a turn off the main Faro–Portimão road, 15 kilometres from the airport. This wonderful coastline, running west to east and facing south, has the best winter climate in Europe. The clean, restless Atlantic sweeps in from Africa, there are impressive rust-red cliffs and massive dark rocky headlands and miles and miles of fine-sanded yellow beaches. In January the countryside is pale pink with almond blossom and the oranges and lemons glow on the dark-leaved trees along the roadside like Christmas lanterns. Despite its rapid development over the last twenty years the Algarve is somehow less raddled by tourism than Spain's Costa del Sol. There are very few high-rise buildings and despite the large luxurious villa complexes with their florid sporting amenities, there are still good small restaurants tucked away up side roads and in hill villages, still people catching fish and growing oranges and almonds, and obstinately wearing traditional old black felt and straw hats instead of golf visors.

VALE DO LOBO
This is the oldest of the courses in the Almancil area and one of the most attractive, with three loops of nine holes all running through eucalyptus, cork, sea pine, mimosa and fig trees right down to the pale-sanded beaches and the surging Atlantic and back to the clubhouse.
It has some memorable holes like the 5th on the Yellow Course, which calls for a drive from a high tee, down a valley over the corner of the bordering umbrella pines, and an uphill shot to the green. Two holes on, the 7th is the most spectacular hole on the Algarve, a 204-yard par 3, across a series of russet chasms in the cliffs overlooking the sea, to a narrow green.
The 5th on the Orange Course is a beautiful hole with bunkers and trees threatening the drive and the flag set against the bright ocean a few yards behind the green. The 7th on this nine is the longest hole on the course, 548 yards with an uphill drive, a gap between trees to negotiate with the second shot and a pitch up to a green hemmed in by cork oaks. The 9th, another par 5, uphill all the way from the eucalyptus trees around the tee to the large but skilfully bunkered green makes a testing finish.

QUINTA DO LAGO
East of Vale do Lobo, Quinta do Lago has four nines which provide a fine variety of golf, whirling dog-legs, shots carrying water and downhill par 3s across valleys among the pines. The fairways are exceptionally well cushioned and most of the greens are flat so that you can easily hit woods for second shots and run your putts straight at the hole—provided you have had a close look at the grain which is important on these Pencross surfaces. The 9th on the White Course is a good finishing hole, needing a drive across a lake and then a powerful shot into a high shelf green and the 16th on the Red Course is a par 3 with a long carry across water which needs a well-struck and exactly placed tee-shot.

SAN LORENZO
On the eastern edge of the Quinta do Lago estate, this is a Joe Lee design in a perfect peaceful setting along the Ria Formosa estuary and the salt-water

lagoons, cut through the bushy-topped sea pines over rolling territory and around a large lake.

It opens quietly with a long but not fierce par 5, followed by a par 3 to a kidney-shaped green with a large bunker in front. The 3rd is a tight tree-lined dog-leg punitively trapped on the corner and with a difficult shot into the three-bunker green. At the second of the par 3s, the ultra-short 129 yard 5th, there are wonderful views over the long beaches and the Atlantic. Then you had better stop looking at the scenery and concentrate on the next two rigorous holes along the estuary and the demanding finish to the first half. The 8th is a double dog-leg, along and over water for the best part of 600 yards, before you turn inland again up the hill towards the clubhouse.

There are some lovely inland holes with views over the blue mountains of the Serra de Caldeirado and then you head back towards the sea and the great nerve-tingling finish where water and staying out of it must stay firmly focussed in the mind. The 18th is a masterpiece, where even the most perfectly struck drive leaves you with an approach of about 150 yards, almost all the way across water, to a peninsula green with three bunkers around its fringe. A memorable course.

Floresta, on the road between Almancil and Vale do Lobo **
Very much a Vale do Lobo local but outside the estate on a corner leading up towards the main road. On the Algarve you have to choose between the elegant upmarket international restaurants like The Outside-In or Casa Velha, where prices are comparable to top UK restaurants, and the others at which you eat well and cheaply but simply off a limited menu of local produce.

Floresta comes into the second category but, of course, some of the local products such as clams, sea bass, sole, langoustines and the like would almost come into the luxury class elsewhere. Here you eat well—soup, pâté, seafood starters, pork cutlets or chicken *piri-piri*, beautifully fresh vegetables and fruit and the only two Portuguese puddings *pudim* (crème caramel) or something made with almonds, usually tart or cake. The house wine comes from the Algarve and is powerful but drinkable. Wines from elsewhere in Portugal are a better choice.

Sergio's, 30 Rua do Correio, Almancil 8100 tel: (089) 95154 ***
Sergio's, opposite the post office in Almancil, is owned and run by an English couple, Roger and Gay Evans, and has a menu which combines local and international dishes. You can start with deep-fried camembert cubes with cranberry jelly; crêpes filled with mussels, clams and shrimps with a seafood sauce; chicken salad with pineapple and oranges; smoked salmon or garlic mushrooms and move on to baked sole with a crabmeat filling and seafood sauce; breast of chicken stuffed with prawns and camembert; cataplana, pork and clams in a garlic, onion and tomato sauce; roast duckling with a fresh peach and liqueur sauce, tenderloin of pork with asparagus or monkfish kebabs marinated in cumin and mint served with yoghurt and a break-out into the British pudding menu

with trifle, profiteroles, peach flambé, apple crumble and pancakes as well as the inevitable *pudim*. Pleasant atmosphere and good service and a well-selected list of good Portuguese wines and liqueurs.

Casa Velha, Quinta do Lago, Almancil tel: (089) 9472 ＊＊＊＊
This 300-year-old farmhouse in the middle of the Quinta do Lago estate was beautifully converted into a restaurant by Portuguese artist Pedro Leitão and was a roaring success even before the golf courses opened for play.
The beamed ceilings and the dark wood tables, light walls and the tiled floor and the logs stacked by the open fire preserve the old country atmosphere with added elegance; the menu is Portuguese and international so you can have *ameijoas à cataplana* or *caldeirada* and tournedos Rossini, *pudim* or bombe surprise in the certainty that they will be made of the finest ingredients and beautifully cooked and presented. The list has some excellent Portuguese wines carefully chosen from the best growers.

A Tranca, Almancil tel: (089) 94237 ＊＊
A pink-washed building with iron grills over the windows on a corner of the main road in Almancil, A Tranca is a haven of genuine Algarvean cooking among the 400 restaurants spread along this coast, whose styles have been culled from culinary influences ranging from Austria to Zanzibar.
Here you can get some of the 365 different *bacalhau* dishes which other places ignore, variations on the use of the *cataplana* which is a cooking pan and not a recipe, lots of excellent fresh fish and shellfish served in the style of the province and charcoal-grilled meat and seafood. There is *caldo verde*, the green soup of the Minho, good wine and, on certain days of the week, first-class *fado* passionately sung by professionals.

Outside-In, Sitio de Valados-Santa Bárbara de Nexe
tel: (089) 91443 ＊＊＊＊
This ambitious and stylish restaurant on the road between Faro and Loulé is run by an Englishman, Mike Gilhooley, but offers French cooking of a high standard based on ingredients available locally. You might begin with cream of langoustine soup with brandy; shrimp mousse with fresh tomato puree; lobster and monkfish terrine with avocado sauce or pâté with cranberry sauce.
Main course fish dishes could be pastry-wrapped John Dory filet stuffed with shrimps and fresh herbs; turbot with spinach and orange; sea trout en papillote; scallops of monkfish with mushrooms in a crayfish sauce. There are also tournedos Rossini; fantail of duck breast with baked pear; chicken breast stuffed with crab with langoustine sauce; sirloin steak with a light mustard sauce and noisette of Alentejo lamb. Desserts break through the *pudim* barrier with a trio of seasonal sorbets with fresh fruit; chocolate truffles filled with ice cream; lemon mousse and whisky ice-cream cake. The list is meticulously selected from the very best growers

and winemakers in Portugal and offers some quite exceptional wines. Not an easy restaurant to find but worth searching for.

VILAMOURA, 8125 Quartiers, Algarve
tel: Vilamoura Um (089) 313652   *6923 yards SSS 72*
     Vilamoura Dois (089) 315562   *6771 yards SSS 71*
     Vilamoura Três (089) 880722   *6439 yards SSS 71*

RESTAURANTS
Castelo do Bispo, Albufeira ✳✳✳   O Elegante, Quartiera ✳✳

Vilamoura now has three courses imaginatively named Um, Dois, Três (which you have probably worked out means One, Two and Three). The original course, opened in 1969 and designed by Frank Pennink, is a kind of subtropical Wentworth, cut through narrow gorges of pines with sloping fairways and cunningly bunkered greens.

There are some intriguing short holes, particularly the 4th, where you have to float an approach delicately through the air over a double pond to a raised green on what is virtually an island, and the 6th, downhill from the clubhouse, where a formidable area of brush in the valley below stands between you and the green.

Of the longer holes eight are dog-legs with three really tough par 5s, all more than 500 yards in the back nine and another more amiable one at the final hole leading back to the most elegant clubhouse in the Algarve.

Vilamoura Dois was also designed by Pennink and used to be known as the Dom Pedro but it has been altered in the last few years by Robert Trent Jones. It is much more open than Vilamoura Um and from the first nine there are fine views over the sea and the Vilamoura development. A sentinel pine tree in the middle of the fairway at the par-4 2nd dictates the line of the tee-shot and there is water in front of the 3rd green. At the 12th you have to carry a stand of pines to reach the flag. You must keep straight on both these courses, because if you get into the trees, you will find that the short bushy sea pines will not only block your shot but often prevent a proper swing under their low heavy branches.

Vilamoura Três has twenty-seven holes and eleven lakes and was designed by Joe Lee close to the Vilamoura Marina. It opened for play in 1991.

Castelo do Bispo, Albufeira, Algarve ✳✳✳
On a hill overlooking the bustling town of Albufeira and its beaches, this smart restaurant is about 8 kilometres from Vilamoura. Albufeira is the St Tropez of the Algarve, full of show-biz people and good small restaurants, bars and discos but not entirely spoiled, just a little tarty in its spider web of streets, woven up the sides of hills and cliffs.

Everyone has his own favourite Albufeira restaurant but this one is run by Portuguese and has a menu with a vital mixture of traditional Portuguese dishes like stuffed squid and huge prawns grilled with garlic, pork marinated in a green-pepper paste; suckling pig and *cabrito* (spit-roasted kid), and international recipes for sole, turbot and lobster thermidor.

Have an orange. Watching a Portuguese waiter peeling an orange in one cut and laying it out like a flower for your dessert is an artistic as well as a gastronomic experience—and the oranges here come fresh from the trees and taste quite different from the gas-preserved fruit we get in the UK.

O Elegante, Avenida Infante de Sagres, Quartiera tel: (089) 65339 **
Quartiera is the exception to the Algarve rule. On the coast between Vale do Lobo and Albufeira it looks as if it had been imported from one of the less tasteful costas, an ugly splotch of high-rise buildings along the seashore.
It has its compensations, however, in the fact that it has a wonderful market for fish and vegetables at its western end and O Elegante at the other on the road running out towards Vale do Lobo. This small hotel has a restaurant renowned for its Portuguese dishes: superb fresh seafood; pork Alentejo; *caldo verde, caldeirada* and fish soup made with crayfish, rice and almonds; boned sardines in pastry with stoned olives and tomato; clams with ham; smoked sausages, onions and white wine and tuna steaks with bacon.

PENINA, PO Box 146, Penina, 8502 Portimão, Algarve tel: (082) 415415
Championship: 6889 yards SSS 73   Monchique: 3500 yards SSS 35
Quinta: 2278 yards SSS 31

RESTAURANTS
Penina Hotel **** Tropical Beach, Praia da Rocha ***

Much farther west, 12 kilometres beyond Portimão, Penina was the Algarve's first course designed by Sir Henry Cotton, created from rice paddy fields in 1966. It is magnificent—if you like that sort of thing—very long, playing 6889 yards from the medal tees (championship tees stretch it to 7480 yards), very flat and cunningly designed to call for every golf shot in the book. There is usually plenty to write on the exceptionally handsome score cards with coloured maps of each hole, spaces for everything and carefully measured distances to all hazards.
There are some very good holes. The 549-yard, par-5 11th starts down a narrow, tree-sentinelled fairway and only becomes a dog-leg 365 yards from the tee, when you have to try to hit your second shot round the corner over a massive bunker right across the elbow to give you a reasonable chance of getting to the green in 3. The 13th, with its 170-yard carry across water on the right as the best line to the green, is a splendid short hole, even if the brightly coloured ducks on the pond do fall about laughing if you fail to make it. Finishing the back nine with two par 5s can seem verging on sadism.
However, it is a very beautiful course, rather over-long, over-lush and over-manufactured for my taste. The two nine-hole courses on the other side of the main road, Monchique and Quinta, are much less demanding but have the same large smooth greens, dog-legs, water and mimosa, pine, eucalyptus and orange trees. Monchique has two par 5s, two 3s and five 4s—all interesting. Quinta has five par 3s and two 5s in its rather staid make-up. All the courses are beautifully kept.

Penina Hotel, 85500 Portimão, Algarve tel: (082) 22051 ****
The only piece of rising ground in the golf-course area is occupied by
the luxurious white slab of the Penina Hotel, now owned by Trusthouse
Forte, dominating everything rather like a modernised Turnberry but
with nothing like the views you get from Turnberry when it is not
raining.
The international menu in the grill room and dining room makes good
use of local produce but without much emphasis on Portuguese cuisine.
There is excellent meat as well as fish, pâté de foie gras rather than the
local chopped-pig terrine, T-bone steaks, duckling à l'orange, smoked
salmon and turtle soup, steak au poivre and tournedos and trolleys of
elaborate puddings. The list extends beyond Portugal but it is worth
remembering that expensive imported wines are not necessarily better
if you choose well.
If you stay at Penina, it is very well worth while going into Portimão not
only for its fine shops but to eat sardines on the quayside just under the
bridge which crosses the river estuary. Freshly grilled on charcoal and
served with salad and a bottle of extra-crisp local white wine, they make
as good a cheap lunch as you will get anywhere.

Tropical Beach, Areal, Praia da Rocha tel: (082) 26738 ***
Praia da Rocha was the only holiday resort on the Algarve until it was
'discovered' in the 1960s. Tropical Beach has fine views over the sea
especially when the sun is setting behind Cape St Vincent. The cooking
is modern and sophisticated—avocado stuffed with chicken, spiced and
herby kebabs of meat, vegetables and fish, grilled turbot and grouper,
swordfish with anchovies, tuna steaks, monkfish tails and cunningly
flavoured casseroles. Good Portuguese list.

PARQUE DA FLORESTA, Budens 86650 Vila do Bispo tel: (082) 6533
6476 yards SSS 72

RESTAURANTS
A Tasca, Sagres ** Fontanario, Espiche **

Parque de Floresta is another typically eccentric creation by the Terror of
Torrequebrada, former Spanish Amateur champion, Pepé Gancedo. At first
sight it looks rather like one of those jokey golf calendars which have you
play from tees on cliff ledges across volcanos to greens on mountain peaks
but, although endlessly fascinating as Pepé develops his canvas of one
quirky hole after another, it turns out to be perfectly and most entertain-
ingly playable.
However, this is not the image which imprints itself on the eye as you stand
quaking on the first tee. Before you, succeeding waves of fairway slope
menacingly from right to left. On the left, yawing in front of the green on
the hillside 501 yards away, is what appears to be a bottomless pit. The
initial emotion is one of stark terror. But a couple of long irons and a man-
or-mouse approach hit solidly will get you there, albeit with heart in
mouth.

The 5th is a short hole where the green appears to be farther below you than from you—and so it meanders madly and merrily on. Mercifully, there are three par 3s in the first nine. The second half opens with another transversely rolling hill fairway, followed by a beautiful downhill par 3 with a lake behind and left and guardian mimosas on the right. There is not a dull hole on the course and the long par-5 14th is one of the toughest anywhere, uphill all the way, needing radar to get near the green with your second—plus a missile-like three wood.

Parque de Floresta is one of the most dramatic courses in Europe and I have not had as much fun playing a new course in years. The stupendous views over the rolling hills are wonderfully exhilarating, the air is like wine and the problems set concentrate the mind wonderfully. A course to play again—and again.

If you are as intrigued by Parque de Floresta as I was after playing it, the people, who know about the course and the far west of the Algarve are Vicente and Brown Lda (Rua das Alegrias, 21, 8600 Lagos, Algarve), who arrange golf holiday packages for individuals or groups from clubs or societies and are property, golf and leisure consultants. Michael Brown was formerly with Eurogolf and he managed Parque de Floresta when it opened before going into business on his own.

A Tasca, overlooking the bay at Sagres tel: (082) 64177 **

This fishermen's restaurant, just below the cliff-top fortress where Prince Henry the Navigator trained his captains before they sailed their caravels out to explore the unknown oceans, looks over Baleeira Bay and serves just about the best fish on the coast. Live lobsters and crabs are kept in sea-water tanks; the decor of nets and creels and other marine objects is simple, service is good and friendly, the food is delicious and very moderately priced. Cooking is not fancy and there is little in the way of sauces and such fripperies, but with fish as fresh as this nothing extra is needed. There is a good list, helpings are generous and as value for money A Tasca is incomparable.

Fontanario, Espiche **

Espiche is on the main EN 125 road between Lagos and Sagres and this restaurant by the village fountain serves an interesting mixture of local and north European food.

There are several steak dishes, excellent grilled prawns, sole, bream and hake cooked to Portuguese recipes as well as swordfish, barbecued pork ribs, calf's liver, and veal in Madeira sauce and some unusually exotic puds. The list is surprisingly long and there is good inexpensive house wine and plenty of choice from Portuguese growers and vintages.

SPAIN

There was a time when the image of Spain was made up of proud matadors swirling their capes across the blood and sand, Don Juans lusting musically after mantilla-swathed señoritas on balconies and the click, flash and skirt froth of flamenco. All this drama and intensity in the spirit of *duende*, the dark Spanish philosophy of blood and death, was a bit hard to live with, despite the sun and the paella and, although a traditionalist by nature, I cannot find much to regret in the fact that *Death in the Afternoon* has been supplanted in many parts of Spain by *Another 18 in the Morning*? nor that my memories of Andalucia and Catalonia are partly of blossom-lined fairways under the sun, smooth treacherous Robert Trent Jones's greens and bunkers full of crushed marble on some very beautiful golf courses.

Time and tourism have wrought many changes in this part of the world, some of them a lot less pleasing to the eye than the green mottling of the brown landscape with golf courses. A couple of decades ago if you had offered a typical Spaniard a 7 iron, he would not have known whether to use it to beat his *burro*, hoe his stony vineyard or try to improvise it into a fishing rod. Today any Iberian of modest educational pretensions would recognise the golf club as an important contribution to his national economy.

A lot has happened to golfing in Spain since 1976 when a nineteen-year-old ex-caddy with a (then) unpronounceable name led the Open Championship at Royal Birkdale for three rounds, tied with Jack Nicklaus for second place and resolutely refused to be a nine-day wonder. Severiano Ballesteros has had a considerable influence on golf in Spain but there was golf before Ballesteros. It is probably true to say however that before his appearance, it was a game most Spaniards regarded as strictly tourist-trap material rather in the category of flamenco mantillas and castanets.

There were a few golf clubs in Spain before the last war, mostly around Madrid and the San Sebastian area (homeland to both Ballesteros and Olazabal), but they were principally for rich Spaniards to say they belonged to. Only a few eccentric foreigners and some well-heeled natives who had caught the bug in Britain and America actually *played*. Today golf in Spain is a major part of the tourist industry.

Nowhere is this social phenomenon more evident than on the Costa del Sol. Ever since the 1960s golf courses have grown like bindweed along this coast between Malaga and Gibraltar as the increasingly wealthy Spanish tourist business discovered that the game provided a potent winter lure for northern and transatlantic visitors.

Today there are around ninety courses in Spain and the Balearic islands and another five in the Canaries. Although the Costa del Sol remains the prime area for holiday golfers with twenty courses, other golfing *costas* include the Costa Brava, north of Barcelona, the Costal del Azahar around Valencia, the Costa Blanca between Alicante and Cartagena and the Balearic islands of Majorca, Ibiza and Menorca.

Costa Brava

The Costa Brava stretches from the French frontier at Porthou to Blanes, 60 kilometres north of Barcelona. It was the first of the Spanish *costas* to surrender to the blandishments of tourism and the universal mediocrity which inevitably follows, but except at certain resorts it has perhaps managed to survive it better than most. The rugged coastline beginning in the foothills of the Pyrenees in the north and quite a number of the rocky headlands and the dramatic small coves and inlets have managed to keep their charm and something of the unspoilt littoral it once was is retained and inland Catalonia remains pretty inviolate.

PALS, 17256 Pals, Girona tel: (34 72) 66 77 40   *6804 yards SSS 74*

RESTAURANTS
La Costa, Playa de Pals, Girona * * *   Hotel Aigua, Blava * * *

Set in a pine forest next to the Playa de Pals beach, this course circles its clubhouse, sometimes following the shoreline, sometimes in and out of corridors of scented umbrella pines. Designed by F W Hawtree in 1966, it quickly established its reputation as a stiff test of golfing ability and it is a regular venue on the Spanish circuit for national and international tournaments.
Straight hitting is essential here and although the opening holes are not too demanding of anything but accuracy, the 7th is a tight and densely wooded dog-leg and the 8th is long and tough. The second nine need both power and precision particularly at the tricky short 15th and the par-5 16th. The course is well-maintained and the rustic clubhouse has good facilities, including a restaurant and a bar.

La Costa, Hotel Golf Playa de Pals, Girona tel: (34 72) 66 77 36 * * *
In the restaurant of this smart hotel, Catalan specialities like *cocido*, a stew combining beef, ham and chicken with spicy *chorizo* sausages; Serrano cured ham, calamares and spiced eels may be on offer but there is also a menu of international specialities, including well-hung and expertly grilled steaks and a variety of chicken and game dishes as well as fish. The list has a wide range of excellent Spanish wines, with a natural emphasis on Riojas from the north of Spain, but not ignoring other regions where good wine is now being produced as the rule rather than the exception.

Hotel Aigua Blava, Playa de Fornells, Begur, Girona
tel: (34 72) 62 21 12 * * *
This fine hotel is set above a rocky creek 4 kilometres east of Begur in a position secluded from the package tour beaches. In its handsomely panelled Catalan-style restaurant game from the Pyrenees, the mountain soup made with onions, cured ham, eggs and garlic; trout from the hill streams; lamb from foothills of the sierras, beef from the great plains of

central Spain and a wide variety of fish and shellfish dishes form the main part of the menu. Cooking and presentation standards are high and there is a well-selected wine list.

MAS NOU, 17250 Platja d'Aro, Girona tel: (34 72) 82 60 84   *6800 yards SSS 72*

RESTAURANT
Guitart Platja d'Aro, Girona   ∗∗∗

This fine course designed by Spanish golf architect Ramón Espinosa in 1987 is in the Sierra de las Gavarras, 1000 feet above sea level and 35 kilometres south-east of Girona, with spectacular panoramic views over the Costa Brava. Although there are pines and cork trees and two man-made lakes which come into play, it is a fairly open course with sculptured bunkers round the greens and some quite punishing rough off the fairways. The air is exhilarating, the views are marvellous and although the course is built on a mountainside, the fairways are mostly flat and there are no stiff hills to climb. There is also a nine-hole, par-3 course.

> *Guitart Platja d'Aro*, Platja d'Aro, Girona tel: (34 72) 81 72 20   ∗∗∗
> This comfortable restaurant in an hotel on the coast has a fairly conventional menu with a few local items like prawns in garlic and fish stew, the inevitable paella and whatever the day's catch provides, but the steaks, chicken dishes, lamb and pork are well cooked and attractively presented with style and flair and the usual boring Spanish puddings have been superseded by an enticing trolley of desserts. Excellent Spanish wine list and an attractive setting with an outdoor bar by the hotel fountain.

Costa del Azahar

For some time now Spain has badly needed another 'costa del golf'. The prime favourite among European golf coasts, the Costa del Sol between Malaga and Gibraltar, is badly overcrowded with golfers from many European countries from November to April. Tees and hotels are often overbooked as more and more people get into the profitable off-season golf holiday business and the situation will almost certainly be exacerbated as Gibraltar once again becomes fully operative as a through-put airport for the south of Spain.

An amiable alternative is the Costa del Alzahar (the Orange-Blossom Coast) which lies in a kind of no-man's Costa between the Costa Brava in the north and the Costa Blanca to the south between Denia and Cartagena.

This costa centres on Valencia, the city where El Cid died in battle against the Moors in 1099, an agreeable and elegant non-touristic city in a region famous for oranges, shoes and other leather goods, and renowned for having more variations on the paella theme than anywhere else. There are six good courses within 60 kilometres, all very different, interesting and agreeable to play.

EL SALER, Parador Luis Vives 46012, El Saler, Valencia
tel: (96) 161 11 88 *7092 yards SSS 75*

RESTAURANTS
Galbis, Valencia ∗∗∗ Civera, Valencia ∗∗∗∗

Just 16 kilometres from Valencia, El Saler is certainly one of the best courses in Spain and probably one of the most under-rated. Venue for the Spanish Open and other important tournaments, it provides a curious but intriguing mixture of links and parkland, flanked by the Mediterranean on one side and a mixed forest of pines and ilexes on the other.
It is a tough test of golf for there is no mercy off the fairways and it is vital to keep straight. If you are not on grass you will almost certainly be playing from scrubland sand and possibly under trees and the sandy off-fairway lies make recovery shots difficult.
Only two of the par 4s in the front nine and only one in the inward half are under 400 yards; all the par 3s but for the 9th are over 200 yards and all the 5s are substantially more than 500 yards. The par 5 3rd at 530 yards is a classic with a long carry over rough ground to the fairway and heavy bunkering around the green. The last of the 5s, the 569-yard 15th, a double dog-leg, begins the highly testing finish where the short 213-yard 17th has an ominously familiar look, bearing a strong resemblance to the 11th on the Old Course at St Andrews.

Galbis, Marva 28, Valencia tel: (96) 325 88 13 ∗∗∗
Valencia and the area around it is known as the thousand rice dishes country. The most famous of these is of course paella Valenciana which is made with chicken, lobster, garlic sausage, peas, prawns, mussels and tomatoes. Real paella is cooked in olive oil and the minimum of stock is added. In the Valencia area where shellfish is an essential ingredient the stock is usually made from mussels but chicken or another kind of stock is sometimes used and in addition to the ingredients already mentioned it can be made with snails, eels, broad beans, artichokes, green beans, and of course garlic, onions, saffron, herbs and pimentos.
At Galbis not far from the Plaza España there are most elegant variations on the paella theme, including some in-house creations and also specialities such as sea bass with the local all i pebre (eels cooked with garlic and pepper). Roast suckling kid with garlic is another regional dish and there are excellent sardines or anchovies, smoked swordfish and charcuterie served as starters as well as fried rice soup and the cold garlicky gazpacho, originally a Moorish recipe. Game dishes are also popular here.
A great improvement has been made in the wines from the Valencia district. In recent years they have been made less heavy and more delicate without losing their flavour and local character; the white and rose wines from Utiel-Requeña and the red Jumilla from farther down the coast are worth drinking and, of course, all the fine Spanish wines from Rioja, Torres in Penedes, Ribiero and the splendid Vega Sicilia are listed.

Civera, Lerida 11, Valencia tel: (96) 347 59 17 ****

This restaurant by the River Turia specialises in seafood. In addition to fresh anchovies; baked tunny fish; bream with almonds and aladroch tortilla, a Spanish omelette made with the fry of anchovies; hake stuffed with eggs and ham and various fish baked in rock salt, there are all kinds of shellfish and various fish stews like zarzuela and risotto made with shellfish and squid. There is a good choice of wines from all over Spain as well as some interesting local bottles.

MEDITERRANEO, Urb, La Coma, Borriol tel: (964) 32 12 27 *6604 yards SSS 72*

RESTAURANT
Brisamar, Castellon **

About 60 kilometres north of Valencia, up in the mountains above Castellon de la Plana, lies Mediterraneo, a delightful even if most inappropriately named course, as it is set in a charming valley, ringed with purple-grey mountains, without so much as a glimpse of the sea.

This glorious isolation is very peaceful and makes an ideal setting for a golf course, as, tranquil and trouble-free, you stroke your way around this Shangri-la like glen among the blue water lakes and the blossoming bushes and trees.

Mediterraneo (which it seems is the new name the publicity boys have dreamed up for this whole costa) is a gentler examination of your golfing skills than El Saler but, winding through almond, mimosa, pines and ilexes with the occasional not very demanding water hazard, it has great charm and is kept in beautiful condition.

In fact I enjoyed it so much that on completing my round there I promptly went out and played another nine holes.

Brisamar, avenida Buenavista 26, Castellon de la Plana tel: (964) 184 **

Overlooking the harbour of Castellon, an important centre for wine and oranges, this unpretentious but attractive restaurant offers all the local specialities, not only variations on the paella theme but dishes of rabbit and game from the mountains and some of the good local wines like Teruel, Cheste and Utiel-Requeña.

ESCORPION, Apartado Correos, 1 Betera tel: (96) 160 12 11 *6939 yards SSS 73*

RESTAURANTS
See El Saler

Just 15 kilometres north-west of Valencia, Escorpion is built around a picturesque 200-year-old farmhouse and the course is cut through groves of oranges and lemons with the fruit glowing against the dark-leaved trees. It is long and tough with lots of demanding water hazards and some awkwardly positioned trees.

The par-5 9th, for example, is 586 yards long and has a 200-year-old tree in the middle of the fairway which turns it into a really difficult double dog-leg. This is the second massive par 5 in the last three holes of the outward half in which the 8th is a par 3 of 247 yards!

The second half opens and closes with 5s and at the 18th you have to carry one arm of the lake with your drive and another with your second shot. This scorpion certainly has a sting in its tail.

Costa Blanca

Alicante and Murcia in the Costa Blanca are the garden areas of Spain, producing dates, carnations and citrus fruits, almonds and all kinds of vegetables in a long tradition dating back to the Moors, who introduced many of the first irrigation systems.

LA MANGA, 30385 Los Belones, Cartagena tel: (968) 56 45 11
North: 6423 yards SSS 72   South: 6822 yards SSS 73

RESTAURANT
Rincón de Pepé, Murcia ***

South beyond Alicante in the province of Murcia is La Manga, two superb golf courses, away from the bustling beaches, but with good water sports available and plenty of other activities nearby. Several Spanish Opens have been played here and for some years it was the place where aspiring pros trying to get on the European Tours qualified for their playing cards.

Both courses are rated par 71 but the South Course is 400 yards longer and offers more tricky problems of length and direction among the 3000 palm trees and fourteen lakes which make up the complex—to say nothing of the *barrancas*, the stony ravines which carry away the storm water from the mountain streams, a hazard not encountered too often elsewhere.

At the 1st on the South Course you drive over one of those ravines to a clutch of bunkers on both sides of the dog-leg to set up a downhill approach to a flat green. At the 390-yard 2nd there is water on both sides with the right-hand lake flirting with the edge of the green. The first par 3 at the 3rd demands a shot across water to a green with a bunker eating into its centre. There are two 3s and two 5s on each half.

Once you get out round the turn, the *barrancas* and the water really begin to close in on you. The 510-yard 9th has water all round the drive area and a ravine in front of the green; at the 10th the *barranca* runs across and all up the right-hand side and there is also water on the left—just to ensure you do not lose concentration. Other *barrancas* at the 11th and 12th make the straight path of virtue even more imperative.

After that it is a comparatively gentle run home, although there is another lake to be flown at the short 17th and a very long par 5 at the 18th with water to the right and a bunker virtually on the green in front.

The North Course is considered easier but it has more *barrancas* which come into play at ten of the holes, wriggling like stone-faced worms across and along fairways. Six of the holes which do not have *barrancas* involve water. The two remaining short holes just have bunkers.

Both La Manga courses are a rewarding experience to play but this is a place for serious golfers. The courses are beautiful and fascinating but tough. There are other things to do—sailing, swimming, water-skiing, wind-surfing and fishing—in and around the lagoon of the Mar Menor to the immediate north and the narrow strip of land which separates it from the Mediterranean but the nearest towns, the ancient naval port of Cartagena and the provincial capital of Murcia are 20 and 50 kilometres away.

El Rincón de Pepé, Apostoles 34, Murcia tel: (968) 21 22 49 ***
This famous taverna is celebrated all over Spain for its rich and varied traditional cuisine. Ham from Jabugo; the cold soup gazpacho made here with ripe tomatoes, garlic, cumin seeds, bread, garlic, olive oil, cucumber and green peppers; pigeon stuffed with artichokes; thick yellow tortillas, omelettes made with eggs, onions and potatoes and flavoured with langoustine tails or ham, asparagus or mushrooms. *Fabada*, the bean stew of Asturias in the far north with pig's trotters and kiln-cured sausages and sweets flavoured with limes, oranges and the juice of pomegranates (which take their name from the Andalucian city of Granada). This is the place to drink the famous strong wines of Murcia (in recent years made mercifully slightly less alcoholic) such as Jumilla, Yecla and Rocote.

Costa del Sol

This south-facing coast stretches from Cabo de Gata, east of Almeria to the Punta Marroqui at Tarifa, west of Gibraltar. For almost half the length it is southern Europe's Costa del Golf, with some twenty courses between the provincial capital, Malaga and Gibraltar. For much of its length it can seem like wall-to-wall building sites along the ill-tended and scruffy beaches served by one of the most dangerous roads in Europe, the N340, along which the Beautiful People and their acolytes tend to drive like lunatics. There is rather too much of everything on the Costa del Sol, including con-crete, pubs, tourists, restaurants, expatriates and the dread creeping fungus of *urbanizacion* has been allowed to spread its stifling algae almost every-where. However, there are places away from the coast where things are still recognisably Spanish but even they are being colonised.

If you want to play golf there is plenty of it about, but you must make sure you have booked a tee-time and that you have a pocket full of pesetas. Some courses on this coast have now become private and are available only to property-owners, members and their guests. Many are constructed in American-resort style and most of them seem to have been built by Robert Trent Jones.

TORREQUEBRADA, Apartado 67, 29630 Benalmadena
tel: (52) 44 27 42 *6411 yards SSS 72*

MIJAS, Apartado 138, Fuengirola tel: (957) 47 68 43
Los Lagos 7040 yards SSS 73   Los Olivos 6448 yards SSS 71

RIO REAL, Apartado 82, Marbella tel: (952) 77 17 00   *6778 yards SSS 72*

RESTAURANTS
La Plaza, Fuengirola *** El Balcon, Coin-Alhaurin **
Valparaiso, Mijas-Fuengirola *** El Corzo, Hotel Los Monteros ****

These four courses are all within a few miles of each other, the two Mijas
courses in the flat plain below the steep bluff on which stands the pretty
whitewashed town from which they take their name; Torrequebrada on the
hills above Benalmadena and Rio Real on the river bank 5 kilometres east
of Marbella.

TORREQUEBRADA

This is one of the few courses on this coast *not* designed by Robert Trent
Jones. It is the work of former Spanish Amateur champion, Pepé Gancedo,
one of the most original minds in golf design today. It is a marvellous,
highly individual course full of menacing invention, not long but one of the
most testing courses in Spain, carved out of the hillside and lined with
palms, pines, yuccas and olive trees and offering not only challenging golf
but fine views of the mountains and the sea.

It begins with a par 5 and a drive over a lake, always an intimidating prospect from the first tee, then a second shot which must avoid a group of
olive trees and a pitch into a right-to-left sloping green. There is more
water at the next hole and at the 3rd it really makes its mark.

You must drive over the corner of a large lake to the bend of the dog-leg
and then cross it again with your shot to the rolling green. Then it is downhill at the 4th and uphill to the dangerously-bunkered 5th green. The 6th
continues the climb and needs two long strong uphill shots even to catch
a glimpse of the two-tier green tucked round a corner on the left.

From the 7th tee, with its marvellous high view over the course and coast,
you have a long carry to the fairway and a difficult shot to a two-level green
sloping in front and flat at the back. It takes seven holes to get to a par 3
and when you do it, is only just a shade over 100 yards. But the narrow
putting surface is sternly defended by deep bunkers and you must put your
ball on the same level as the flag on the three-step green to make sure of
par.

The par-4 9th seems almost a gift with its wide and open fairway but it is
quite a long carry from the tee to get there and the big green slopes
towards you and is tightly bunkered on the left and terraced. The 538-yard
11th is downhill but the fairway narrows at drive length and your approach
shot has to be well struck to the elevated green. The 400-yard 13th is a 90-
degree dog-leg, starting over water and there is more water at the back of
the short 14th and the 15th is one of those tricky uphill holes where you
have to fade your drive and draw your approach to reach the flag. The short
16th is all the way over a lake and the water threatens the left-hand side

of the long narrow green at the par-5 17th. This a course which demands all the shots in the book and a firm and confident putting stroke to negotiate the contoured greens.

MIJAS

The original Mijas course Los Lagos is typical Trent Jones, long and flat with bunkers in which you could bury a bus, and lakes clustered round many of the large greens. The second course is on a less massive scale with some holes carved through olive groves and a lavish use of sand and water hazards. In the wide bowl between the Sierra de Mijas and the Sierra de Ojen, the stately background of the sheer dusty-blue mountains give it an air of drama which is not altogether borne out by the course design which seems almost overawed by its impressive setting. Technically, however, all the standard golfing problems are here: length accuracy, long and short shots out of sand, no shots at all out of water and very long putts on the huge greens.

You begin with a long par 5 towards the gleaming mountains. The lakes begin to come into play at the 3rd and affect judgement and distance at the next five holes. After a dryshod finish to the first nine, the water returns at the 10th and is an important hazard at the 11th and the 13th. There are two par 5s in the outward half and two more on the homeward leg and this is an enjoyable if not exactly inspiring place to play golf.

RIO REAL

This delightful course, a few kilometres east of Marbella, runs along the banks of the river from which it takes its name, climbing the Mediterranean shore up into the foothills of the Sierra de Ojen. It belongs to the Hotel Los Monteros, one of the most elegant in Spain, 3 kilometres up the road towards Malaga, and guests at the hotel play on the course without charge. The swift-flowing river provides an interesting hazard and comes into play at six holes, most notably perhaps at the 161-yard par-3 3rd and the par 4s at the 5th and the 11th, where you have to play across it. There are no 5s in the first nine holes but two of more than 500 yards in the inward half. One of the long-established courses on the Costa del Sol (it was opened in 1965), Rio Real has a comforting air of tranquillity and maturity and a charming and original clubhouse with a swimming pool.

La Plaza, Plaza de la Constitucion 9, Fuengirola tel: (52) 46 33 59 ∗∗∗
This restaurant, overlooking the main square in Fuengirola in one of the original old houses of the town, has a tapas bar downstairs and a restaurant above where you can dine on the terrace at the back to the gentle splash of an artificial waterfall or within. The menu is not very Spanish (as is often the case on this coast) but the food is good, well prepared and attentively served.

Smoked salmon, smoked swordfish, mussels or *langostinos* in cream sauce, salmon steaks with dill sauce, gratin of lobster, sliced veal tongue with pepper sauce, duck breast with muscatel and apples, fillet of sole with prawns and good desserts like chocolate tart with a raspberry coulis, raisin tart and crêpes with fruit and ice-cream make up the menu. A selection of Spanish wines.

El Balcon, Coin-Alhaurin el Grande crossroads, 9 kilometres from Mijas tel: (52) 49 11 94 ✳✳✳
This white-painted restaurant out in the sticks on the high plain beyond Mijas manages to get away from the smooth international *carte* in both food and atmosphere. Here you can get the excellent white garlic soup, a speciality of the region, served cold and made with Malaga almonds and sultanas as well as chicken stock and garlic, an alternative to the universal gazpacho.
There could also be kid roasted on a spit or casseroled with vegetables; quails plain grilled and stuffed; rabbit roasted and in a rich stew as well as hare, pheasant; fish dishes including eels and squid, and desserts such as the special Ronda apples called *peros* and Andalusian pastries, candied pine nuts and prickly pears.

Valpairaiso, Carretera de Mijas. km 4 tel: (52) 48 59 96 ✳✳✳
This vivacious restaurant halfway between Fuengirola and Mijas offers dancing to live music as well as a suave international menu, including regional specialities, steaks, veal and chicken dishes, shellfish and other sea food, plus such sophisticated in-house dishes as baked avocado with prawns and lobster sauce. Good selection of mainly Spanish wines. Dinner only, closed on Sundays.

El Corzo, Hotel los Monteros, Carretera de Cadiz tel: (52) 77 17 00 ✳✳✳✳
The grill room at the elegant and popular Hotel los Monteros offers a distinguished international menu which ranges from Beluga caviar, pâté de foie gras de Landes and snails bourguignonne to Weiner schnitzel, chicken in whisky, entrecôte Mirabeau and charcoal-grilled T-bone steaks, lobsters, shashlik and monkfish kebab in addition to something called oeufs frites Yorkshire with which I am not familiar. The service is superb and the cooking matches it, as does the wine list, in which there are some concessions to being in Spain. If you do not wish to flirt with the Spanish kitchen, you will not eat better anywhere, but that is exactly where it could be—gastronomes' anywhere.

LAS BRISAS, Apartado 147, Urb, Nueva Andalucia, Marbella
tel: (952) 81 08 75 *6778 yards SSS 73*

LOS NARANJOS, Apartado 64 29660, Nueva Andalucia, Marbella
tel: (952) 81 52 06 *7090 yards SSS 75*

RESTAURANTS
The Yellow Book, Estepona ✳✳✳ La Rana, towards Estepona ✳✳
La Fonda, Marbella ✳✳✳✳

Farther down the coast around Marbella there is a wide choice of courses at Guadalmina, Atalaya Park, El Paraiso, La Duquesa and the new Ballesteros-designed Los Arqueros.

There are an awful lot of holes involving water at Las Brisas, the senior of the Trent Jones's courses on the Nueva Andalucia estate. Lakes, ponds, rivers and streams, often hidden from tee and fairway, exert their baleful influence at twelve of the eighteen holes and I once played there with an American who lost sixteen balls in one round—five of them mine! This is one of the breed of courses on this coast and others which you can come to believe were designed to mock your temerity for indulging in anything as frivolous as a golf holiday. Almost without exception Spanish courses are made to rigorous championship standards, fraught with daunting hazards ranging from duck-filled ponds to ravines, as if the prime purpose in their creation was to hold the Open Championship there once a month. Even from the forward tees many of these courses are truly intimidating and for the ordinary golfer whose vanity, swing and score-card resolutely refuse to support the idea that he is a budding Ballesteros or a future Faldo, they can seem unduly punishing for the higher handicappers who are at least 90 per cent of holiday golfers.

Los Naranjos is even longer than Las Brisas and a formidable challenge to the accurate long hitter. Apart from a few uncharacteristically merciful holes where you dally in and around orange groves, the rest is typical Trent Jones malevolence: fairways running down hills into streams at drive length, landing areas for shots of all kinds, plastered with bunkers like bomb craters. The only problem about playing well here is that when you go for a drink in the evening to the gilded artificial harbour of Puerto Banus down the road, you will be surrounded by the Beautiful People, who are so hitched up to hype that they will not recognise the truth when they hear it.

The Yellow Book, Carretera de Cadiz km 161, Estepona
tel: (952) 80 04 84 ✳✳✳✳
One of the most celebrated restaurants of the Costa del Sol, the literary fancifulness of its title does not extend to the menu which melds the best produce of the region in a skilful and imaginative way. Roast baby lamb, excellent steaks and soufflés, deep-fried mushrooms, cauliflower soup flavoured with tarragon, smoked meats and fresh river, lake and sea fish are typical dishes with elegant and original sweets and a finely selected wine list. Dinner only, closed on Sundays.

La Rana, on N340 between San Pedro de Alcantara and Estepona
Small friendly Scandinavian-run restaurant which offers well-cooked uncomplicated dishes like fish pie, steaks, grilled shellfish, fish pancakes, stuffed cabbage and good salads and sweets. Well-chosen short Spanish wine list.

La Fonda, off market square, Marbella
tel: (952) 77 18 99 ✳✳✳✳
In the heart of old Marbella this old and polished restaurant offers a highly sophisticated international menu, using Spanish produce in classical dishes like entrecôte marchand de vin, lobster with crab sauce and

pernod, turtle soup, stuffed artichoke hearts, venison fillets, spit-roasted lamb, seasonal game and fish like turbot and halibut with traditional French sauces. Good and extensive wine list and courteous and attentive service.

SOTOGRANDE, Paseo del Parque, Sotogrande (Cadiz) tel: (956) 79 20 50
Old Course: 6849 yards SSS 72

VALDERRAMMA, Sotogrande, Cadiz tel: (956) 79 27 75
6918 yards SSS 72

RESTAURANT
Manolo, La Linea **

The Old Course at Sotogrande was Robert Trent Jones's first design in Europe and it remains one of his finest, matured now over thirty years, a lay-out of a kind not seen in Europe before his arrival and if now too often copied, nevertheless representing a benchmark of golf-course architecture. Here the natural landscape has been used and not adapted, bull-dozed and remade. Even the created water hazards look as indigenous as the apple tree in the Garden of Eden. This, like Pevero in Sardinia, shows Trent Jones at his imaginative and majestic best, one of the great golf courses anywhere, patrician, unfussy, challenging and fair to look upon.

You begin with the great brown-purple rock of Gibraltar hunched behind you on the first tee and wind through palms and cork trees, around lakes up towards the Sierra Almenara and back again to the white clubhouse by the beach.

The soft springy fairways give beautiful lies and are gloriously untiring to walk upon, the greens are quicksilver fast but very true, the sand in the eighty-eight bunkers is crushed marble. On the way home you can see the dark bronze peaks of the Rif mountains of Africa across the narrow entrance channel to the Mediterranean.

The 1st introduces you to one of the two very natural-looking lakes on the course, running up the right-hand side of the fairway as it approaches the green. The dog-leg, 527-yard 2nd is cunningly trapped on the inside of the curve and there is more sand in front of the green but the 3rd, also a dog-leg, presents even more precise problems. The green is shaped like a four-leaf clover with a bunker between each leaf. This means that if the pin is anywhere but in the centre of the green, you have to play a second shot of great accuracy if you are not to have a dog-legged putt.

Probably the best hole on the course is the 422-yard 7th. You drive down a narrow valley lined with cork trees and are then faced with a shot which combines power and delicacy in almost equal proportions: for the target is a narrow green sloping from the woods on the left towards two bunkers and a pond on the right. The 14th too is a spectacular hole, which can be shortened by the courageous, prepared to take on a long carry across a big lake to set up the chance of a birdie at this par 5. At the par-5 17th too there is a route across water to the peninsula green, but in each case there is an alternative track to the hole for the less steely-nerved, not a choice often offered on some other Trent Jones courses. There is also an intriguing par-3 course in the corner between the clubhouse and the beach.

Trent Jones's second course at Sotogrande, on the other side of the main road to Gibraltar, was bought by a Spanish millionaire and a group of investors a few years ago to make a kind of Costa del Sol Augusta and it has been much altered (and much criticised) since its original design and is now known as Valderamma.

It looks much more like the Trent Jones courses all over the world which we have come to know (and love or hate) and if you like that sort of thing, you may well share the old maestro's own opinion that it is the finest thing he has ever done. On the other hand you might subscribe to Irish Ryder Cup player David Feherty's view after the 1989 Volvo Masters was played there, that it is 'Walt Disney's last creation'. On golf courses, as Dr Johnson said of lapidary inscription 'no man is upon oath'. At least not that kind of oath

Manolo, Plaza del Sol, Paseo Maritimo, La Atunara-La Linea
This fish restaurant on the ring road which takes you around La Linea towards Gibraltar is opposite the beach on which the fishing boats are pulled up and offers what are probably the best bargains on the Costa del Sol. The fish is the freshest you will find anywhere and it is sold sometimes by the kilo and sometimes by the plate. Sea bream, fans of fried fresh anchovies, prawns, squid, mussels, clams, tuna steaks and swordfish, everything the sea outside the door has on offer today is here. There is a daily set menu, including fish, wine, bread, salad and fruit, which is definitely worth study.

ITALY

I n Italy golf is not a national sport in the sense that the results of tournaments are eagerly scrutinised and newspapers blazon forth the deeds of its heroes. It is what it was always meant to be—a recreation, to be enjoyed by the people who play it for its demands on skill and temperament and the beautiful settings in which it is played.

That said, there are now around one hundred courses in Italy and in recent years a few Italian golfers have begun to make an impression on the European tournament scene. Golf in Italy still tends to be *un poco snob* but there are some very beautiful Italian courses and the popularity of the game is growing and facilities for playing are improving fast.

Most of the courses are in the north within easy reach of the big industrial cities, for it is very much a businessman's sport, but you can play on the Gulf of Taranto, next to the ruins of the seventh century BC Greek city of Metapontum; there is a charming nine-hole course at Aquabona on Elba and a stunning course on the Costa Smeralda in Sardinia.

GARLENDA, via Golf 7, 17030 Garlenda, Savona tel: (0182) 580012
6532 yards SSS 71

RESTAURANTS
La Meridiana **** L'Hermitage **

Garlenda is one of the best-kept secrets of the Italian Riviera. It is not on the coast and foregoes strenuous efforts to promote itself. It lies 15 kilometres north of Alassio and was designed by John Harris; a three-level course with most of the holes situated in the floor of the valley, climbing up to different levels among the vineyards and orchards, chestnut and pines and flowering bushes.

One of its pleasures, in addition to its beautiful tranquil setting, is that it offers several holes presenting a driving challenge, one of golf's most agreeable sensations when well accomplished. From the 3rd tee you are faced with what looks like a formidable drive across the road which runs up into the village of Garlenda and the *torrente*, a rocky dried-up river bed for most of the year, which nevertheless carries a considerable volume of water from the Alpine foothills in the north into the River Arroscia when the snows melt in the spring. The intimidation is more psychological than actual but it is still a matter for deep satisfaction to place your drive securely on the fairway (slightly to the right so that you are in good shape to get on in two) off this early tee.

At the 320-yard 10th, descending from the second level, there is a somewhat similar downhill shot threaded through trees, but a real man-or-mouse test comes when you encounter the *torrente* again at the 13th on the way home. This is a par 3 of 196 yards, all carry across the river to a green set sombrely against a cypress hedge which hides the course from the road. However the real test of nerve comes—as it often does on good courses—at the end. From the elevated tee of the 18th among the pines, you must drive to carry a hedged road leading up to the clubhouse, 50 feet below and 180 yards out. There you need to find a fairway veering right to put yourself theoretically in an unemcumbered position to hit a 7-iron into the well-bunkered green, overlooked by the Campari-sippers on the terrace.

Trees on the right inhibit the straight path, the cypress hedge on the left menaces any suggestion of a hook. It is a splendid and attractive finishing hole, where if you get a par 4, you can amiably forget any traumas you may have picked up on the way round.

For the belt-it-straight-and-long-off-the-tee holes are by no means all there is to Garlenda. The 15th is a thought-provoking hole, where the shot into the green is threatened by a valley on the left. The 9th demands a solid drive out of the vineyards past a venerable converted farmhouse belonging to an Italian motor millionaire. There are arboreal problems at most holes and visual distractions almost everywhere among the densely wooded hills, the apple orchards, the mimosa and the mind-spinning scent of the mountain pines.

Garlenda is a wonderfully peaceful haven away from the clatter and bustle of the Italian Riviera coast down the road. There is accommodation on the course, a few rooms in the clubhouse and villas on the hill behind; secretary Gianfranco Costa will help in making arrangements. The clubhouse serves excellent food; there is a swimming pool, a good pro-shop and practice and teaching available from maestro Zanini and his staff. A fine course and a delightful place to spend a peaceful and invigorating week. The course is closed on Wednesdays.

La Meridiana, via ai Castelli, 17033 Garlenda tel: (0182) 580271 ****
This part of Piemonte is one of the best eating areas in Italy. In and around Asti they make not only the famous Italian sparkling wine Asti Spumante but also Barbera, Grignolino, Muscat, Barolo and Barberesco. Southwards to the coast, this is a countryside unashamedly devoted to food. Alba is the chief truffle town and at the village of Roddi there is a 'university' for the dogs which hunt out the aromatic white Italian truffles. Half Europe's confectioners are supplied with hazelnuts from Langa, delicious *torrone* (nougat) is made at Canelli, there are chestnuts, walnuts, peaches, mushrooms, game, trout and several local cookery schools to tell you what to do with them. La Meridiana in the elegant restaurant of its small luxurious hotel makes the most of all these ingredients in a very upmarket way.

Sometimes in striving to be international it loses the contact with local flair and tradition and the richness of the earth which produces it. This can make for over-finesse and a leaning towards blandness. However, the food is meticulously prepared and beautifully cooked and the service and attention of a very high order.

Hermitage, Villanova **
This small hotel and restaurant belongs to Nino Barbera who used to be responsible for the food and wine side of Garlenda. It provides a dinner

menu which would be the envy of most Italian restaurants in London—delicious home-made pasta of all kinds; salads with day-fresh vegetables with a dressing made with his own olive oil (everyone round here has olive groves and vineyards), excellent veal and beef, fish and pork and real chickens, superb salami with figs, local cheeses and fruit. The list has some of the best wines in Italy, ranging from the brisk, very local white Pigato, to the great red wines from Piemonte and the Valtellina, Barbera, Barberesco, Spanna, Grumello and the best Valpolicella I have ever tasted.

RAPALLO, via Mameli 377, 16035 Rapallo tel: (0185) 26177
6227 yards SSS 70

RESTAURANT
Elite **

Rapallo, on the other side of Genoa along the Ligurian coast, was a favourite spot of the master of the beady-eyed epigram, Sir Max Beerbohm. It is an endearing town, which is not so much a resort as somewhere which provides weekend homes for the *Milanesi*, as all city-dwelling northern Italians are called, whether they come from Milan or not.

You see the golf course as soon as you come off the autostrada from Genoa, laid out enticingly along the banks of the River Boate, which provides the town with one of its most celebrated historical monuments: a bridge that Hannibal crossed after descending from the Alps with his elephants.

The river has been diverted since 218 BC and you will not encounter Hannibal's bridge on your round but you see plenty of the river because it and its tributaries are crossed no less than seven times. Rapallo has the amiable style of being longer on the first nine than the second with two par 5s on the outward half (one of 570 yards) and none on the way home.

The 5th hole is a tough par 4, just on the edge of being a 5, with water to cross with the drive and continuing all along the left, and a well-defended green. The 10th also has water threatening at the angle of the dog-leg and the final hole is a par 3 across the river and up to the clubhouse. As well as water there are lots of tall trees. Although not long, Rapallo is a course on which you must be straight to score well. It is very easy on the eye and kept in excellent condition.

Elite, via Milite Ignoto 19 tel: (0185) 50551 **
The great specialities of the Ligurian coast are burrida, the Genoan answer to bouillabaisse, a fish stew with wild mushrooms but served as a rule without shellfish; any kind of pasta with pesto, the delicious basil sauce which is one of the hallmarks of Ligurian cooking; cappon magro; tuna; lobster; sea bass; prawns; lettuce and herbs with anchovies; artichokes; celery; olives; boiled eggs and fennel-flavoured mayonnaise; stuffed lettuce in broth. These are available in this smart restaurant, but also more rarified items like sea bass with grapes and artichokes; marinated wild boar in sour-sweet sauce; and good veal and beef dishes.

There is a good list of local and other Italian wines with particularly excellent dry Cinque Terre from the cliff-top vineyards above La Spezia for the sea food dishes. Closed Thursday and all of November.

FIRENZE UGOLINO, via Chiantigiana 3, 50015, Grassina
tel: (055) 205 1009   *6327 yards SSS 70*

RESTAURANTS
Cantinetta Antinori, Florence ✻✻   Cammillo, Florence ✻✻✻✻

This splendid rolling course, laid out in the Chianti hills 8 kilometres to the south of Florence, manages to be a testing place of golf skills while retaining all the enchantment of the Tuscan countryside. Tall cypresses, olives, fruit trees, cork oaks and pines line the fairways and it is rather like playing golf through the background to a Renaissance painting.
There are some quite steep hills to be climbed in the first nine. The 5th, a long par 4 through an olive grove, is a test of straight hitting and accurate approach play and the previous hole is one of those par 3s where you hang a shot in the air from a high tee and have difficulty in visualising the 220 yards you have to carry.
After the 11th, a tough up and down par 4, you are on more level territory. However, the 14th at 572 yards and the 17th at 519 yards provide an exacting finish, interspersed with some par 4s demanding concentration and careful shotmaking, of which only the 18th is substantially under 400 yards. The club has a bar and restaurant, a swimming pool and tennis courts and is open all the year round.

Cantinetta Antinori, Palazzo Antinori, Piazza degli Antinori 3, 50123 Florence tel: (055) 292234 ✻✻
There are dozens of good restaurants in Florence but this elegant wood-panelled wine bar in the Palace of the Antinori, one of the most famous winemaking families in the world dating back to the fourteenth century, is particularly attractive, both for the elegant quality of its straight-forward menu and, naturally, for its wine list. The antipasti are superb and simple—marvellous cured ham with figs, delicately flavoured salami; mortadella and bresaola; artichokes dressed with green Tuscan oil; classical Florentine game dishes in season; veal and papardelle; fruit and intriguing local cheeses.
On the list all the wines are from Antinori vineyards; from the sparkling Marchese Antinori Nature, a dry *méthode champenoise* made from pinot noir and chardonnay grapes, a fine alternative to champagne, through the fruity fresh pale-gold Galestro from central Tuscany to the really splendid reds like Tignanello, made from the Chianti sangiovese grapes blended with cabernet; Sassicaia from the Tuscan coast near Bolgheri south of Livorno made with cabernet sauvignon and Solaia, another nobly aged cabernet from the heart of Chianti country. Very much a businessman's restaurant in the centre of the city but well worth finding in the imposing internal courtyard of the Palazzo Antinori.

Cammillo borgo Sant' Jacopo 57, Florence tel: (055) 212427 ****
On the south side of the River Arno, just a short walk from the Ponte
Vecchio, this traditional Florentine taverna combines the great virtues
of the Italian style of freshness and flavour in typical Tuscan dishes. On
the menu are tripe cooked with fresh sieved tomatoes, marjoram and
Parmesan; chicken breasts in butter with rosemary; veal scallopine in
wine sauce with herbs; the famous Florentine beefsteak, a T-bone
hanging over the edge of its large oval plate, grilled on charcoal to pink
tenderness and dressed simply with butter and herbs. There are also
seafood pasta and risotto; red mullet with tomatoes and olive oil, cac-
ciucco, the great Livornese fish stew; partridge and pheasant in season;
rabbit and hare; and the sheep's milk cheeses from the Apennines. The
list has good dry white wines like Arbia, Bianco Vergine dei Colli Aretini
and Procanico from Elba and a splendid range of Chiantis and the Vino
Nobile di Montepulciano.

BOLOGNA, via Sabatini 69, Monte San Pietro tel: (051) 969100
6674 yards SSS 72

RESTAURANTS
Battibecco, Bologna **** Papagallo, Bologna ****

Bologna's golf course was designed by Henry Cotton in 1959 and is a
delightful, well-matured and well-tended parkland lay-out set in the
foothills of the Apennines, 17 kilometres from the centre of the oldest
university town in Europe. It is hilly in a gentle undemanding kind of way
and through the poplars, oak trees, cypresses and pines which border the
fairways, there are fine views over the Appenines and the hill vineyards on
the lower slopes.
Despite this gentle classical ambience, there is plenty of interest in the
golfing problems set. There are four par 5s, two in each nine but none is
under 500 yards and the 5th is almost 600 and, to add agony to injury, has
quite a severe right-hand dog-leg. This is compensated for by a number of
short par 4s at the finish of the first nine (although some of them are across
valleys) and three 3s in the same half. However, the inward nine is almost
600 yards longer than the first and has only two 3s. Henry Cotton did not
believe that you should think this is an easy game. The pleasant clubhouse
has a restaurant and bar, tennis courts and a swimming pool. Open all the
year round.

Battibecco, via Battibecco 4, Bologna tel: (051) 275845 ****
Bologna as well as having the oldest university is also the finest eating
town in Italy and it is almost impossible to eat badly anywhere, if you
except the slab-concrete chain hotels out near the exhibition complex.
But in the beautifully preserved and tranquilly arcaded ancient town in
the centre, there are fine restaurants galore. Off the Piazza Galileo,
round the corner from the immense Piazzo Maggiore, you will find the
Trattoria Battibecco.

Nico and Paolo epitomise the continuing fascination of the Bolognese with food and the richness which Emilia Romagna provides. But the food here is not traditional Bolognese—heavy sauces, zampone and cotechino sausage, lots of cream, butter and cheese are eschewed. Something more subtle but nevertheless distinctly indigenous is offered instead. Not *nouvelle cuisine* (the Bolognesi are too fond of their food for that) but dishes that are typical without being heavy. Yellow penne with wild mushrooms and herbs, risotto with celery, gnocchi made with semolina and spinach in a light gorgonzola and walnut sauce, squid salad to whet the appetite. Main courses might be monkfish tails grilled with tomato; breast of duck cooked with balsamic vinegar; rabbit with herbs; lamb with aubergines or turbot with an aromatic tomato and basil sauce. The ingredients are natural and fresh and put together in a simple and masterful way with the highest level of culinary skill.

The list is extensive and covers the country but particularly interesting are the fine cabernet sauvignons from the Zola Predosa, out near the golf course, and crisp, full-bodied chardonnays from Umbria. Open Monday to Friday. Closed 1–25 August, 24–31 December and public holidays.

Pappagallo, piazza della Mercanzia 3, Bologna tel: (051) 232807 ＊＊＊＊
This elegant mirrored restaurant, hung with photographs of film stars, opera singers and musicians who have eaten here, has long been one of the ornaments of Bologna. As the gastronomic capital of Italy in the heart of food-rich Emilia-Romagna: home of countless variations on the theme of pasta, as well as the supreme kinds of sausage, wild mushrooms from the autumn-tinted forests, ham from Parma, cheese from Reggiano, game from the Apennine hills, fish from the Adriatic, duck and geese from the marshes of the Po valley and wine from the vineyards of the plain. Bolognese restaurants have an enviable larder to plunder. The manner in which they avoid over-elaboration is masterly. Among the Pappagallo's antipasti are chicken galantine; rabbit terrine with olive oil and herbs; breast of duck with green beans and lemon; slices of raw sturgeon with fresh tomato and black olive sauce. The pasta dishes include lasagne and tagliatelle with traditional Bolognese sauce but also fusilli with turnip tips and tomato; small ravioli stuffed with aubergines with courgette sauce; tagliatelle with turbot and sweet peppers; rigatoni with shrimps and wild mushrooms and spaghetti with clams and mullet roe. Main dishes include fillet of veal in balsamic vinegar with courgettes; sea bass baked in foil with rosemary-scented vegetables; rabbit with wild mushrooms and potatoes with thyme; veal kidney with armagnac and tarragon; swordfish with fresh tomato and mint. For dessert there can be ricotta pastry with strawberry and peach sauce, various sorbets and ice creams; cherry pie with rum and custard cream or lemon and raisin foam with mint sauce. And on the menu page opposite the sweets, there is a list of dessert wines—a very commendable idea.

The list has a long selection ranging from Sicily to the Alto Adige including some fine wines from Emilia Romagna, notably the Sauvignon di Monte San Pietro made by Vallania in the Zola Predosa and some excellent Sangiovese di Romagagna from Braschi. Closed on Mondays.

VENICE, via del Forte, 30011 Alberoni, Lido di Venezia tel: (041) 731015
6700 yards SSS 72

RESTAURANTS
Antico Martini, Venice * * * * Taverna La Fenice, Venice * * *

Golf is not an activity usually associated with Venice but there has been a course here at the south end of the Lido island, which protects the Pearl of the Adriatic from the sea, since 1928. It is rather like a Scottish links with trees because the Adriatic and the Malamocco Channel, the southern entrance to the Venetian lagoon, lap round it.

You start from a high tee next to an ancient Venetian fort with a drive across a moat to a fairly straightforward par 4. A tricky par 3 to a well-bunkered green follows and on the next short par 4 you have to avoid a bunker on the left to set up your shot into the closely-bunkered green with another bit of the moat at the back.

At the 4th things get abruptly tougher with a 410-yard par 4 and the 5th, heading along the Adriatic, is a tough par 3 of 220 yards with not much in front of the green except bunkers. The 6th is a 494-yard 5 well trapped on the right and with quite a large bunker in front of the green; the 7th is almost as long but just manages to be a par 4, with a difficult shot to an angled fairway from the tee and a well-protected green.

The 8th is a monster, almost 600 yards long, dog-legged right with water threatening on the left and two strategically placed bunkers on the run in to the green. At the 9th you have another shot across the moat from out of the trees.

The sea pines, ilexes, olives and poplars crowd in a bit more on the second nine and water impinges on the wayward shot at the 10th, and the two par 5s, the 548-yard 11th and the 546-yard 13th. On the 11th the water is on your left from the tee with an extra little lake on the right to menace the second shot. On the 13th it is on the same side almost all the way down from drive length to the green.

The 14th is a tough dog-legged par 4 and then you cruise in on four par 4s, all under 400 yards, although demandingly bunkered, and all playing in different directions, to cross the moat once more to the final green.

The Alberoni course is an agreeable test of accurate golf, the Scottish links feel about it extending to the sandy lies you find if you stray from the fairways. The Hotel Cipriani on the Giudecca in Venice runs golf holidays and provides you with a boat to take you from the hotel to the course and back. Quite apart from the uniqueness of the idea of playing golf in Venice, this is a course worth anyone's attention and it has been the venue for the Italian Open.

Antico Martini, campo San Fantin tel: (041) 5224121 ✶✶✶✶
This elegant and venerable Venetian restaurant in the square outside
Venice's eighteenth-century opera house, Teatro La Fenice, has been
one of Italy's great restaurants for decades. Traditional Venetian food is
often a mixture of the local and the exotic, harking back to the great
days of the past when Venice controlled the spice trade.
Bottarga, Venetian caviar, dried and compressed tuna or grey mullet
eggs, seasoned with lemon juice, oil and pepper and served on grilled
polenta; brodetto, fish soup with fennel and saffron; fried squid stuffed
with garlic, parsley, chopped tentacles, ham and breadcrumbs
moistened with wine and egg yolks; fried soft-shell crabs; sardines split
and marinated in lemon juice, onion and oil; eel soup; liver alla
veneziana; *risi e bisi*, rice with mange-tout peas and ham; turkey in pever-
ada, a sauce made with livers, parsley, rosemary, garlic and thinned with
pomegranate juice, are ancient recipes of the water-city as are all the
variety of sauces with anchovies, artichokes with fennel garnished with
onions, garlic and salami; leaves of sage dipped in batter and fried and
borracciate egg whites whisked with almonds, sugar, pine and pistachio
nuts and flavoured with lemon and cinnamon. At Antico Martini the
menu offers a changing selection of such dishes, together with modern
cuisine like filo parcels of salmon; boar ham; chicken stuffed with wild
mushrooms and pine nuts; jugged hare as well as veal, beef and fish. To
all kinds of cooking the same delicacy and finesse is given. The list of
wines, particularly from Friuli, the Veneto, Lombardy and Piemonte, is
outstanding. Closed on Tuesday and Wednesday from March to November for lunch.

Taverna la Fenice, San Marco 1938 tel: (041) 5223856 ✶✶✶
Just across the piazza and around the corner of the opera house is this
fashionable restaurant named after the theatre which housed the
premières of *Rigoletto*, *La Traviata* and many other operas which are still
warbling with us and during the season it is patronised by many of the
Fenice stars. What is fresh is on display; the odours of sizzling scampi
and squid from the grill, the scent of saffron and wild mushrooms,
rosemary and thyme perfume the air as you give yourself to the serious
matter of drinking your aperitif and examining what the menu has to
offer today.
Excellent pasta with subtle and traditional sauces, aubergines stuffed
with veal, mushrooms, Parmesan and garlic; roast loin of pork with
chestnuts; guinea-fowl with juniper berries, brandy, grapes and madeira;
risotto alla finanziera with chicken livers, lemon, mushrooms and
marsala; clams with tomatoes, onions and polenta; large shrimps grilled
with oil and lemon; scampi risotto with celery and herbs, roast lamb
with anchovy sauce and wild duck with marsala and oranges are among
the dishes which could be there.
Oranges reappear in one of the most famous of the Taverna Fenice's
specialities, along with the cane sugar, which Venetian traders brought
from the East to Europe. Aranci Caramellizzati are oranges briefly

cooked in their own kirsch-flavoured syrup, decorated with their caramelised peel and served cold.

The list favours the Veneto but there are wines from all over Italy and even some from France. The Fenice, theatre and restaurants are two of the many glories of this fabulous city.

PEVERO, 07020 Porto Cervo, Sardinia tel: (0789) 96210
6765 yards SSS 72

RESTAURANTS
Pevero **** Rosemary's ***

Robert Trent Jones, the renowned American golf architect, has been accused of many things in the design of his many courses world wide, from 'hating golfers' to inventing artificial landscapes. At Pevero on the Costa Smeralda on the north-east coast of Sardinia, he has created his masterpiece, the most beautiful golf course in the world.

This is, of course, a big claim but it is based on my own experience of playing on more than 500 courses in every continent and on not a little checking for other claims among my colleagues. Only one, a very much travelled golf writer, Michael Gedge, has ever demurred; entering a plea in favour of a course on a Pacific island where I have never played. But, on the last occasion we played together at Pevero, we stood on the 10th tee looking down over the green and across the course to the 15th century straggle of the Cala di Volpe Hotel along the bay and the islands and mountains beyond and he said 'I give in—this is the most spectacularly beautiful course in the world.'

The 1st hole runs down towards the exquisite gold and turquoise arc of the bay of Pevero, its shining waters decorated with elegant yachts and the swift, brightly coloured slash of windsurfers. The 2nd and 3rd climb towards the amazing Sardinian mountains, jagged, seemingly restless peaks, whose talons scrabble at the sky. The 4th, from on high, swoops to a dramatic valley towards the sea; the 5th is a short hole cloistered by trees with the bay gleaming beyond; there is a lake at the 6th and 7th and a fig tree which provides a mid-morning snack at the 8th and the most succulent wild mushrooms grow in the rough alongside the 9th fairway.

From the 10th you get one of the most beautiful golf views in the world, down over the falling fairway to the dramatic Cala di Volpe Hotel. Jacques Couelle, the French architect who designed Cala di Volpe, used to love people asking him what it was before it became an hotel. It looks like a fifteenth-century Italian castle, one of those rambling unplanned buildings of truncated towers and spreading low-eaved roofs, desultorily pink and amber washed and pantiled, fitting the landscape as naturally as an oleander bush.

Set against the Bay of Foxes glinting in myriad blues and greens in the sun, from outside and within it offers an ever-changing visual excitement and satisfaction and is the most perfect place to stay for lots of money I have ever been. It was built in 1964.

Beyond are the purple and blue islands and the spoon-shaped Capo Figari and the silver granite cliffs of the massive island of Tavolara which tower 1500 feet above the sparkling sea and strike the light back at you.

Then you turn towards the holes where the rugged mountain crests line the green fairways like torn stone lace, and the tees and greens, where your eye is drawn irresistibly to the sweep of a sapphire bay edged with a pale-gold arc of sand, a cluster of cobalt islands, a dark-shadowed headland. All this enveloped in the perfume of Sardinia, the *macchia*, that heady tangle of rosemary, cistus, wild thyme and myrtle, whose scent floats on the warm breeze from the wild and rocky hills.

This is what you wake to in the morning, just before the first plunge into the blue pool with the little bright birds, zooming chattering from the olive trees and the hibiscus and bougainvilles as you hit the water, the geraniums spilling pink red and white foam from the terracotta pots on the walls.

In addition to the breathtaking views from every tee and green, this course, set between its two sea bays, poses a very real golfing challenge. At the 562-yard 3rd your drive should carry the spur of herb-scented shrubland which thrusts into the fairway, to set up your second shot towards the flag on the brow of a green hill outlined against dusty mauve crags. At the par-4 4th you must detach yourself from the view from the high tee to steer your drive far enough right to be able to come in from a good angle to the shelf of green cut from the hillside. At the 6th and 7th and the 16th and 17th there is water to cross and the 16th is probably the most difficult hole on the course.

You drive downhill through a narrow valley, rockstrewn on either side, with a lake in front of the green and another, almost invisible from the tee on the hill-top, into which a pulled shot will vanish with a splash. At only 316 yards, club choice is crucial and the tee-shot has to be struck with great accuracy to come up just short of the water and give you a comfortable chip to the angled green.

Pevero has a sumptuous clubhouse, with an excellent pro-shop and bar, a luxurious swimming pool on the terrace commanding wonderful views of the course and one of the very few places in the world where I would recommend you eat in the clubhouse restaurant. There are golf carts and trolleys for hire, tuition available and golf holidays are arranged from Britain by Costa Smeralda Holidays Ltd, 140 Walton Street, London SW3 2JJ; tel: (071) 493 8303.

Pevero Golf Club, 07020 Porto Cervo, Costa Smeralda
tel: (0789) 96210 ****
Eating out in Sardinia gives you the flavour of the island in a very real way. Although this is a restaurant of *gran classe*, it offers some Sardinian specialities and the excellent local wine, once labelled *giustamente alcoolico* (although that accurate definition is now considered too unsophisticated). The food tends to have a wild and mountainous flavour: smoked wild-boar ham, suckling lamb, boar and kid roasted on a spit with myrtle and other hillside herbs. There is good seafood, including the Sardinian version of *bottarga*, caviar-like mullet roe and a curious kind of fish pâté made from minced octopus.

There are different kinds of pasta too, such as malloredus, bullet-shaped dumplings rather like gnocchi, and a kind of African cous-cous called *sa fregula*. Vegetables are very good in Sardinia, particularly artichokes, and there are excellent cheeses and special forms of bread, including the famous paper-thin *carta da musica*.

In elegant candle-lit luxury at Pevero the menu offers smoked salmon and Beluga caviar among the starters, along with foie gras from Strasbourg and cured goat ham from the Valtellina.

There is pasta in rock-lobster sauce, seafood risotto with truffles and fettucine flavoured with salmon and garlic; you can have broiled rock-lobster from Tavolara or sea bass poached with Vernaccia for the fish course and as a main course goose liver and truffles, veal kidneys in gorgonzola sauce, loin of lamb or *carpaccio*, the Italian version of steak tartare.

The list is comprehensive and includes many wines from outside Sardinia, but the local bottles are well worth trying—Vernaccia di Oristano is an excellent aperitif rather like a non-fortified fino sherry and the well-aged Cannonau reds can be magnificent.

Rosemary's, Pitrizza, Porto Cervo tel: (0789) 91185 ***
This restaurant above the Hotel Pitrizza and on the road to Baja Sardinia from Porto Cervo was opened in the 1960s, when the Costa Smeralda was developed, by a group of English women which included the Duchess of York's mother. It is still English owned and is very much a centre for Costa Smeralda life, popular with both the British and the Italians. It has a very agreeable and friendly atmosphere, the food is good—seafood, pasta, meat and game in traditional cuisine, the wine is excellent and prices are reasonable.

SCANDINAVIA

Anyone who has ever devoted any thought to what Swedes do in summer when they are not pursuing lissom ladies through the birch trees in a promise of wistful Nordic orgy as suggested by their film industry, have probably got the answer wrong. What more and more Swedes of both sexes do in the long days of their relatively short summer is—play golf.

This was powerfully underlined in 1991 when the Swedes won both of the major international team trophies, the Dunhill Cup at St Andrews and the World Cup in Rome. There are more golf courses per head of population in Sweden than in any country in Europe outside Britain, despite the fact that in a country which stretches for 1000 miles from inside the Arctic Circle to the more hospitable waters of the Oresund Strait in the Southern Baltic, it is not possible to play all the year round. That is why if you go to the Costa del Sol or the Algarve in winter you will find hotels which give *smorgasbord* parties and why the oaths rising from bunkers and woodland sound more like ancient Viking curses than the mutterings of matadors.

When you can play in Sweden—April to October in most places—the golf is excellent and the welcome very heartening. Way down south at Falsterbo is the most interesting and challenging seaside course in Scandinavia: a tough 6400-yards links, on a promontory looking across the Oresund to Denmark.

In Denmark the pace is gentler. This is sweet dairyland country; even the roadside deer warnings come down the scale. In Sweden and Norway they depict elks, in Denmark bambi-like fallow deer. There are several good golf courses however: Rungsted, near Copenhagen, Ebeltoft and Silkeborg, in Jutland, and St Knuds, at Nyborg in Funen.

There are a dozen courses in Norway where just about the daftest golf in Europe is played in the Midnight Cup held on the nine-hole course in Trondheim in the midnight sun on Midsummer's Night. There are good eighteen-hole courses at Bogstad outside Oslo and at Stavanger on the west coast and a nine-hole course at Bergen, where you start from a tee the size of a billiard table hung precipitously about a hundred feet above a lake, across which you are expected to urge the ball towards a green shrouded in cloud somewhere below.

Between the 6th green and the 7th tee you could be pardoned for thinking that you had lost the course altogether, halfway through hauling your clubs for the best part of a mile over a mountain. Bergen was clearly designed by the Norwegian Ski Association to discourage golf but it serves well enough as a kind of toughening-up process before braving the maddening glare of the midnight sun at Trondheim. Golf in Scandinavia is different.

Sweden

LYCKORNA, PO Box 66 45900 Ljungskile tel: (0522) 20176
6392 yards SSS 72

RESTAURANTS
Lyckorna Havbad *** Mortens Krog, Uddevalla ***

On Sweden's beautiful west coast near Ljungskile, 20 kilometres south of Uddevalla, this fjordside course cuts through a forest of beech, pine and oak. Both nines have the classic lay-out of two 5s and two 3s. All the 5s are over the 500-yard mark and the 16th is almost 600 yards from the back tees. At the 546-yard 8th you have to fly a ravine with water in it and you have to cross it again at the par-4 10th.
Several holes run down to the fjord and there are enchanting views over the wooded islets and the bright-sailed yachts. A fine testing golf course in a quiet, relaxing, old-fashioned, little resort town with its nineteenth-century wooden-gabled Nordic houses and segregated nudist bathing beaches.

Lyckorna Havbad, Lyckorna ***
This bright and agreeable restaurant near the bathing beaches in the village serves good seafood lunches, including the large and succulent prawns found on this coast and the generous and mouthwatering west-coast sea salad. There are also steaks, other salads, pastries, fruit and coffee. Swedish cooking is strong on delicious pastry, puddings and bread like saffron bread, brandy ring twists, chocolate dream cake, gingersnaps and marzipan apples, as well as the endless varieties of different flavours and textures in pickled herring and fresh fish served in all its simple untrammelled magnificence. Swedish beer is excellent, crisp, nutty and refreshing but, owing to licensing restrictions, not all restaurants have wine lists.

Mortens Krog, Kungsgatan, 17 451 30 Uddevalla tel: (0522) 11003 ***
Uddevalla is one of Sweden's most important ports and this inn, while serving all the celebrated west-coast delicacies also caters for an international clientele. The crayfish and the elk casserole are particularly recommended.

LYSEGARDENS, Box 82 44221 Kungälv tel: (0303) 23426
6270 yards SSS 71

RESTAURANTS
Langedrag, Gothenburg *** Societshuset, Marstrand ***

This spectacular very man-made course near Kungälv, 19 kilometres outside Gothenburg, is set in a valley with views across the course to a wooded ridge from which tumbles a waterfall. It begins with a par 3 and the 4th is also a short hole with water threatening on the right; there are two long holes of over 500 yards at the 5th and the 9th. At the 10th the main feature of the course, a huge artificial lake filled with trout, first comes into play and remains there for all the holes on the back nine, except the 14th and 15th. The most vaunted hole is the 13th, where, after the dog-leg 230 yards out, the second shot is threatened by a deep ravine on the right and the eye enlivened (or distracted) by a waterfall beside the green.

The 601-yard 16th takes you back to the lake; at the par-3 17th you must fly your tee-shot over it all the way to the green but the short par-4 18th offers a more merciful conclusion with only a stream to cross with the drive and a simple shot on to a generous green.

Langedrag, Langedrag outside Gothenburg tel: (031) 272070 ***
Gothenburg, Sweden's second city and its largest port, is where the Swedish golf story really began. The game formally started in Sweden in the same year as in the United States, 1888, when a private course of just six holes was laid out on the Ryfors estate, near Jönköping at the foot of Lake Vattern, right in the centre of Sweden. In 1891 in Gothenburg, where Scottish influence was strong, an English vicar, the Reverend A V Despard founded a club which failed to survive his departure after missionary work lasting six years. However the virus had been planted and the Gothenburg club was formed in 1902 and a Swedish Golf Union in 1904.

Overlooking the route which all these pioneers took into Sweden is the famous summer fish restaurant at Langedrag, on the Göta estuary 10 kilometres outside Gothenburg with superb views over the fjord and the entrance to the harbour.

Here, there is the best and most varied assortment of pickled herring I have ever eaten—with sour cream, mild mustard sauce, red smoked, with dill and bayleaves, sliced with red pepper and in the famous *gafelbiter* marinade to name but a few. Wonderful fresh fish like turbot, hake, codling, halibut, haddock and mackerel, crustaceans like crab, lobster, prawns and molluscs, and freshwater fish such as salmon, sea trout and lake and river trout adorn the menu. Desserts include the Scandinavian speciality, cloudberries. The Swedes, who are mad about statistics, calculate that there are 88.32 cloudberries per inhabitant, so you can eat your fill. Good list, mostly French and mostly white, but there are some well-chosen reds from France and Italy.

Societshuset, Langgggatan, 1 44 30 Marstrand tel: (0303) 60600 ***
This restaurant at the beach resort and yachting centre of Marstrand is open only during the summer but it is much more than just a holiday restaurant. In addition to the usual Swedish seafood dishes, *smorgasbord*, there are smoked meats and exotic salads together with substantial hot dishes and grills.

TYLÖSAND, 30273 Halmstad tel: (035) 30077
6838 yards SSS 74   6294 yards SSS 72

RESTAURANTS
Restaurang Klubbhuset, Tylösand ** Stefan Holmstrom, Halmstad ***

This important and imposing golf complex at the beach resort of Tylösand, 9 kilometres from Halmstad, has two impressive courses: one, cut through a close-knit pine forest with overtones of Wentworth in its tightness, calls for accuracy as well as considerable length; the second has more space but also more bunkers round its American style greens.

On neither is there much room to spare for, when the forests are not pressing in upon you and the hole opens out a little, there is always some watery hazard or a maliciously sited bunker or just a few trees detached from the thousands crowding around you but plumb in the wrong place.

Down in this part of south-west Sweden the coastline is not as rugged as farther north and the golf problems are less affected by the terrain than by man's fiendish ingenuity.

There are two kinds of golf architecture—strategic and penal. Penal design in essence means that you are confined to a narrow or perilous route to the green from which you depart at your penal peril. Strategic means that alternative routes are offered and you can choose the one that suits your game best. The great Bobby Jones's definition of a good course was that it should offer 'problems a man may attempt according to his ability. It will never become hopeless for the duffer nor fail to concern and interest the expert.' Tylösand offers lots of concern and interest to the expert but I am not sure that it falls into the category of the more generous half of Mr Jones's definition. However, in a masochistic sort of way, it is fun to play—if you have a sense of humour and take plenty of golf balls.

Restaurang Klubbhuset, Tylösand, 30273 Halmstad tel: (035) 30077 **
The golf explosion in Sweden over the past thirty years has changed the original image of the game.

The rather aristocratic, up-market ambience in which the game is played in Germany, Austria, France and Italy has largely disappeared from Swedish golf. Kids have taken it up; about 30 per cent of Sweden's active golfers are women and champions in other sports popular in Sweden—skiing, skating, ice-hockey and tennis—have taken to the links with avidity. They say that when Sven Tumba, Sweden's top ice-hockey star a generation back, began to play golf he doubled the country's golf population overnight.

This means that with a five-month season (the most you can expect in many places) there is a lack of country club elegance at the 19th hole, which tends to be some functional shack rather than a home from home. To this, Tylösand is an exception. It has an elegant clubhouse with all the usual amenities, including accommodation for visitors and a good restaurant in which I had one of the best clubhouse lunches in many years. To the typical Swedish menu of *smorgasbord* are added good grilled and baked fish, hamburgers and steaks, chicken in sour-cream sauce, baked ham and that marvellous mix of potatoes, anchovies, onions, butter and cream, Jansson' Temptation, excellent beer and a reasonable choice of wines.

Restaurang Stefan Holmström, Strandgatan, 6 302 46, Halmstad tel: (035) 111711 ***
In the middle of Halmstad, on the bank of the River Nissan opposite the castle, Stefan Holmström's restaurant has the reputation of being one of

the finest in Sweden, serving a menu which combines the best of
Scandinavian produce from sea and mountain, farm and woodland with
a stylish level of accomplishment in the best European cuisine.

FALSTERBO, PO Box 71, Fyrvägen 23011, Falsterbo tel: (040) 470078
6400 yards SSS 72

RESTAURANT
Kaptensgarden, Falsterbo * * *

This superb seaside course, at the south-westernmost tip of Sweden, is 35
kilometres south of Malmo, just 48 from Copenhagen across the Oresund
but almost 500 from Stockholm. It is one of the few true links in mainland
Europe but maintains its particularly Swedish character by having more
lakes in its lay-out than any other links I know.
It also has more than a hundred bunkers and although the weather down
here can often be benign in the summer, when the wind comes there are
plenty of places for it to blow from; for open sea surrounds the course on
three sides. Whether from Russia across the Baltic or over the flat farm-
lands of Denmark from the North Sea or down the Kattegat from Norway
and the Atlantic, it can howl across here.
But this is a golf course site you cannot invent, you have to discover it. The
1st hole moves deceptively inland, turning its back on the shoreline and the
hordes of migrant birds which populate its emptiness in spring and
autumn, but it is quite a tough par 4 with out-of-bounds on the right, the
old striped lighthouse in its copse over your shoulder and trees and sand
crowding in as you aim for the green. The danger of water can be seen
glinting in the tall reeds at the back of the second green and the only par
5 in the outward half comes at the 3rd. The 4th, with its green out on a
spur jutting into the huge lake which forms the eastern boundary to the
course, is a difficult hole on which to judge the approach and there is water
all round at the 5th where the drive must be straight or the second will be
soggy.
After the 6th, a short hole with more water to carry, bunkers provide the
danger until you reach the 11th, another par 3, which is all flight across a
corner of the lake to a peninsula green.
At the 12th you turn back to the south-west and a series of inland links
holes, prolifically bunkered, until you come to the 16th and Falsterbo's all-
along-the-shore finish. Out to the westernmost point on the headland on
the par-4 16th with dunes on the right and bunkers to the left, then a turn,
back south-eastwards, at the 17th, a cunningly plotted 377-yard dog-leg
with a ridge to carry with the second shot, the beach on the right and some
strategically placed bunkers.
And so to the par-5 18th, 498 yards, a boomerang inland and back to the sea.
The tee is almost on the beach, bunkers lie on the inner angle of the dog-leg;
then you have a long shot back east into the green as the hole turns again
towards the shore and the four bunkers which guard the flag in front of the
clubhouse. A highly individual, challenging and invigorating golf course.

Kaptensgarden, Kaptensgatan, 1, PO Box 14, Falsterbo
tel: (040) 470750 ***
Although the captain may have come ashore, he has brought the know-ledge of harvest of the sea with him, and it arrives daily from the local harbour. What Scandinavians call shrimps but what are in fact quite large prawns, crayfish, crab, lobster; smoked herring from the Danish island of Bornholm to the south-east; fresh sea fish like turbot and halibut, cod, monkfish and haddock; game like ptarmigan from above the snow-line, reindeer steaks as well as beef, pork and lamb dishes and Arctic berries and the rich sticky Swedish pastries make up the menu. There is a good list with well-chosen reds and a large selection of white wines.

Denmark

Across the Oresund in Denmark things are different. The clubhouse is a place of social gathering and the golf is played around it. Cashmere sweaters with eagles, panthers and crocodiles on them, tight-bottomed slacks in well-known Scandinavian tartans, kids in designer jeans and T-shirts bearing up-to-the-minute rock-group or save-the-planet slogans make you conscious that here golf is a social relaxation not an obsession.
Nevertheless Denmark has some good and testing golf courses and more are being built. There are at present fifty-five courses, by the seaside of Denmark's 7250 kilometres of coastline, on parkland, heathland and in forests of spruce and pine. There are even courses with hills (the highest point in Denmark is 561 feet), like the Hvide Hus course at Ebeltoft in East Jutland (5632 yards SSS 67) which starts uphill from the clubhouse next to the comfortable modern hotel to which it belongs and has most of its holes on a windy plateau above the pine woods overlooking the Kattegat, until it descends to the valley at the 16th for the last three.
The landscape is homely rather than dramatic, full of the green smell of growing in the spring and summer in the fields around the low-hunched farmhouses with deep-eaved roofs like medieval helmets pulled right down over the ears. The drama is in the castles, like the one at Helsingor, under whose massive walls the ferry comes in after its 20-minute crossing from Sweden. In the echoing halls of Kronborg Castle the drama is easy to catch—for this is Shakespeare's Elsinore, home of Hamlet, the moody Dane, and you watch the tapestries stirring in the breeze for a rat behind the arras or half catch the wailing of Ophelia's last song for her lost senses.

RUNGSTED, 2960 Rungsted Kyst tel: (42) 863444 *6452 yards SSS 72*

RESTAURANTS
Krogs Fiskerestaurant, Copenhagen *** Escoffier, Copenhagen ***

There is a pleasant golf course at Helsingor but Rungsted, halfway down the coast between Helsingor and Copenhagen, is a much more serious course set amid splendid beech woods with narrow fairways threading their ways between the trees and the punishing rough and streams networking the course for good measure.

A typical Rungsted hole is the 5th: 450 yards with the fairway sloping to a stream and a huge oak tree effectively blocking off the right-hand side just at drive length. You must hit your second shot high and straight to avoid the bunkers encroaching on the green and stay on to get a regulation 4. There are only two par 5s on the course but both are in the last three holes: the 16th at 526 yards and the 18th at 488 yards. However, you have the consolation that these are almost the only holes at which water does not come into play.

Krogs Fiskerestaurant, Gammel Strand 38 K, Copenhagen
tel: (01) 158915 ***
Like the rest of Scandinavia, Danish food centres very much around the harvest of the sea, and this fish restaurant overlooking the old harbour offers not only outstanding shellfish dishes like prawns and lobsters but magnificent fresh cold-water fish from the North Sea like turbot, cod, halibut, hake, herring, eel smoked and fresh and new-smoked Bornholm herring and salmon, fish soups and stews and original versions of pickled herring and sild. There is a good wine list and a wide choice of Danish lagers.

Escoffier, Dronningens Tvaergade 43 K, Copenhagen
tel: (01) 150554 ***
This international restaurant near the Rosenborg Palace presents a change from the pickled herring circuit with a menu of European dishes from France and Italy, some of them offering seafood but cooked in very different ways from the traditional Danish methods. It also has plenty of good dishes involving beef, ham, pork and the dairy produce for which Denmark is famous, with pasta dishes and veal Italian style, duckling and goose cooked à la française and an extensive and well-chosen European wine list.

SILKEBORG, Sensommervej 15C 8600 Silkeborg tel: (86) 853399
6506 yards SSS 72

RESTAURANT
Kongensbro Kro, Ans by ***

In the heart of Jutland, Silkeborg is famous for the macabre almost perfectly preserved corpse of a second-century man, the Tollund Man, found in a local peat bog in 1950: the 1700-year-old victim of a ritual murder, probably a sacrifice at the winter solstice. You can see him and the extraordinarily peaceful expression on his ancient leathery face in the Silkeborg Museum. More cheerful viewing is the splendid golf course created in 1966, 5 kilometres east of the town, set in heathery hills and soft-wood forest, perfumed with the scent of pine and bog myrtle. The clubhouse has a convivial atmosphere and the course is one of the best in Scandinavia, often used for important tournaments. Most of the fairways demand very straight shots and the forest is dense enough to cause real problems and the rough grows long and tangled.

A couple of lengthy par 5s in the back nine will test anyone and there are two intriguing short holes in each half. The woodland and lake district around Silkeborg is considered to be the most scenic area in Denmark and despite its difficulty and challenging qualities, the spacious lay-out and isolated calm of this course is certainly very easy on the eye and soothing to the nerves, giving that sense of peace and tranquillity which is the keynote of true relaxation.

Kongensbro Kro, pr Ans tel: (06) 870177 ∗∗∗
Kro is the Danish word for inn and this beautifully restored eighteenth-century inn, once a favourite watering hole of Hans Christian Andersen, is just the place to continue the relaxation which the Silkeborg golf course and its beautiful setting inspires. On the quiet bank of the Gudenaa river, along which barges of merchandise and foodstuffs used to be towed from the fjord port of Randers to Silkeborg, it offers old-fashioned standards of modernised comfort and attention in its rooms, and magnificent food and wines in its pine-boarded restaurant.

The menu is more countryside orientated than in most Danish restaurants although seafood starters like prawns and other shellfish are on offer. But there is also game and river and lake fish, delicious pork with red cabbage and chops with pickled cucumber and lots of other traditional Danish farm recipes and a wine list which could be the envy of many a multi-starred city restaurant in European capitals. Playing Silkeborg and dining here makes as perfect a golf day as you will find.

ST KNUD'S, 5800 Nyborg Strand tel: (09) 311212   *6555 yards SSS 70*

RESTAURANT
Hotel Hesselet ∗∗∗∗

By contrast at St Knud's, reached by driving across the Little Belt bridge to the island of Funen, all is ultra-cosmopolitan to the point of being bizarre. On the way to Nyborg you pass through the charming town of Odense, which as well as being the birthplace of Hans Christian Andersen (who, by way of being the Queen Elizabeth or George Washington of Denmark, crops up everywhere), also has a eighteen- and a nine-hole course at Hestehaven.

Nyborg can claim some historical interest because its castle is the oldest secular building in the country and within its ancient walls, the first Danish constitution was signed in 1282, but the Hotel Hesselet and the St Knud's Golf Club are very firmly twentieth century.

The course was designed by English architect Frank Pennink on a wooded peninsula which sticks out into the channel separating Funen from Sealand, called, not inappropriately, the Great Belt. You need a couple of those to get to the flag at the 16th and the 18th which continue the sadistic Scandinavian habit of having two 5s in the last three holes.

The 530-yard 16th, a dog-leg along the curve of the bay is a particularly good hole for the wind comes in off the sea and makes judging its effect as well as hitting the length a tidy problem. There is only one par 5 in the outward half but the par 3s are all interesting and the 422-yard 5th is a fine testing hole. The rough is not as tough nor the fairways as narrow as at Silkeborg but there are some demanding holes and the greens are very fair and beautifully maintained.

Hotel Hesselet, 5800 Nyborg tel: (09) 313029 ****
The creator of the Hesselet, metal-container millionaire Carl Haustrop, shared the venture with a friend who lived in Tokyo. The result, in the middle of Hans Andersen country is a beautifully styled luxury hotel with its own beach, swimming pool, library, sauna, tennis and golf course, which serves Japanese food in its elegant restaurant, has Japanese servants and an exquisite Japanese masseuse to take the kinks out of your muscles when you come off the golf course.
The *sashimi*, *sukiyaki* grilled eel filets and seaweed-flavoured *sushi* are also delicious. This is one of two addresses which all Japanese business-men have with them when they arrive in Denmark; the other is a bar in Copenhagen.

Norway

The national sport of Norway is enjoying Norway as nature made it with as little interference as possible. Thus ski-touring as well as organised downhill skiing (the Norwegians invented skiing), sailing (there are 250,000 privately-owned pleasure boats for a population of 4 million), fishing and tramping about from one hut to another in the rugged mountains which make up most of this country, where two-thirds of the land is over 1000 feet. A third is within the Arctic circle and only 3 per cent of all Norway is cultivated, so you can see there is not much room for golf courses.
However, you can't keep down a good game which you can play from the ages of six to ninety-six, and there are twelve courses in Norway, almost half of them nine holes, eight within easy reach of Oslo and four built within the last twenty years.

TRONDHEIM, PO Box 169 7001 Trondheim tel: (07) 531885
6159 yards SSS 72

RESTAURANTS
Naustloftet, Trondheim *** Teatergrillen, Trondheim ***

At Trondheim it is difficult to know what to expect from a sub-Arctic golf course—a bit of tundra, perhaps the odd elk or reindeer, scrub-grass fairways, greens to be treated with well-bred tolerance?
That is what I thought when I went to play in the Midnight Cup there. In fact I found a beautiful nine-hole course set high above the port with breathtaking views across the medieval capital of Norway and the Trond-heim fjord. Alternative tees make a real test of the second nine—there are differences of more than 50 yards at several holes, some tees are hidden deep in forests and others set at angles which completely alter the hole.

It winds most intriguingly through forest and up and down into gullies and along hills. There is a lake mirroring the dark pines beside the 2nd and 3rd holes, two splendid dog-legs where you have to put your drive well within sight of the green to have a chance of a par 4 and a final hole, past the ox-blood-painted old wooden farm which serves as a club-house and a towering group of trees, which needs a bit of highly skilled negotiating.

The Midnight Cup was something else, a golf folly which is a true collec-tor's piece, recognized as such by a certificate testifying to your partici-pation in this charming piece of nocturnal solacy. Played over eighteen holes as a Stableford, it begins at the witching hour of Midsummer's Day and continues in the tepid glare of the midnight sun until around four o'clock in the morning.

Other than being encompassed in the general Scandinavian midsummer euphoria—drinking *akavit*, being fondly embraced by strange wild-eyed ladies, being careful not to spoil the lies of younger members of the per-missive society in the brushwood—it is played straight.

Well, that is a relative term. The Rules of Golf are not bent is what I mean. Anyone of average ability playing absolutely straight would have won by about twenty points. It was a very jolly occasion, with roars of disparate laughter punctuating the golfing progress, an occasional swing-steadying glug from a bottle, the occasional halt in the proceed-ings while some diaphanous Nordic nymph floated through the silver birches.

It could have been the powdery diffused light of the midnight sun which made distances on chips and putts very hard to judge on the first few holes. It could have been because when you adjusted to this, the light had strengthened and the ground dried out and second judgements proved no better than firsts. It could have been the beguiling carroway flavour of the *akavit*, the disturbing stirrings in the birch forests, the midnight birds piping. It could also have been that I was having such a good time, I was not concentrating. Anyway, The Midnight Cup is still there to be won by an invader from the south.

Naustloftet, Prinsensgate 51, Trondheim tel: (07) 31500 ***
Near the magnificent Norman cathedral in the old town, its walls hung with ancient Norwegian fishing tools and gear, Naustloftet claims to be the northernmost top fish restaurant in the world.

Certainly, in the setting of a typical Norwegian boathouse, it does its best to sustain that boast. Norwegian fish chowder, smoked salmon with scrambled eggs, herring fillets, cured and pickled, served with raw onions, beets and boiled potatoes, shrimp omelette, fillet of sole in white-wine sauce, escalope aux mer, fried sole with pineapple and béar-naise sauce, pan-fried prawns with mushrooms, with rice and with sauce remoulade, salmon with pepper sauce keep up the seafood side.

There is also pork fillet with nuts, raisins and pineapple with rice, steak with béarnaise, chicken, veal and a Norwegian smoked-meat platter. Norway's wines are bought by a central government agency and this can result in some rather peculiar lists. Here it offers claret and burgundy, Chianti, Rioja and Bull's Blood and a more ambitious range of whites, including wines from Alsace, Yugoslavia, Germany, the inevitable Portuguese pink and champagne.

Teatergrillen, Prinsensgate 18, Trondheim tel: (07) 24000 ∗∗∗
This smart grill room has a more international menu than most Trondheim eating places. Smoked salmon with scrambled eggs, west-coast seafood cocktail and mussels with whisky mayonnaise are accompanied by artichoke hearts with pimentos and mushrooms, Norwegian cured ham with asparagus, ox-tail and turtle soup on the starters menu. There are, of course, fish dishes but they have French titles like filet de carrelet Marguery and à la Grecque, which is flounder cooked with wine, mussels, shrimps, lobster, crab, asparagus and mushrooms or with rice pilaff, pimentos and onions as well as a fry-up of fish and shellfish; scampi and halibut with shrimps, pimentos and mushrooms with remoulade sauce. Meat and poultry also come in foreign styles, beef filet with stuffed tomatoes, mushrooms and sauce béarnaise, châteaubriand, pepper steak, veal and pork brochettes and other kinds of kebab and a number of surf 'n' turf dishes, involving veal, pork, shrimps and crab. Well-cooked food and a standard Norwegian wine list.

BERGEN, PO Box 470, 5001 Bergen tel: (05) 182077   *4922 yards SSS 66*

RESTAURANTS
Bryggen Tracteursted, Bergen ∗∗∗   Ole Bull, Bergen ∗∗∗∗

Bergen's nine holes 10 kilometres north of the town is within a salt whiff of the sea and surrounded by mountains. Although short by conventional golfing standards even when two rounds are played, it certainly offers enough exercise. Not only are there often considerable distances between one hole and another (between the 6th green and the 7th tee a walk over a small mountain of about a mile!) but there is good deal of tramping up and down hills and, I suspect, you could add a few hundred yards to the course if it were measured over the ground.

The 1st is a par 3 of 103 yards, always a nasty start to a round because everything depends on the tee-shot. Here it is played over a lake from a hill platform high above, which is so small you feel if you over-swing you may be in for an early bath.

You reach the second by walking along a road and it is another, simpler, slightly longer par 3 with no water. At the 3rd you are into the big time on a tricky hole of 350 yards with a stream to the right, a humped fairway and encroaching trees. There is a long carry across a dip at the dog-legged 4th and you continue through a series of varying lengths of par 4s. The 400-yard 5th is the most testing, as a golf hole, a long dog-leg round a rocky bluff.

After the 6th you take to the hills but play no more golf until you hit your drive down the narrow valley of the 7th. At the 8th you play up to a platform green, seemingly little bigger than the tee you started from.

Then it is back to the lake, all carry over the water to a green high above the tee, below the clubhouse. As much an adventure trek as a golf course but an experience, probably designed by trolls.

Bryggen Tracteursted, Bryggen, Bergen tel: (05) 314046 ***
Along the eastern shores of Vagen, the inner harbour, is Bryggen, the picturesque restored wooden quayside quarter of the merchants of the Hanseatic League, the consortium of German merchants who formed a trading association which was an important force in North European politics from the thirteenth to the sixteenth centuries.
This ancient cluster of trading houses, assembly rooms, offices and chandlering stores, some of which pre-date the Hanseatics, are the most romantic part of old Bergen. Some of the town's best eating places are here, including the only purely fish restaurant Enjorningen (The Unicorn), where all the traditional Norwegian specialities are served.
Tracteursted has a mixed indigenous and international menu with *Bergens Kjottesuppe*, a beef broth made from marrow bones, beef and vegetables, a complete meal and not just a starter; broiled trout with almonds; spare ribs with curry sauce; lamb fricassee with celery, carrots and green peas; fillet steak; hamburgers with sour cream; smoked ham with peppers. desserts include apple pie, ice cream and pastry filled with cloudberry cream. There is a short wine list from France and Hungary.

Ole Bull, Norge Hotel, Ole Bull Plass, 4, N-5001 Bergen
tel: (05) 210100 ****
Ole Bull was the famous Bergen nineteenth-century violinist who put Norway on the cultural map by his virtuoso performances in Europe and America, the discoverer of Grieg and the founder of Norway's first theatre in Bergen where Henrik Ibsen made his name.
The Norge is the top hotel in Bergen and here in the Ole Bull and the Grillroom you can have Norwegian specialities like Bergen fish soup, *smorgasbord*, smoked fish, poached cod served with the liver, boiled potatoes and parsley butter, cured ham and mutton, salmon and sea trout, ptarmigan fried in butter and sour cream or elk steak with a sauce made from the brown Norwegian goat's cheese gammelost. There is a distinguished list which covers not only Europe but most of the winemaking world.

STAVANGER, Longebakke 45, 4042 Hafrsfjord tel: (04) 555431
5566 yards SSS 68

RESTAURANTS
Antique, Stavanger ****   Skagen, Stavanger ***

Stavenger is the oil capital of Norway and houses a curious international mixture of hard-nosed, high-tec oil men, back-packing sightseers about to take boat to the inner fastnesses of the vast south-western fjord system which extends fan-like for 250 kilometres around the town, Chinese restaurants and architecture and institutions which reflect a sentimental attachment to the old fishing days. These include the best-preserved wooden-house settlement in Northern Europe, a thirteenth-century cathedral and, among a rash of museums, one devoted to the sardine canning industry.

The eighteen-hole golf course, set alongside the Stokka lakes, 6 kilometres to the south-west, owes more to oil than history. Opened in 1956, it is cut like so many Scandinavian courses through a pine forest. Although not long, it is tight and a test of accurately struck irons to thread the ball through the dark, slender and dense pines. There are several interesting holes which skirt Lake Stokka where the conjunction of dark trees and bright water make distances particularly hard to judge.

Antique Restaurant, Atlantic hotel, Jernbaneveien, 1 Stavanger
tel: (04) 527520 ****
The Atlantic is Stavanger's top hotel, just above the harbour in the centre of town facing the thirteenth-century cathedral across Lake Breiavatnet. The luxuriously appointed Antique, the hotel's gourmet restaurant, has views across the lake, a stylish international menu which honours Norwegian specialities such as reindeer steaks and ptarmigan, the Arctic grouse braised in sour cream with goat's cheese, marinated and cured ham and fish but also offers French cuisine with spit-roasted chicken, duck, game birds, beef and lamb served with the appropriate sauces.
Member of the Chaine des Rôtisseurs. There is a distinguished wine list with one of the best choices in Norway.

Skagen, Skagenkaien, Stavanger tel: (04) 526190 ***
This restored wharf warehouse on the quay where the ferries leave for the fjords has a spendidly old-fashioned air, with unpainted wooden walls and balconies, tables and chairs. It is very near the fishmarket, so whatever is on the quays this morning will be on the table today. After a dish of fresh prawns, smoked leg of mutton with *flatbrod*, Norwegian crispbread and *akavit*, Norwegian schnapps could also be on the menu along with marinated salmon, *gravet laks* or *farikal*, delicious mutton, cabbage and black pepper stew, as well as international dishes like hamburgers, steak and chicken.

OSLO, Bogstad 0757 Oslo 7 tel: (02) 504402 *6719 yards SSS 72*

RESTAURANTS
Continental, Oslo **** Blom, Oslo ***

The eighteen-hole course at Bogstad is ringed by wooded hills with the tall finger of the huge Holmenkollen ski jump on the horizon. There is a lake in the middle with a number of good holes around it and there are some long tough ones like the 480-yard, par-5 2nd among these rolling hills (they use them to ski on in the winter). There are two par 5s in each half, with the two longest the 11th at 557 yards and the 18th at 577 yards, helping to make a real challenge of the second half. On the whole it is quite an open course, although trees come into play now and again.

After the turn and the big par-5 11th followed by a long par 3, there is a run of demanding 4s all round the 400-yard mark before another 3 at the 17th and the almost 600-yard finish back to the welcoming clubhouse. Considering that it spends many months under snow, it is not surprising that the fairways can be a bit uneven but the greens are very well looked after and run very truly.

Continental, Stortingsgade 24–26 0161 Oslo 1 tel: (02) 419060 ✶✶✶✶
The Continental is one of Oslo's more old-fashioned hotels and it retains an old-fashioned attachment to Norwegian food. This was the scene many years ago of my induction into the delights of beyond the cold table; a sight and a meal of some magnificence but one which can become a bit of a bore if you are confronted with it every day and almost all day. You can get to the point where the prospect of yet another even more ingeniously pickled herring is more than flesh and blood can stand.

The young deputy manager of the Continental, whose assistance I had implored as a journalistic gourmet to try to break through the *negladt sild*, pickled fish curtain, introduced me to *rakorret*, a well-aged fermented trout (three months in the barrel), smoked ptarmigan, delicious reindeer steaks in sour-cream sauce, a wide variety of stews of superb simplicity and haunting flavour, fresh salmon with dill, and sundry smoked meats.

There were also golden cloudberries and other desserts with provocative names like Veiled Peasant Girls and Linje *akavit*, the Norwegian schnapps which travels across the equator and back to improve its flavour.

The most modern and up-to-date hotel in the Norwegian capital is the Oslo Plaza, the highest building in Scandinavia, in Sonia Henies Plass, tel: (47) 2171000, which offers a different kind of escape with a French brasserie, an Italian restaurant and an English pub.

Restaurant Blom, Karl Johansgate, 41b Oslo tel: (02) 427300 ✶✶✶✶
This charming nineteenth-century restaurant, all dark wood and copper, lined with pictures of eminently bearded gentlemen, most of whom look like Ibsen or Grieg and some of whom are, has been the artists' restaurant of Oslo for many years. It has a fish tank in the centre so you can choose your fish live and have it netted by the waiter and cooked to whatever recipe you choose. There are good steaks and native Norwegian dishes and a bohemian spread of cuisines from all over Europe. Excellent and comprehensive wine list and the most endearing ambience in Oslo. Open Monday to Saturday, 11.30am to midnight.

BENELUX

In his splendidly researched book *Early Golf* the great Dutch golf historian, the late Steven JH van Hengel quotes well-substantiated documentary evidence for the theory that the game began in the Low Countries as early as the fourteenth century but he always said (to me, at any rate) that there was no real proof as to whether the Dutch traders who came to the twelfth-century Senzie Fair at St Andrews, one of the largest trading markets in Europe which continued for 300 years, brought the game with them or took it away from the linksland that is now the Old Course.

At all events the documentary evidence, all of it relating to complaints about the game being played to the nuisance and alarm of non-golfers, certainly gives the Netherlands a prior claim, but the game vanished altogether in that part of Europe at the end of the seventeenth century and only reappeared at the very end of the last century as an import from Britain.

Netherlands

There are some fifty courses in the Netherlands, half with only nine holes but others like Nunspeetse near Zwolle, Nijmegen by the border with Germany and Kennemer on the coast near Haarlem, having twenty-seven holes while a number also have par-3 courses.

KENNEMER, PO Box 2040 AB Zandvoort tel: (02507) 12836
Van Hengel: 3227 yards   Pennink: 3188 yards   Colt: 3206 yards SSS 72

RESTAURANTS
Ile de France, Amstelveen ✳✳✳   Excelsior, Amsterdam ✳✳✳✳

This, with Falsterbo in Sweden and Le Touquet in France as its only rivals, is probably the finest links course in Europe. Its twenty-seven holes are named after two celebrated English golf architects and Steven van Hengel, the great Dutch golf historian, who was a member here. The main course has two loops of nine rather like Muirfield, one running round the outer perimeter and the inward half varying its route in several directions. If you think Holland is flat, you will change your mind when you have played Kennemer.

H S Colt laid out Kennemer in the late 1920s among the huge sand dunes and the spinneys of pine, but it became a defence zone against invasion for the Germans in the 1939–45 war, and it was only in 1947 that the course was restored to its former challenging splendour by Frank Pennink.

The 1st hole requires a drive down a broad fairway between pine-crested dunes but it is after the short 2nd that Kennemer begins to sort out the men from the boys. There is a long carry from the tee to the fairways at the 3rd and the dog-leg is well bunkered on the corner. At the 4th the drive through a gap in a stand of pines is testing, as is the cluster of bunkers waiting to receive it and the tight and fearsome sand around the green. The only 5 on the outward half is at the 6th, where there is a lot of rough between tee and fairway, and there is another long carry for the tee-shot at the 7th and a long cross-bunker in front of the green set against the pine-fringed sandhills.

The inward half is longer with three par 5s, two of them substantially over 500 yards and begins with a glorious driving chance at the 10th over a tangled valley to an invisible fairway with the chance to fly some more wild country with the second shot to the green, tucked around a right-hand, last-minute corner at the hole's end.

You need a handsome second shot to the 13th green set high in the dunes and better than that to get on at the short 15th, its green on top of a steep-edged plateau from which anything not accurately struck will roll away to disaster. The 16th and the short 17th zig-zag across the landward side of the course to give a fine finish at the par-4 18th with its tightly-trapped green.

Ile de France, Pieter Lastmanweg 9, Amstelveen tel: (20) 453509 * * *
On the way back to Amsterdam this pretty restaurant has an original touch with classic dishes such as halibut in pastry, turbot steamed with sorrel, warm salad of quail with goose liver, duck breasts with red peppers and crab claws with spring onions. A good list of wines from France and Germany.

Excelsior, Hôtel de L'Europe 2–8, Nieuwe Doelenstraat, Amsterdam tel: (020) 234836 * * * *
Although tourists are encouraged in Amsterdam to eat at the Indonesian restaurants, this kind of food is now served in most large cities and in this elegant dining room overlooking the Amstel the emphasis is not Eastern but top French. Wild duck with gooseberries and shallots, turbot with butter sauce, sweetbreads with truffles, salmon steak with vermouth and spring onions, scallops in pastry, truffled goose liver with calvados, guinea-fowl with wild mushrooms are among the dishes which may be on offer. There is a distinguished list with some good vintages, particularly in claret and burgundy. The service is exceptional.

UTRECHTSE 'DE PAN', Amersfoorstweg 1, Lj Bosch en Duin
tel: (03404) 55223   *6642 yards SSS 72*

RESTAURANT
Hoefslag, Zeist * * * *

This is one of the oldest golf clubs in the Netherlands, founded in 1894, and as its parkland lay-out is popular, it is wise to ring first to make a booking. This is one of the few forest and heathland areas of the Netherlands and some of the holes will look like familiar territory to anyone who has played on the courses to the south-west of London. Long enough to offer a substantial challenge to the straight hitter, De Pan demands accuracy in the short game as well as power to stay out of its woods and bunkers.

De Hoefslag, Vosseniaan 28, 3735 KN Bosch en Duin
tel: (030) 784395 ★★★★
This is one of the greatest restaurants in Holland. A beautiful woodland inn where you might expect to get a friendly welcome but would hardly hope for an elegant restaurant decorated with the works of distinguished modern painters and a menu and cellar which vie with the most renowned in Europe.
The cooking is light and delicate but accomplished and satisfying, alive with fascinating variations on the classic approach. Salmon with fennel; smoked turbot with caviar and lemon vinaigrette; oysters marinated with sorrel; quails stuffed with creamed truffles; noisettes of roebuck with wild mushrooms; shellfish lasagne with lobster sauce; slices of guinea-fowl with foie gras and beer-braised sauerkraut are some examples.
A very distinguished list completes the impression, wines from France, Germany and farther afield, chosen to match the originality and distinction of the cuisine. This is a restaurant which not only is worth a detour but merits a special journey.

Luxembourg

GRAND-DUCAL DE LUXEMBOURG, 1 route de Treves,
2633 Senningerberg tel: 34090   *6304 yards SSS 71*

RESTAURANTS
Saint Michel, Luxembourg ★★★★   La Marmite, Luxembourg ★★★

The Grand-Duchy of Luxembourg has only one golf course, just 7 kilometres outside the capital on the way to the airport, an attractive parkland lay-out through woods where each hole is isolated from the others. The trees bordering the holes make for tight fairways and tee-shots must be accurately placed to open up the well-bunkered, generally narrow greens. The 4th and the 7th, both par 3s of more than 200 yards, demand very exact shots to stay out of trouble and the 462-yard 4th is a tough 4 needing two precise and powerfully struck shots to reach the tiered green in two and have a chance of a par.
There is a welcoming creeper-covered clubhouse with a bar and restaurant where good meals are served and there are good practice facilities.

Saint Michel, 32 rue de l'Eau, Luxembourg tel: 23215 ★★★★
This small restaurant, under the arches of the precipitous city of Luxembourg, has a particular reputation for fish. Its sea-urchin salad with chive butter and its saffron-coloured langoustine soup are famous; other dishes like the pink sea bass flavoured with beetroot butter; the sole fillets with fresh noodles and foie gras and rabbit with shrimps deserve to be. Here too you are back with the great Benelux addiction to the sweet tooth and desserts are imaginative and enticing.
There is an excellent wine list full of good choices, including some very good fish wines from the Luxembourg Mosel.

La Marmite, 6–12 place d'Armes, Luxembourg tel: 24125 * * *
This handsome restaurant overlooking the Place d'Armes offers the good, tasteful upper bourgeois food which is typical of Luxembourg—fine ingredients, meticulously chosen and prepared and presented without too many frills, other than those of attentive service and good culinary judgement. Scallops with a purée of broccoli; saffron-flavoured John Dory with cucumber; sweetbreads with tarragon; entrecôte with wild mushrooms from the Ardennes; pork fillets with cream and calvados; sumptuous, filling sweets and a discreet list including some fine Luxembourg riesling.

Belgium

Belgium has thirty-seven golf courses and eleven of them have 'Royal' in their titles, a reflection of the exceptional interest taken by the Belgian royal family in the game. King Leopold is the only reigning monarch ever to have played in a national championship, at Le Zoute, and, after his abdication, he played in several tournaments and reached the quarter final of the French Amateur Championship at St Cloud in 1949. His son, King Baudouin, has played for Belgium in international matches.

ROYAL ANTWERP, Georges Capiaulei 2, 2950, Kapellen
tel: (03) 666 8456   *6715 yards SSS 73*

RESTAURANT
De Bellefleur, Ekeren * * * *

This is the oldest club in Belgium and the second oldest on the continental mainland of Europe, founded in 1888—the same year that the St Andrews Club at Yonkers became the first in the United States—by British businessmen in the port. It moved from an army training ground around the turn of the century to its present woodland site 20 kilometres north of Antwerp and was originally laid out by Willie Park, son of the man who won the first Open Championship, then re-designed by Tom Simpson in the 1920s, although some of Park's original holes remain in the nine-hole course.
Today Royal Antwerp makes its way up and down avenues of tall pines and silver birch, shrubs and heather, not profusely but cunningly bunkered so that even on such a flat course the choice of club is crucial to playing a hole well. Because the fairways are broad, it tends to look easier than the courses west of London, which it closely resembles, but almost all the par 4s are on the long side, demanding something more than just a pitch to the green for the second shot and there are two 5s in the first nine and three in the second.
The short 7th where the ball must be struck precisely through a narrow funnel of trees over a mound, keeping to the left to avoid the single greenside bunker is a strict hole and there are long carries over the heather and scrub to the fairways at the 3rd, the 8th, the 10th and the tight dog-leg of the 14th. Indeed dog-legs are a feature of the holes around the turn, often restricting or dictating the line of the drive to give room and sight for the next shot.

De Bellefleur, 768 Kapelsesteenweg, Ekeron tel: (31) 646719 ∗∗∗
Ekeron is on the road south to Antwerp about halfway between the golf
course and the city. In Belgium eating is *très sérieux* and the Bellefleur
has the reputation of being one of the best restaurants in the country.
Classic cuisine with original touches are what marks a great chef and
they are here in abundance.
Almond-stuffed oysters; calf's liver with hop sprouts and quail's eggs;
monkfish in pastry; lobster with passion-fruit juice; saddle of rabbit with
dumplings; pigeon and woodcock in addition to more traditional dishes
give the idea. The list is formidable, wide-ranging and selected with
care.

ROYAL ZOUTE, Caddiespad 14 8300 Knokke-Heist
tel: (050) 601227   *6750 yards SSS 73   3845 yards SSS 60*

RESTAURANT
L'Aquilon, Knokke-le-Zoute ∗∗∗∗

The outer course is a championship lay-out with the short eighteen-holer
of just under 4000 yards at its heart. The undulating parkland of the main
course has some challenging holes, although it looks fairly open to begin
with, until you realise that these stands of birch and pine, gentle mounds
and innocent not-very-deep patches of sand occupy strategic positions.
The circular design means that the wind off the sea down the road can have
a considerable effect on your game because there are seldom two holes in
succession played in the same direction. A much more testing course than
first appearances might suggest and kept in excellent condition. The comfortable clubhouse has a restaurant and bar.

L'Aquilon, 306 avenue Lippens, Knokke-le-Zoute
tel: (050) 601274 ∗∗∗∗
In this Louis XVI-style restaurant not all the refinement and flourish is
in the decor. Naturally, with salt water on the doorstep there is a strong
accent on marine dishes—North Sea soup, seafood boudin and langoustine soufflé bring the sea to the table, but there are also dishes
featuring wild duck, goose liver, game and pan-fried steaks and chops.
A famous wine list complements the standard of the cooking.

Firms and organisations providing information about golf travel

Belgium
- North Sea Ferries, King George Dock, Hedon Road, Hull HU9 5QA tel: (0482) 795141
- Leopold II Dam (Havendam) 8380, Zeebrugge, Belgium tel: (050) 543430

Denmark
- Scandinavian Seaways, Scandinavia House, Parkeston Quay, Harwich CO12 4QG: tel: (0255) 554681
- Sterling Airways, 209 Edgeware Road, London tel: (071) 706 2778

England
- English Tourist Board, 4 Grosvenor Gardens, London SW1W 0DU tel: (071) 730 3400
- Trust House Forte, Grosvenor House, Park Lane, London W1A 3AA tel: (071) 499 6363

France
- BDH Golf, 362–364 Sutton Common Road, Sutton SM3 9PL tel: (081) 641 6060
- Longshot Golf Holidays, Meon House, Petersfield, Hants GU32 3JN tel: (0730) 68621
- Air France, 158 New Bond Street, London W1Y 0AY tel: (071) 499 8611
- Eurogolf, 41 Watford Way, London NW4 3JH tel: (081) 202 4744

Holland
- North Sea Ferries, Hull
- Noordzee Veerdiensten BV, Beneluxhaven, Europoort (PO Box 1123 3180 AC Rozenberg ZH), Netherlands tel: (01819) 55500

Ireland
- Irish Tourist Board, Ireland House, 150 New Bond Street, London W1Y 0AQ tel: (071) 493 3201
- Northern Ireland Tourist Board, 38 High Street, Sutton Coldfield, West Midlands B72 1UP tel: (021) 354 1431
- Aer Lingus Holidays, Aer Lingus House, 52 Poland Street, London W1V 4AA tel: (081) 569 4001
- Longshot
- Eurogolf

Italy
- Costa Smeralda Holidays, Ltd, 140 Walton Street, London SW3 2JJ tel: (071) 493 8303
- Alitalia, 205 Holland Park Avenue, London W11 4XB tel: (081) 745 8361

Norway
- Norway Airlines, 209 Edgware Road, London W2 1ES tel: (071) 706 2778

Portugal
- The Travel Club, Station Road, Upminster, Essex RM14 2BR tel: (04022) 25000
- Vicente & Brown Lda, rua des Alegrias, 8600, Lagos, Algarve, Portugal tel: (0) 82 62176
- TAP, Gillingham House, 38–44 Gillingham Street, London SW1V 1JW tel: (071) 828 2092
- Longshot
- Eurogolf

Scotland
- Scottish Tourist Board, 23 Ravelston Terrace, Edinburgh EH4 3EU tel: (031) 332 2433
- Sibbald Travel, 9 Hope Street, Edinburgh EH2 4EL tel: (031) 226 7613

Spain
- Sibbald Travel
- Longshot
- Eurogolf

Sweden
- Swedish Tourist Board, 29–31 Oxford Street, London W1R 1RE tel: (071) 437 5816
- Transwede Airways, 209 Edgware Road, London W2 1ES tel: (071) 706 2778

Wales
- Wales Tourist Board, Brunel House, 2 Fitzalan Road, Cardiff CF2 1UY tel: (0222) 499909

Index